# GREEK
# CIVILIZATION

# GREEK CIVILIZATION

## An Introduction

edited by
Brian A. Sparkes

Ltd

K

Blackwell Publishers Inc
350 Main Street
Malden, Massachusetts 02148, USA

*British Library Cataloguing in Publication Data*
A CIP catalogue record for this book is available from the British Library

*Library of Congress Cataloging in Publication Data*
Greek civilization : an introduction / edited by Brian A. Sparkes
p.    cm.
Includes bibliographical references and index.
ISBN  0–631–20558–6 — ISBN  0–631–20559–4 (pbk)
1. Greece—Civilization. 2. Greece—Civilization—Influence.
I. Sparkes, Brian A.
DF77.G793     1998                          97–24389
949.5—dc21                                  CIP

Typeset in 10.5 on 13pt Galliard
by Graphicraft Typesetters Limited, Hong Kong
Printed and bound in Great Britain
by T. J. International Limited, Padstow, Cornwall

This book is printed on acid-free paper

# CONTENTS

# PLATES

# FIGURES

# TABLES

# CONTRIBUTORS

Dr Robin L. N. Barber, Department of Classics, University of Edinburgh, Scotland

Dr Sue Blundell, Birkbeck College, University of London, England

Professor Alison Burford, Cambridge, England

Dr Averil M. Cameron, Keble College, Oxford, England

Professor Richard Clogg, St Antony's College, Oxford, England

Dr Oliver T. P. K. Dickinson, Department of Classics and Ancient History, University of Durham, England

Sir Kenneth Dover, St Andrews, Scotland

Dr Nick R. E. Fisher, School of History and Archaeology, University of Wales College of Cardiff, Wales

Dr Lin Foxhall, Ancient History Division, School of Archaeological Studies, University of Leicester, England

Professor Michael Greenhalgh, Faculty of Arts, Australian National University, Canberra, Australia

Edward L. Hussey, All Souls, Oxford, England

Professor Olga Palagia, University of Athens, Greece

Professor Robert C. T. Parker, New College, Oxford, England

Dr Helen Parkins, Fitzwilliam College, Cambridge, England

Professor Friedrich Sauerwein, Modautal, Germany

Dr Graham Shipley, Ancient History Division, School of Archaeological Studies, University of Leicester, England

Professor Brian A. Sparkes, Department of Archaeology, University of Southampton, England

Professor Malcolm J. Wagstaff, Department of Geography, University of Southampton, England

# PREFACE

The chapters which comprise this book have been organized into four parts. The first part (Landscape, Seascape) sets the scene by outlining the geological make-up and environment of the Greek peninsula and the surrounding islands. The second part (The March of the Past) is concerned with the history of the peoples of Greece up to the end of antiquity, starting with the prehistoric and protohistoric periods and then surveying the thousand and more years until the transfer of the Roman imperial court from Rome to Constantinople. The third and longest part (Classical Mosaic) deals with different aspects of the classical period, to give a kaleidoscopic picture of some of the more important elements in Greek life: the country, politics, religion, the spoken and written word, philosophy, art, craftsmanship and social behaviour. The historical direction is taken up again in the fourth part (Continuity and Change) in which the history of Greece after antiquity is sketched from the early Christian generations through the centuries of Ottoman control to the recent years of independence. The final chapter gives a glimpse of what Greece has meant, particularly in the West, in the centuries since the classical period.

The book is intended to provide an introduction for students, both professional and amateur, who wish to know why Greece and the Greeks have been of interest and importance to us in the past and are still so today.

The illustrations have been chosen to assist in understanding the text; they are not intended to act as decorative accessories. Lists of Further Reading close each chapter with a selection of books and articles that may act as a second (or even third), more detailed stage of study for those seeking to augment what they have learnt in the brief chapters of this book. Books organized in the form of dictionaries have been omitted from those lists, but they obviously prove useful by allowing immediate access to specific items. Mention might be made here of M. Avi-Yonah and I. Shatzman *Illustrated Encyclopaedia of the Classical World* (Maidenhead: Sampson Low, 1976), M. Howatson *The Oxford Companion to Classical*

*Literature* (Oxford: OUP, 1989), A. P. Kazhdan (ed.) *The Oxford Dictionary of Byzantium* (New York: OUP Inc., 1991), D. Sacks *Encyclopedia of the Ancient Greek World* (New York: Facts on File Inc., 1995), G. Speake (ed.) *A Dictionary [The Penguin Dictionary] of Ancient History* (Oxford: Blackwell, 1994/Harmondsworth: Penguin, 1995), S. Hornblower and A. Spawforth (eds) *Oxford Classical Dictionary* (third edition, Oxford: OUP, 1996), and S. Hornblower and A. Spawforth (eds) *Oxford Companion to Classical Civilization* (Oxford: Oxford University Press, forthcoming).

Most ancient Greek names are given as close to their original form as proved feasible; those that have become familiar in English are retained in their familiar form (e.g. Alexander, Athens, Cyprus, Plato). Total consistency was, however, beyond the editor's grasp. An added complication was created by the medieval and modern Greek chapters into which different inconsistencies forced themselves.

The editor wishes to thank the contributors for their patience and the following for general help and for assistance with translations and technical advice: Nick and Babis Gouraros, Kathy Judelson, Timothy Potts, Commander Desmond Scott, Professor Malcolm Wagstaff and Jane and Henk Wijsman. My wife Diana has given me her usual wholehearted support. John Davey proved an admirable editorial director in the initial stages, and Tessa Harvey has been a worthy successor. I also wish to thank the copy-editor Anna Oxbury for her professional expertise.

The publishers and editor are grateful to the museums, agents and private individuals named in the Illustration Acknowledgements (pp. xvii–xxi) for prints and permissions, and they apologize for any oversights. The maps and plans drawn for the book were executed by the members of the Cartographic Unit, University of Southampton, under the direction of Tim Aspden.

Brian A. Sparkes

# ILLUSTRATION
# ACKNOWLEDGEMENTS

Plates 1.1–5: photos: author; figure 1.1 and table 1.1: drawn from information supplied by the author; plates 2.1 and 2.2: photos: author; plate 2.3: Volos, Museum, after D. R. Theocaris (ed.), *Neolithicos Politismos* (Athens: National Bank of Greece, Cultural Foundation, 1981), ill. 268; plate 2.4: London, British Museum A17, photo: Museum; plate 2.5: Athens, National Museum inv. 4974, photo: Museum; figures 2.1a–b: based on *The American Journal of Archaeology* 91 (1987), p. 62, fig. 3a and p. 64, fig. 5; figure 2.2: after C. Renfrew, *The Emergence of Civilization* (London: Methuen, 1972), fig. 18.1; figure 2.3: Syros, Museum; after R. L. N. Barber, *The Cyclades in the Bronze Age* (London: Duckworth, 1987), p. 111, fig. 87; figure 2.4: after M. S. F. Hood, *The Minoans* (London: Thames and Hudson, 1971), p. 142, fig. 127; plate 3.1: Crete, Heraklion Museum, after M. S. F. Hood, *The Minoans*, fig. 63; plate 3.2: Athens, National Museum 624, photo: Museum; plate 3.3: Crete, Heraklion Museum, photo: Museum; figures 3.1–2: adapted from O. Dickinson, *The Aegean Bronze Age* (Cambridge: Cambridge University Press, 1994), p. 62, fig. 4.12 and p. 50, fig. 5.26; figure 3.3: Crete, Heraklion Museum, after Arthur Evans, *The Palace of Minos* I (London: Macmillan, 1921), p. 276, fig. 206; figure 3.4: after O. Dickinson, *The Aegean Bronze Age* (1994), p. 156, fig. 5.31; plate 4.1: photo: Mervyn J. Popham; plate 4.2: photo: author; plate 4.3: photo: editor; plate 4.4: photo: Istanbul, Deutsches Archäologisches Institut (66.130); plate 4.5: Los Angeles (California), Collection of the J. Paul Getty Museum 96.AE.98 (Partial Gift of Barbara and Lawrence Fleischman), attributed to the Berlin Painter, photo: Museum; plate 4.6: Athens, Epigraphical Museum 5384, after J. Kirchner, *Imagines Inscriptionum Atticarum* (Berlin: Mann, 1935), pl. 15; plate 4.7: photo: author; figures 4.1 and 4.3: drawn for this book; figure 4.2: after *Cambridge Ancient History* III, part 3 (Cambridge: Cambridge University Press, 1982), p. 168, fig. 28; plate 5.1: Naples, National Museum 6149, photo: Rome, Deutsches Archäologisches Institut (85.11.29); plate 5.2: London, British Museum 1857, photo: Museum; plate 5.3: photo: American School of Classical

Studies, Agora Excavations; plate 5.4: photo: Athens, Ecole Française d'Athènes (Ch. Avezou); plate 5.5: photo: Berlin, Staatliche Museen, Preussischer Kulturbesitz, Antikensammlung PM 6866 and 8013; plate 5.6: photo: Athens, Deutsches Archäologisches Institut (Ath. Bau. 607); figures 5.1 and 5.3: drawn for this book; figure 5.2: after W. Radt, *Pergamon: Archaeological Guide* (Türkiye Turing ve Otomobil Kurumu, 1984), pl. 1; plate 6.1: photo: Hamish Forbes; plates 6.2a–d: Paris, Louvre F 77, photo: Museum (Patrick Lebaube); plate 6.3: Cambridge, Fitzwilliam Museum GR 9–1917, attributed to the Pig Painter, photo: Museum; plate 6.4: photo: Hamish Forbes; plate 6.5: Boston (Mass.), Museum of Fine Arts (Henry Lillie Pierce Fund) 99.525, photo: Museum; plate 6.6: photo: Hamish Forbes; table 6.1: drawing: Debbie Miles; plates 7.1–2: Athens, Agora Museum I 6524 and B 822, photos: American School of Classical Studies, Agora Excavations (Craig Mauzy); plate 7.3: photo: Athens, Deutsches Archäologisches Institut (Ath. Bau. 583A); plate 7.4: London, British Museum 1929.10–16.6, photo: Museum; plate 7.5: Berlin, Staatliche Museen, Preussischer Kulturbesitz, Antikensammlung F 2298, attributed to the Triptolemos Painter, photo: Museum (Jutta Tietz-Glagow); figures 7.1–2: American School of Classical Studies, Agora Excavations; plate 8.1: Boston, Museum of Fine Arts 03.997 (Francis Bartlett Collection), photo: Museum; plate 8.2: Ferrara, National Museum inv. 2897 (T 128 VT), attributed to the Group of Polygnotos, photo: Museum; plate 8.3: Brauron, Museum 1151, photo: Museum; plate 8.4: Boston, Museum of Fine Arts 95.24 (C. P. Perkins Fund), manner of the Chrysis Painter, photo: Museum; plate 8.5: photo: Athens, Ecole Française d'Athènes (Ph. Collet); plate 8.6: Athens, National Museum 3369, photo: Museum; plate 9.1: after *Oxyrhynchus Papyri* V (London: Egypt Exploration Fund, 1908), no. 841 pl. II; plate 9.2: London, British Museum E 270, attributed to the Kleophrades Painter, photo: Peter Corbett; plate 9.3: Los Angeles (California), The Collection of the J. Paul Getty Museum 82.AE.83, photo: Museum; plate 9.4: Berlin, Staatliche Museen F 2285, attributed to Douris, photo: Museum; plate 10.1: Oxford, Bodleian Library MS. Auct. F.6.23, fol 15r, photo: Library; plate 10.2: photo (fragment 19 Smith): Professor Martin F. Smith; plates 10.3a–b: Athens, National Museum 15087, after D. J. de Solla Price *Gears from the Greeks* (New York: Science History Publications, 1975), figs. 11 and 12; plate 10.4: Florence, Biblioteca Medicea Laurenziana MS Laur. Plut. 74, 7, fol. 203v, after E. D.

Phillips, *Greek Medicine* (London: Thames and Hudson, 1973), pl. 13; figure 10.1: Vienna, Austrian National Library MS med. gr. 1, fol. 187, verso (Codex Vindobonensis), after R. T. Gunther, *The Greek Herbal of Dioscurides* (New York: Hafner, 1959), p. 477, no. 79; plate 11.1: Athens, Agora Museum I 7396, photo: American School of Classical Studies, Agora Excavations; plate 11.2: photo: Alison Frantz Collection, American School of Classical Studies at Athens (AT-41); plate 11.3: Berlin, Staatliche Museen F 2294, attributed to the Foundry Painter, photo: Museum; plate 11.4: Boston MFA 61.195 (William Francis Warden Fund), attributed to the A. D. Painter, photo: Museum; plate 11.5: Athens, National Museum 29, photo: Alison Frantz Collection, American School of Classical Studies at Athens (AT-221); plate 12.1: Olympia, Archaeological Museum, photo: Alison Frantz Collection, American School of Classical Studies at Athens (PE-184); plate 12.2: photo: Alison Frantz Collection, American School of Classical Studies at Athens (AT-2); plate 12.3: Rome, Villa Albani, photo: Alinari 27595; plate 12.4: London, British Museum 303, photo: Museum; plate 12.5: London, British Museum 1000, photo: Museum; plate 12.6: Delphi, Museum 369, photo: Athens, Deutsches Archäologisches Institut (Delphi 368); plate 12.7: Reggio, National Archaeological Museum, photo: Florence, Soprintendenza Archeologica per la Toscana 35492; plate 12.8: Piraeus, Museum, photo: Athens, Deutsches Archäologisches Institut (70/1310); plate 13.1: Boston, Museum of Fine Arts 01.8035 (Henry Lillie Pierce Fund), photo: Museum; plate 13.2: Oxford, Ashmolean Museum 1885.502 and 482, photo: Museum; plates 13.3a–b: London, British Museum 601, photo: Museum; plate 13.4: Oxford, Ashmolean Museum 1948.104 and 1874.409, photo: Museum; plate 13.5: Brussels, Musée d'art et d'histoire A 717, painted by Smikros, photo: Museum; plate 13.6: Athens, Agora Museum P 1231, photo: American School of Classical Studies, Agora Excavations; figure 13.1: Athens, National Museum, after E. Pfuhl, *Malerei und Zeichnung der Griechen* (Munich: F. Bruckmann, 1923), fig. 35; plate 14.1: London, British Museum 1920.12–21.1, attributed to the Marlay Painter, photo: Museum; plate 14.2: New York, Metropolitan Museum of Art 36.11.1 (Fletcher Fund, 1936), photo: Museum; plate 14.3: Cambridge (Mass.), Harvard University Art Museums, Arthur M. Sackler Museum 1960.342, photo: Museum; plates 14.4a–b: New York, Metropolitan Museum of Art 07.286.40 (Rogers Fund, 1907), attributed to the Sabouroff Painter, photo:

Museum; plate 14.5: Paris, Louvre MA 738, photo: Alison Frantz Collection, American School of Classical Studies at Athens (EU-243); plate 14.6: Munich, Antikensammlungen und Glyptothek inv. 2645, attributed to the Brygos Painter, photo: blow up; plate 15.1: Naples, National Museum 127.929, attributed to the Pan Painter, after E. Pfuhl, *Malerei und Zeichnung der Griechen* (Munich: F. Bruckmann, 1923), fig. 477; plate 15.2: Brussels, Musée d'art et d'histoire R 351, painted by Smikros, photo: Museum; plate 15.3: Boston, Museum of Fine Arts 08.292 (gift of E. P. and Fiske Warren), photo: Museum; plate 15.4: London, British Museum E 815, attributed to the Nikosthenes Painter, photo: Museum; plate 15.5: Munich, Antikensammlungen und Glyptothek 2654, attributed to Makron, photo: blow up; plate 15.6: Berlin, Staatliche Museen F 2095, attributed to the Group of Berlin 2095, photo: Museum; plate 16.1: Rome, Palazzo dei Conservatori; photo: Deutsches Archäologisches Institut Rome (59.1720); plate 16.2: photo: Alexander and Haris Kalligas; plate 16.3: after S. Kadas, *Mount Athos* (Athens: Ekdotiki, 1991), p. 37; plate 16.4: after D. Talbot Rice, *Art of the Byzantine Era* (London: Thames & Hudson, 1963), fig. 77; plate 16.5: after P. Hetherington, *Byzantine and Medieval Greece* (London, John Murray, 1991), fig. 1; plate 16.6: photo: J. Allen Cash; figures 16.1–2: drawn for this book; plate 17.1: from F.-M. Tsigakou, *The Rediscovery of Greece* (London: Thames & Hudson, 1981), pl. 8; plate 17.2: Athens, Benaki Museum, from F.-M. Tsigakou, *The Rediscovery of Greece* (London: Thames & Hudson, 1981), pl. 72; figures 17.1 and 17.4 drawn for this book; figure 17.2: based on *Osmanisches Reich – Die Provinzerwaltung am Ende des 19. Jahrhunderts*, sheet B IX 13 of the *Tübingen Atlas des Vorderen Orients* (Wiesbaden: Dr Ludwig Reichert Verlag, 1979); figure 17.3: based on J. Cvijić, *La Péninsule balkanique: géographie humaine* (Paris: Armand Colin, 1918), p. 223; plate 18.1: photo: Athens, Hellenic Literary and Historical Archive; plate 18.2: after *National Geographic Magazine*, November 1925; plate 18.3: after V. P. Mathiopoulos, *Eikones Katokhis* (Athens: Hermes, 1990), p. 89; plate 18.4: after C. M. Woodhouse, *The Rise and Fall of the Greek Colonels* (London: Associated Press, 1985), opposite p. 84; plate 18.5: photo: Athens, Hellenic Literary and Historical Archive, and Manuscripts Division, J. Willard Marriott Library, University of Utah; plates 19.1–2: photos: Rome, Deutsches Archäologisches Institut (72.2400 and 57.1085); plate 19.3: Rome, Vatican Library MS Chigi F.v.110 fol. 39v, after R. Weiss, *The*

*Renaissance Discovery of Classical Antiquity* (Oxford: Blackwell Publishers, 1969), pl. 11; plate 19.4: after *The Iliad of Homer,* *engraved by T. Piroli from the compositions of John Flaxman* (London, 1793), pl. 27; plate 19.5: after Thomas Major, *The Ruins of Paestum* (London, 1768), pl. 7.

# PART 1

## Landscape, Seascape

# 1 / THE PHYSICAL BACKGROUND

## *Friedrich Sauerwein*

### INTRODUCTION

Greece lies on the southernmost spur of the Balkan peninsula, like a springboard pointing in the direction of Asia Minor and Africa. For thousands of years it has been an intermediary for the cultural currents flowing from East to West and vice versa. Greece is also a land open to, and penetrated by, the sea. In addition to its current territorial area of *c.*132,000 sq km (almost identical with that of England (131,500 sq km)), it has 3,054 islands. This results in a coastline of 15,000 km, whereas Italy, which is a much larger country (301,000 sq km), has a coastline of only 8,700 km. But Greece is also a mountainous country. Twenty mountain summits rise over 2,000 metres, and the highest elevation is reached with the mountain of the gods, Olympos, at 2,917 metres.

In order to present this area as a platform on which to set the history that has shaped our world, it is necessary to depict its fundamental structures – geological, tectonic, morphological, climatic and botanic.

### GEOLOGICAL AND TECTONIC PROCESSES SHAPE THE STRUCTURE OF THE GREEK HABITAT

An old legend is often told in Greece. When God created the earth, he used a sieve to distribute good soil everywhere, keeping back the stones in the sieve. He then threw the stones over his shoulder and created Greece. In reality, this means that only 30 per cent of Greek soil can be used for agriculture: the rest of the terrain is stony and mountainous.

In a geological sense, like all southern European peninsulas, Greece is numbered among the youngest parts of the continent. In the deep basins and channels of the original sea (Tethys), debris from adjacent continental masses accumulated from Palaeozoic times and portions that broke off formed huge chalky deposits in the sea. Lateral pressure on these sediment layers, often several kilometres

**Plate 1.1**   A text-book illustration of zigzag folds in limestone plates, on the road from Igoumenitsa to Ioannina (1974)

thick, compressed, folded and finally lifted them above sea level to form mountains. Extensive overthrust folds indicate the force behind this folding process which started about 140 million years ago in Mesozoic times and continued, in several cycles, up to the Tertiary period, 20–15 million years ago.

The explanation offered by modern geophysicists for the cause of this tectonic upheaval is that the huge African plate collided with the Eurasian and the small Aegean plates, and that during this process the African plate slid beneath the other two as a result of lateral drift. This process is called subduction. As though gripped in a vice, the strata underwent distortion because of the high pressures exerted over a considerable period of time and sometimes too because of high temperatures. In addition to this overall shrinking of the earth's crust, there were also areas of internal expansion. The earth's crust fractured along what are known as fault lines and shifted in both vertical and horizontal directions. Trench rifts were formed, as for instance the Gulfs of Corinth and of northern Euboia, and horsts (raised blocks of land edged by faults) were pushed up, like slabs of earth lifted vertically. In this way a network of faults developed throughout the Greek-Aegean region (see plate 1.1).

The formation of a volcanic chain is a typical occurrence in the vicinity of a subduction (or Benioff) zone, and this is what we find in Greece. From Nisyros via Santorini (Thera), Melos, Methana and Aigina, this chain extends along the eastern coast of Greece to Macedonia. Today only the Santorini volcano remains active (its last eruption was in 1956).

This process in the history of the earth is not yet complete. Subduction continues in the region south of Crete and also along the western coast of Greece. New folded mountains will eventually appear. Dislocations along the fault lines will trigger new earthquakes and the area will undergo change. These processes will, however, take place over periods so long as to be beyond the range of our human imagination. According to geophysical measurements the movement of plates in relation to each other amounts to about 2.5 cm per annum. This might seem microscopic, but in 1,000 years this will amount to 250 m, in 100,000 years to 25 km and, provided the pace remains constant, in one million years it will mean a distance of 250 km.

The collision of the African and the Eurasian continents caused the whole Mediterranean region to become a highly active earthquake belt. Earthquakes originate when static energy, which is built up by tensions in the earth's crust, is converted into kinetic energy and transmitted in wave-like movements. Today these tremors are registered on a seismogram by freely suspended seismographs at earthquake observation points. From the picture of the curve on the graph, the strength of the earthquake and its hypocentre within the earth's crust can be calculated. The point on the surface above this hypocentre where the greatest destruction occurs is known as the epicentre. Ninety per cent of all earthquakes are tectonic quakes, which cause damage over wide areas, 7 per cent (affecting medium areas) stem from volcanic activity and only 3 per cent (affecting small areas) result from the collapse of caves.

The strength of an earthquake is expressed on the Richter scale, which is open-ended. It is a logarithmic scale, which means that each additional point on the scale (e.g. from 4.5 to 5.5) signifies a doubling of the strength of the quake. Greece has an average of about 272 earthquakes per annum. Most of them, however, are not experienced by human beings and only measurable on seismometers.

Despite all this scientific research it is not yet possible to predict earthquakes accurately. This means that there is no reliable early warning system; they arrive unannounced and so cause death and destruction. Often, when buildings collapse, fires break out with nothing to restrain them and devastating conflagrations begin, which cannot easily be extinguished as the waterpipes are fractured at the same time. One solution is the development of relatively 'earthquake-proof' construction techniques using reinforced concrete.

Earthquakes demonstrate particularly clearly how vulnerable mankind is to natural disasters. A quake is capable of destroying the cultural heritage of generations in a few seconds. This has been true from antiquity until the present time, and can be illustrated by a short list of earthquakes:

| | |
|---|---|
| 464 BC | A devastating earthquake in the Eurotas Valley (southern Peloponnese) is said to have cost 20,000 lives – among them was a group of Spartan young men in a gymnasium (Plutarch *Kimon* 16). |
| 426 BC | A strong earthquake in Locris, accompanied by *tsunamis* (Thucydides *Histories* 3.89); the peninsula of Atalante became an island. |
| Sixth century AD | The destruction of Olympia (see plate 1.2). |
| 12 October 1856 | Crete with Heraklion at its epicentre. |
| 9 September 1867 | Off the Mani peninsula, a seaquake with *tsunamis.* |
| 27 August 1886 | Centre in Messenia. |
| 1894 | East Locris. |
| 16 June 1926 | Rhodes. |
| 1928 | An earthquake destroys the city of Corinth. |
| 30 July 1944 | The west coast of the Mani peninsula. |
| 1953 | The Ionian islands. |
| 31 December 1975 | Aitolia and Acharnania. |
| 1976 | Thessaloniki. |
| 1980 | Plataia in Boiotia. |
| 1981 | Corinth. |
| 13 September 1986 | Kalamata in Messenia. |

This list is bound to grow.

In the context of this brief chapter it is impossible to depict the complex geological and tectonic processes within this region in

**Plate 1.2**  The Zeus temple at Olympia brought down in a severe earthquake in the sixth century AD (1984)

exhaustive scientific detail. Nor is this our aim; the object is to demonstrate how varied the factors were which led to the creation of the Greek landscape.

The Greek mountains are characterized by their fold structures, but the effects of the changes resulting from geological faults are much more important. These led to the area being split up and broken into small basins, plains and coastal creeks, which are separated from one another by mountain barriers. These easily defined territories became the sites for the numerous Greek city-states (*poleis*). No large states could be formed in Greece to parallel those created in the broad plains between the Tigris and Euphrates rivers, or on the banks of the River Nile.

Historians often think only in terms of the time in which events take place and geologists often see history only in space. But man lives in both time and space.

## MORPHOLOGICAL PROCESSES MOULD STRUCTURES INTO SCULPTURES

Geological and tectonic processes are caused by the operation of endogenous forces, against which exogenous forces perform. Chemical and biological processes, operating in various combinations,

**Plate 1.3** Grooves caused by the effect of rainwater on a massive limestone block at Plagia (1992)

produce weathering of the earth's surface and lead to a smoothing of the exposed material. Under the influence of gravity as well as water, ice and wind, material is removed ('eroded') or amassed ('accumulated'). Mountains are eroded, plains built up or aggraded, and the sharp edges of basic geological structures are smoothed over and remodelled, just as a sculpture is created by a mason from a block of stone.

As large expanses of Greece consist chiefly of limestones, the formation of karst landscapes plays a very important role. Lime dissolves in water containing $CO_2$. Conversely, lime-saturated water deposits lime when evaporation takes place. This process is followed by the formation of dripstone deposits, which leads to the creation of stalagmites and stalactites in caves, or travertine barriers in waterfalls.

Depending on the location or slope of limestone surfaces rainwater flowing off them creates a pattern of clefts and grooves (see plate 1.3). Where water gathers in small hollows, karst bowls are formed and eventually holes appear and penetrate right through the rock (swallow holes). When these drain, the holes are then enlarged by further erosion to form deep ravines. So, as this process advances, the rock surfaces are carved into a rich mosaic of bizarre clefts and clints, which, as a result of the sharp ridges and ribs between the concave landforms, are difficult to walk across. Between the karst rocks insoluble residual deposits are found scattered, and these form skeletal soils that support sparse vegetation.

In addition to these small-scale karst phenomena, larger karst depressions exist such as *dolines* and *poljes*. *Dolines* are mostly conical depressions, generated by the collapse of a rock-ceiling above a cave, or by far-reaching erosion of the rock. They may have a diameter varying from a few metres to several hundred. When the floor is sealed by residual clay, lakes are formed in them, which are drained by subterranean *katavothres* (swallow holes) on the karst edges. In karst areas these are used as rainwater reservoirs, or cattle drinking troughs. Where extensive collapse has occurred, the resulting features are called *uvalas*.

By contrast, *poljes* are large phenomena of karst morphology, several square kilometres in size; mostly they are elongated basins with flat floors and steep enclosing walls and are created by solutional modification of downfaulted or downfolded blocks. Here too drainage takes place via subterranean *katavothres*. Owing to their size, drainage nets from the surrounding area can flow into such *poljes*. If the *katavothres* cannot drain off all the water that collects during the winter rains, it penetrates the underground karst-hydrographic system. This produces a backwater in the subterranean karst system, and the swallow holes are turned into spouts as they pump additional water into the *poljes*. During the rainy season lakes thus flood the *poljes* and they are only drained away at the beginning of the dry season, exposing fertile soil for agricultural use.

*Poljes* resulting from erosion increase or widen the tectonic basin landscapes. Fluvial erosion and accumulation of deposits lead to intensive moulding of geotectonic base structures. This occurs under the influence of human destruction of vegetation. The morphological processes on the coast have had a particularly strong sculptural effect.

The plain of Lake Kopais in Boiotia provides an interesting example. Here the River Kephisos used to cause flooding every year because the large *katavothres* at the eastern edge of the basin could not contain the volume of water that accumulated in the winter. All ancient and medieval drainage projects failed until at the end of the nineteenth century a tunnel was built forming an artificial *katavothra*, which provided the necessary drainage. A clever solution was, however, devised by the Minyans about 3,500 years ago.

They built their settlements near the fortress of Gla in the plain, surrounded them with powerful embankments and lived as the Dutch do today below the winter sea-level in the reclaimed land behind their dykes.

Due to rapid erosion of the deposits, karst landscapes are among the driest and most sterile areas of Greece. Yet they protect precious rainwater from evaporation by withdrawing it from direct circulation and storing it in the cave system of the karst topography. If this stored water comes into contact with saturated strata or with ground water accumulated in loose basin sediments, this can give rise to karst springs that flow all year round.

Karst caves must have been known to inhabitants of Greece since time immemorial. Otherwise the naturalistic image of the subterranean rivers of the Underworld and the ferryman Charon, as found in Greek mythology, would be impossible to explain. Today they provide tourist attractions.

In addition to the territory of karst phenomena, the activity of water plays another equally important role in the shaping of the Greek landscape. Climate too plays a crucial role. As well as the rivers that flow all year round, there are numerous river beds, which are dry in summer and only fill with water during the rainy season in winter. For this reason the Greeks call these rivers *cheimarroi* ('winter torrents'). The main dividing line in the year falls in the period of summer drought. After this is over, because the earth's pores are filled with air to great depths, the parched soil is incapable of absorbing the heavy precipitation characteristic of the beginning of the rainy season. Water flows over the surface, carrying with it loose material and filling the beds of dried-up rivers and streams with brown cloudy torrents. Huge masses of debris roll down from the mountains and form deposits in the peripheral areas, where lower speeds reduce the river's carrying power.

Some figures serve to illustrate the seasonal erosive power of the water. Depending on the season, the discharge of the Aliakmon River (in Macedonia) varies from 13 to 3,300 cubic metres per second and that of the Axios River (modern Vardar, also in Macedonia) from 10 to about 3,800 cubic metres per second. As a result, they formed huge deltas in the bay of Thessaloniki. Similar data are provided by all Greek rivers.

The small gorges and valleys in the mountains and the broad cones of debris and alluvial deposits building up against mountain

**Plate 1.4** 'Badlands' created by human destruction of vegetation at Eptachorion in the Grammos Mountains (Epirus) (1986)

barriers are clear signs of Mediterranean river erosion. They demonstrate that, due to the high level of land relief caused by the proximity of the mountains to the coastline, the erosive power of the rivers proves very effective. The alluvial plains, which were formed as a result of irregular sedimentation, are partly turned into bogs, particularly when rivers meander widely through flat areas.

Deforestation and the destruction of vegetation, which have been taking place since antiquity up until recent times, especially in the nineteenth century, accelerate the erosion process more than ever (see plate 1.4). The washing off of soil cover and the weathering crusts have transformed the mountains into a skeletal karst landscape. Former important harbours such as Pella, the birthplace of Alexander the Great, silted up and are now situated far inland. In general Greece lacks extensive alluvial plains, because the most recent geological epochs have caused isolated peaks to project above the level ground.

The coasts of Greece are subject to constant change. Here currents transport material eroded by waves, and by this action coastlines are both destroyed and formed. Steep cliffs are undercut and eaten away, spits and lagoons appear, forming graded coasts (where there is a balance between erosion and deposition) or leaving capes

**Plate 1.5** The deep penetration of the land by the sea viewed from the Plagia summit, across Leukas to Kephallonia (1992)

jutting out into the sea. Continuous vertical tectonic movements, as well as fluctuations in the sea level stemming from the Ice Age, have drowned earlier coastlines, or raised them as much as several hundred metres above the present-day sea level. This has resulted in an endless variety, so that every bay and stretch of coast has a character of its own.

The Greek mountains are not friendly to traffic. They make the opening up of the hinterland, consisting as it does of characteristically isolated landscape units, very difficult; communication with other centres is also hard. That is why for thousands of years important thoroughfares have been by way of the sea, making it possible to penetrate far into the interior via the countless bays (see plate 1.5).

The individual character of the various areas within Greece is further enhanced by the numerous islands. Within the border of the modern state, there are 151 inhabited islands, which together with the uninhabited ones make up 19 per cent of the whole country. No island is more than forty kilometres from its neighbour. This serves to underline the role of Greece as a series of stepping stones between East and West more clearly than anything else.

## CLIMATE INFLUENCES MAN'S WAY OF LIFE AND ECONOMY

Greece lies in the Mediterranean sub-tropical zone. Its climate is more often referred to as etesian. Etesian is the name given to dry northerly winds, which start in May, are at their strongest in July and August, and begin gradually to die down in September. They originate from the Azores anticyclone to the north in the region of the trade winds and flow via an endlessly long route to the Mesopotamian low-pressure area in the Persian Gulf, ending in the intertropical convergence zone. In so doing they acquire their dry, continental characteristics above Middle Europe and the Balkans. The relatively high reliability of these air currents bestows upon Greece its dry, hot summers.

The transition to the rainy winter is most abrupt. Heavy thunderstorms with high rainfall announce that this region is being drawn into the westerly wind-drift currents of the damp, temperate zone. Cyclones move along several predictable wind channels from west to east across the Mediterranean basin, though always interspersed with periods of fine weather. Because of the change in pressure conditions, the spring months are unstable, and thunderstorms are a frequent occurrence.

As these changes in the weather do not correspond to the central European seasons, it has been suggested that the year should be divided into three phases:

| | |
|---|---|
| Season of flowering and ripening | c.March to June |
| Dry season | c.June to October |
| Wet season | c.October to March |

The accompanying illustrations (see figure 1.1 and table 1.1) present six climate diagrams showing two profiles moving from east to west over the Greek peninsula. Each profile includes two coastal stations with a mountain station between them. Despite their similar basic structure, the diagrams reveal considerable differences. The amount of precipitation in the western and the mountain areas is much greater than in the dry and arid east. The intensity and duration of the dry summer months increases, as we move from north to south. The shortest and least pronounced phase is recorded at the mountain station of Ioannina. If one takes into

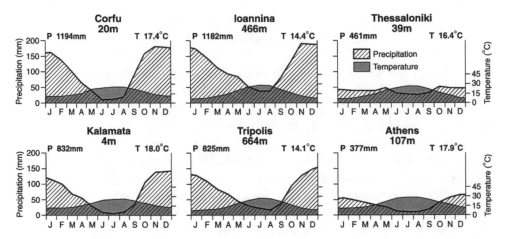

**Figure 1.1** Plan of annual temperature (T) and precipitation (P) at mid-month over a period of thirty years (1951–80)

| | Temperature (°C) | | Precipitation (mm) |
|---|---|---|---|
| | Absolute Maximum | Absolute Minimum | Maximum in 24 hours |
| **Corfu** 20m | 38.8 August | -5.0 January | 161.1 October |
| **Ioannina** 466m | 40.8 August | -9.9 February | 92.0 November |
| **Thessaloniki** 39m | 41.6 July | -9.5 February | 77.2 November |
| **Kalamata** 4m | 45.0 June | -3.4 February | 104.3 October |
| **Tripolis** 664m | 41.0 August | -17.0 January | 91.0 November |
| **Athens** 107m | 43.0 June | -5.5 January | 114.9 November |

**Table 1.1** Extreme values of temperature and precipitation

account the extreme values in the table alongside the mean values, it becomes clear from the range of temperatures that, for instance, winter frosts can endanger the agriculture in the coastal regions. In addition, rainfall is less frequent than in the temperate latitudes, so that, whereas heavy rains occur relatively frequently, persistent rain and drizzle are rare.

In general, the typical Mediterranean climate is limited to the coastal zones, while the mountain regions, particularly in the north of the country, correspond more closely to the continental climate of the Balkan peninsula. This also applies to the last Ice Age. Ice caps in the northern mountains reached significantly lower levels than in the south of the peninsula where rainy seasons determined the climate. Interruptions due to a change in climate in the historical period can be proved to a limited extent.

Despite high temperatures the Greek summer is bearable because of the relatively low humidity which prevents it being sultry. When 2,000 people died in Athens in 1987 during a heat wave, this is more likely to have been the result of the *nephos*, the pall of haze and smog that hangs over the city in the summer months.

The ancient Greeks called the main winds in their country after the wind gods and held fast to these names, notwithstanding the scientific progress made by thinkers, from the Ionian physicists to Aristotle. The specific properties of Notos (south), Zephyros (west), Boreas (north) and Euros (east) could easily be assigned to synoptic processes where the frequency and strength of the winds depend on the general meteorological conditions pertaining over the region at any one time.

Well into the Middle Ages the rhythmic breaks in the etesian climate made sea voyages dangerous during the winter months. Communications – and even wars – were interrupted. Today, however, the high reliability of the summer weather makes Greece a favourite destination for European tourists.

## CHARACTERISTIC FEATURES OF EAST MEDITERRANEAN VEGETATION

Climate is an abstract phenomenon, but it is given visible expression in the vegetation of the landscape. Whereas botanists work with classification methods, it would be as well here to focus on the ways in which vegetation adapts to dry seasons and on its capacity to survive – in other words, to think of outward features or ecological adaptation.

Shortages make economy in water consumption imperative. This can be achieved by evergreen plants which have developed protective measures against water evaporation:

- reduction of leaf surfaces so that broad leaf-like stalks and thorns develop (olive, wild pear, thistle);
- leather-hard leaves covered with a wax-like sheen (laurel, strawberry tree);
- deeper location of epidermal pores in cuticles;
- protection by a tomentum or covering of hair (acanthus);
- enveloping in a cloud of fragrance or essential oils (thyme).

This group of plants is called xerophytes (dry plants). The succulents (storage plants) behave in the opposite way by storing reservoirs of water for the dry season in leathery leaves and stems (opuntia). In addition numerous geophytes survive the dry season underground as tubers and bulbs (tulip), and therophytes, which are annuals, survive as seeds (anemone).

This means that Greek flora is characterized by its enormous variety. As so many species have to flower and bear fruit during a very short season, the 'barren stones' of Greece only blossom for a few short weeks. Then, once the summer heat begins, that splendour is replaced all too soon by withered and dry stems. The bright colours give way to the ochre-brown and grey shades of the dry season under the brilliant blue of the sky and the violet and ultramarine silhouettes of the bare mountains.

Of the original vegetation only a few meagre traces remain. For thousands of years right up to the present day man has exhausted its resources.

*Maquis* is particularly widespread in the damp western and northern areas. It consists of undergrowth and bush, one to five metres high, and is now commonly thought to be a degraded form of vegetation derived from high forest. Even more degraded and characteristic of large areas, especially in the drier east and the eastern islands, is *phrygana*. This is an extensive area of scrubland, with plants reaching ankle- or knee-height, cropped by sheep and goats. The lists below give some of the main plants characteristic of both formations: some can be traced back to the Tertiary period.

Plants of non-Greek origin, which have become well established in the Mediterranean environment, are the agave from Mexico (*Agava Americana*), the fig cactus (*Opuntia ficus indica*), bamboo from the Orient (*Arundo donax*) and the eucalyptus tree from Australia. With regard to cultivated plants, the percentage of exotic species is far higher. As examples mention might be made here of potatoes, maize and tobacco from 'The New World'; these have now developed into an important factor in the economy.

The evergreen Mediterranean vegetation is confined to the lowland and coastal areas. At higher altitudes both *phrygana* and *maquis* dwindle, and in place of evergreen oaks, Aleppo pines (*Pinus halepensis*) or cypresses (*Cupressus semper virens*), deciduous trees appear which reveal a capacity to adapt to two climates, this time to the cold as well. Black pines (*Pinus nigra* and *Pinus pallasiana*) and Apollo fir trees (*Abies cephalonica*) mark the tree line at an altitude of 1,700–2,000 metres duly modified by human intervention. Above this extends a region of alpine meadows with small bushes.

| Typical plants: *maquis* | |
|---|---|
| Holm oak | *Quercus ilex* |
| Kermes Oak | *Quercus coccifera* |
| Strawberry Tree | *Arbutus unedo* |
| Lentisk | *Pistacia lentiscus* |
| Laurel | *Laurus nobilis* |
| Myrtle | *Myrtus communis* |
| Broom | *Spartium junceum* |
| Oleander | *Nerium oleander* |
| Wild Olive | *Olea europea sylvestris* |
| Wild Pear Tree | *Pyrus salicifolia* |
| Cistus | *Cistus villosus* |

| Typical plants: *phrygana* | |
|---|---|
| Kermes Oak | *Quercus coccifera* |
| Thyme | *Thymus capitatus* |
| Blue Globe Thistle | *Echinops graecus* |
| Common Juniper | *Juniper communis* |
| Lavender | *Lavandula stoechas* |
| Asphodel | |
| Heathers | |
| Cistus plants | |
| Spurge plants | |

FURTHER READING

Crouch, D. P., 1993: *Water Management in Ancient Greek Cities*. New York: Oxford University Press.

*Greece Vols 1–3*. HMSO, Naval Intelligence Division, 1944.

Higgins, M. and Higgins, R., 1996: *A Geological Companion to Greece and the Aegean*. London: Duckworth.

Meiggs, R., 1982: *Trees and Timber in the Ancient Mediterranean World*. Oxford: Clarendon Press.

Pe, G. G. and Piper, D. J. W., 1972: 'Vulcanism at Subduction Zones: The Aegean Area', *Deltion Ellinikis Geologikis Etairias* (Athens) 9: 133–44.

Philippson, A., 1950–9: *Die griechischen Landschaften: eine Landeskunde* (4 vols). Frankfurt am Main: Klostermann.

Purcell, N. and Horden, P., 1997: *The Corrupting Sea*. Oxford: Blackwell Publishers.

Rackham, O., 1990: 'Ancient Landscapes', in O. Murray and S. Price (eds) *The Greek City, from Homer to Alexander*. Oxford: Clarendon Press.

Sallares, R., 1991: *The Ecology of the Ancient Greek World*. London: Duckworth.

Sauerwein, F., 1976: *Griechenland: Land, Volk, Wirtschaft in Stichworten*. Vienna: Hirt.

Sauerwein, F., 1980: *Spannungsfeld Ägäis*. Frankfurt am Main: Diesterweg and Aarau (Switzerland): Sauerländer.

# PART 2

## The March of the Past

# 2 / THE HUMAN FOREGROUND

## Robin Barber

### INTRODUCTION

The Early Bronze Age, with which most of this chapter is concerned, saw the beginnings of many of the important social, economic, technological and artistic developments which characterize the sophisticated Minoan and Mycenaean palace cultures of later Aegean prehistory. Study of the buildings and artefacts of this period enables us to build up a broad picture of the overall character of contemporary society and the changes which were taking place in various spheres, e.g. settlements, technology (see below). This in turn contributes to our understanding of the development both of material culture and of social and economic structures in human society as a whole. But investigation of the same buildings and artefacts on which broader conclusions are based also offers us insights into the personal lives and attitudes of individuals. Such insights constitute one of the most compelling appeals of archaeology, inviting us to reassess our own situations and attitudes in the light of what we learn about those of other times and other places. Art too is a primary concern, for Early Bronze Age artefacts are increasingly worthy of admiration for their own sake and aesthetic appeal and not simply as fodder for typological or statistical analysis. Brancusi and Henry Moore are among the sculptors who have found inspiration in the subtle and aesthetically pleasing forms of Early Cycladic marble work.

### HISTORICAL SURVEY

The earliest indications of a human presence in Greece go back to the Palaeolithic period, but it is only from the later phase (*c*.50,000 BC) that there is much in the way of excavated remains. From the Kleidhi Cave in Epirus stone and bone tools and environmental remains show a simple lifestyle based on hunting and gathering. The Franchthi Cave in the north-east Peloponnese, used from the later Palaeolithic until the end of the Neolithic period (*c*.3500 BC), has provided similar information and thrown light on a particularly significant development. This was the importation from the Aegean island of Melos of obsidian, a kind of volcanic glass which was highly valued as a cutting edge for tools and weapons. Although such technology now seems primitive, it is impossible to over-estimate the importance of the discovery of this rich source of material. Readily available, it contributed to greatly increased efficiency in many important activities such as the reaping and processing of grain crops and the working of wood, used for boats amongst other things, and thus to a better standard of living and the improvement of communications. The contact with Melos confirms the existence of sea travel and transport from at least 11,000 BC. This was just as important a step as the discovery of the obsidian, since it opened up avenues for social and economic exchange and progress.

The Neolithic period (*c.*7000–*c.*3500 BC) saw the appearance of settled communities and the domestication of animals and crops. Buildings were permanent and designed to fulfil specific functions.

The introduction of metal technology at the end of the Neolithic and the beginning of the Early Bronze Age has long been used by archaeologists as marking a stage of development which is significant chronologically (the 'Bronze Age') as well as technologically and socially. The quest for sources of raw material and/or finished artefacts stimulated wide contacts between centres of population and thus the exchange of information and ideas in every conceivable sphere of human activity. Specialist crafts developed (metallurgy is a prime example), society became more clearly stratified, and the status of individuals could be reinforced by the acquisition of precious objects (jewellery, vessels of precious metal, etc.).

In the Early Bronze Age (*c.*3500–*c.*2000 BC), the cultures of the Cycladic Islands, Crete and the southern Greek mainland – the three main regional divisions of prehistoric Greece, both geographically and culturally – have some fundamental differences, though within an overall similarity imposed mainly by shared geographical and climatic conditions. The middle phase of the period (*c.*2900–*c.*2300 BC) is particularly important in that interaction between the Aegean regions and with places further afield, becomes more intense, and technological developments and their applications faster and more evident. More complex forms of social organization can be deduced from the range and character of the buildings. In domestic agriculture, the vine and olive were added to the cereals of the Neolithic.

This stage was followed by a period of considerable disruption, most strikingly in the Cyclades, but also on the Greek mainland. Changes of site location and new artefact types suggest hostile movements into the Aegean of peoples from Anatolia (Asia Minor). These disrupted the existence of its inhabitants to varying degrees. One consequence, in the Cyclades at least, was a move towards concentration of the population of each island in one or two 'towns', presumably for security, a move which must have led to the formation of more centralized social organization. Crete was not affected by these threats, but increasing centralization can be seen nonetheless in the important centres with large building complexes which grew up at sites like Vasiliki and Knossos in the middle phase of the Early Bronze Age.

## SETTLEMENTS

In general, the location of settlements is influenced partly by geography and partly by prevailing political and commercial conditions. Hill sites give good drainage, protection from the wind (on sheltered slopes) and defensive advantages, the latter offered also by promontories. Proximity to agricultural land and/or other resources is important, as can be a seaside location for communications and fishing. Inland sites can also be natural centres of communication. Different factors are paramount according to needs at different times, but the most advantageous sites are those where all characteristics are present in some degree. Mycenae, in an elevated and defensible location, was occupied throughout the Bronze Age. The site is on the edge of the fertile plain of Argos and close to important north–south routes. Nor is it too far from the sea. Kastri on the Cycladic island of Syros, occupied at a time of stress and external threat, is a site where defensive considerations take priority over all else. It is high, remote and inaccessible; access to the sea is difficult and agricultural potential limited. Promontory sites, like Ayia Irini (see plate 2.1) in a deep bay on the island of Kea, are also naturally defensible, but here harvesting of the sea and involvement in marine communications must have been the primary reasons for its location. Knossos (see figure 3.2) is some distance inland and out of sight of the sea, but set in a fertile valley and on an important north–south route.

The layout of the buildings is often dictated by the lie of the land, a characteristic of Greek settlements of all periods whose

**Plate 2.1**  The Early Cycladic settlement at Ayia Irini on the island of Kea

conformation to the landscape is often striking – and something for the modern traveller to look for from the air when flying over Greece. Party walls are used where practicable. Construction at some sites such as Myrtos in Crete seems quite haphazard, small houses being squeezed in as and where possible; others such as Zygouries in the north-eastern Peloponnese were more organized, in a layout which approaches the rectilinear. Material varied according to what was available locally. In the Cyclades stone is ubiquitous and the houses of Early Bronze Age Ayia Irini on Kea took full advantage of the neat schist slabs. When a formal plan can be discerned, houses are usually roughly rectangular, sometimes apsidal, with one or two rooms. All probably had hearths. Stone benches could be used also as beds, wall niches as cupboards, perhaps too as places for devotional objects. There may have been wooden furniture, of which evidence only survives in the Late Bronze Age at Akrotiri on Thera, and textile carpets and hangings. A picture of domestic life can be enlarged by reference to more recent village custom where the climate encourages particular habits – outside ovens, dining, sleeping – and interior space is

**Plate 2.2**  A modern village on Seriphos

relatively unimportant for much of the year. The external appearance of these places may not have been so very different from
modern Seriphos, for instance, (see plate 2.2) where a bird's eye
view from the top of the village shows a patchwork of flat roofs
covering houses huddling one against the other.

Distinctively large buildings must point to important functions
and/or reflect the high status of those who occupied or used
them. Thus they can give clues to the nature of social organization.
Even in the Neolithic period, as at both Sesklo and Dimini in
Thessaly, one house in a settlement may stand out for its size and
complexity. It is natural to regard this as the head man's house and
the administrative and religious centre of the community. The
most striking form of main building in the Early Bronze Age is the
so-called 'Corridor House' of which the 'House of Tiles' at Lerna
(see figure 2.1) is the best known example. Central buildings are
important for protecting common resources and providing a focus
for communal activities and organization, which may have been in

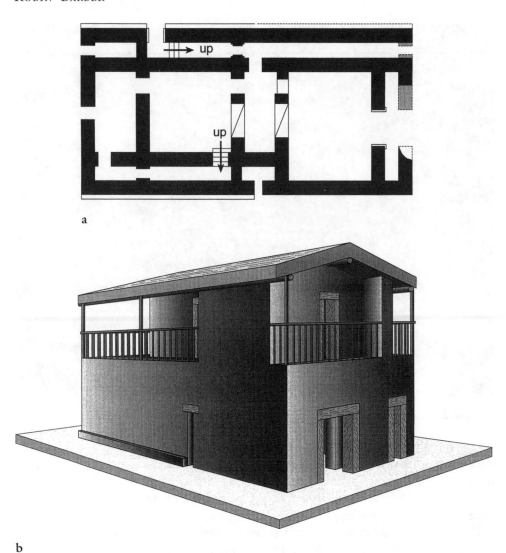

**Figures 2.1a–b** 'The House of Tiles' at Lerna, *c.*2600 BC: plan and restored view from the south-east

the hands of one family or clan. Dimini, Sesklo, Lerna, Kastri and some other sites have substantial protective circuit walls which demonstrate organized communal activity and technical skill as well as affirming the existence of threats to life which must remain to us indistinct. Sites where these relatively sophisticated architectural features are found may have been local administrative centres. Certainly, in the time of the 'House of Tiles', commercial contacts

**Plate 2.3**   Obsidian core, blade and flakes, from Sesklo

between settlements were increasing. To about the same period belongs a large building complex constructed round a courtyard at Vasiliki in Crete, an arrangement which looks forward (in both architectural form and the social organization it represents) to the Cretan palaces of the following period.

## TECHNOLOGY

Food and clothing are the most essential of human requirements, but other needs (e.g. military equipment, votive objects) are consequent on our basic psychological and sociological characteristics. Technology is developed to facilitate these. 'Luxury' products come later in the process unless they serve some higher purpose, for example as votive objects or prestige gifts.

With the domestication of crops in the Neolithic period, improvement of equipment for the harvesting and treatment of grain was a primary concern. Obsidian and flint provided blades for sickles, also probably for threshing sledges, examples of which can still occasionally be seen in use in the countryside. Simple two-part rotary stone querns were used for grinding. The process is little different now in unmechanized rural communities. Obsidian (see plate 2.3) also provided the blades of tools and weapons (arrowheads) even after the appearance of bronze, which did not become widespread until the middle phase of the Early Bronze Age. Even

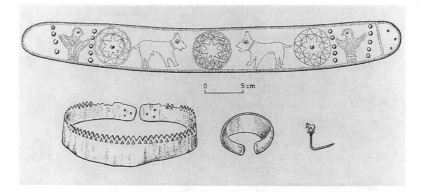

**Figure 2.2** Early Cycladic silver objects

then its use did not displace that of obsidian. Crete and the Cyclades were prominent in developments. Bronze was at first mainly arsenical, later tin. Initially at least it may have been more popular for prestige objects and for swords for which it was essential. The range of types gradually widened and knives, 'razors' and various types of jewellery are found. There are also vessels, and some other objects, in precious metals, e.g. diadems, bangles and pins of silver (see figure 2.2). Obsidian blades were produced by 'pressure-flaking', forcing them off a core with a wooden tool. Copper and silver ores are known to have been mined on Kythnos, Siphnos and in the Laurion area. Mines, with horizontal galleries and vertical shafts to the surface, also smelting furnaces, have been located. The mines sometimes contain discarded tools for extracting the ores. Casting equipment (e.g. moulds and crucibles, see figure 2.3) is known, as from Kastri on Syros. Siphnos was famous in later antiquity as a source of gold, as were certain places in northern Greece (Mt Pangaion), although the latter was not part of the Aegean cultural sphere in the Early Bronze Age and, if raw material was imported from there, it must have been as a commercial venture.

The most commonly used material was terracotta. In particular, ceramic containers were used for a far greater range of functions than we would consider today, when many of them have been subsumed by plastic. The basic processes of pottery production (clay collection and preparation, forming, drying, decorating, firing) are traditional. Early vessels were hand- rather than wheel-made, and fired in simple kilns. Their forms and decoration could be subtle and sophisticated (see below).

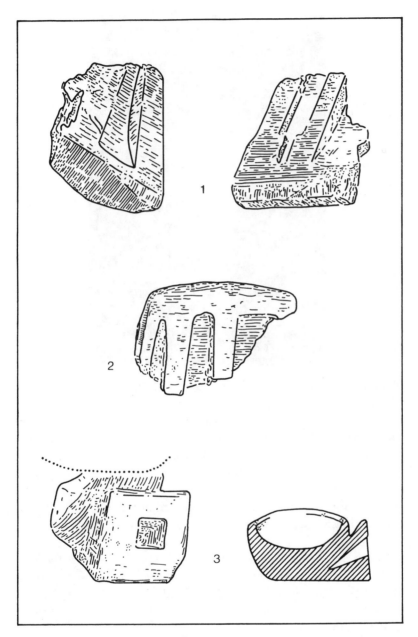

**Figure 2.3** Early Cycladic IIIA stone moulds and crucible, from Kastri on Syros, *c.*2300 BC

**Plate 2.4**  Cycladic marble figure, *c.*2600–2400 BC

Other materials used were marble, as evidenced by stone vases (the Cyclades, Crete) and figures (the Cyclades; see plate 2.4), and wood, the latter for the ships of which we have pictorial evidence and the carts which may be assumed to have existed, as well as many other minor objects (figurines?) which have not survived. The interiors of stone vases were hollowed out by simple reed drills and an abrasive (emery from Naxos), the latter also used for smoothing the surface.

Sheep and goats were the most common animals, kept for food and for their skins and wool. Cattle were probably first prized for their capabilities in terms of traction and transport rather than for food. Spindle-whorls and loomweights testify to the production of woollen fabrics.

## COMMERCE AND INTERACTION

There are plentiful signs of contacts between sites in the form of artefacts characteristic of one place or area found in another. Such finds are more common in some periods (the middle phase of the Early Bronze Age) than others, and it is debatable to what extent they represent direct and deliberate connections between the place of production and the place of discovery rather than haphazard transfer from hand to hand. Some form of commerce can hardly be doubted, stimulated by the want of 'essential' commodities like obsidian, copper ore or tin, or simply by the desirable product (wine) of a particular locality. The discovery of the same seal impression at three different mainland sites (Lerna, Tiryns and Zygouries) hints at a bureaucratic organization of trade, at least in some instances. When 'foreign' elements are found in greater intensity e.g. the Early Cycladic graves and funerary objects at Marathon, different explanations are needed, and it seems more likely that they represent not some form of 'colonialism' but rather a different regional structure in the Early Bronze Age when this part of the mainland coast belonged to the Cycladic cultural area. For the Cycladic figurines in Crete there may be a different explanation, since they are not accompanied by other Cycladic features. They may represent the presence of some settlers within the local community, but just as likely the desire of Cretans to possess exotic objects. Anatolian finds in the Cyclades in the later Early Bronze Age, taken together with clear evidence of disruption (new defensive sites, the disappearance of traditional marble-working) must represent invasion. A much more general indication of 'contact', and thus probably favourable trading conditions, is the wide Aegean spread of the sauceboat pottery form in the middle phase of the Early Bronze Age.

Contact requires transport. Walking and animal transport do not leave direct indications but there is clear evidence of shipping in the form of depictions on vases, and shipwrecks, as at Dhokos near Hydra. The Dhokos wreck was carrying a considerable variety of products, including vases (some presumably with contents) and millstones.

## PERSONAL BELIEFS AND RITUAL PRACTICES: FUNERARY ARCHITECTURE

The mysterious and inexplicable cycle of the seasons, of birth and death in crops, animals and human life, encourages belief in superhuman powers.

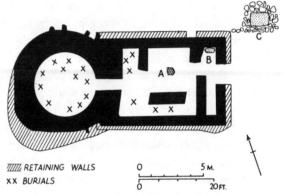

RETAINING WALLS
XX BURIALS

0            5 M.

0            20 FT.

**Figure 2.4** An Early Minoan tholos tomb at Apesokari on the Mesara Plain, Crete, *c.*2000 BC

Concern for the dead, shown in the form of elaborate resting-places and grave goods, betrays beliefs in another life whose details we will never understand. Both Crete and the Cyclades in the Early Bronze Age have substantial, though quite different, funerary architecture and associated objects. In Crete, especially the Mesara area, large circular stone-built tombs (see figure 2.4) were probably family or clan burial places. The burials were accompanied by various and often valuable items (pottery, figurines, stone vases, seals, jewellery, weapons). The remains of the deceased were eventually consigned to ossuaries, also stone-built. Religious rites were conducted at altars close by. In the Cyclades, cist tombs – small box-like stone chambers – were clustered together in cemeteries, like that at Ayioi Anargyroi on Naxos. The amount of burial goods varied greatly but some contained marble figurines and vases which are normally, but not exclusively, found in graves. Over the graves, and sometimes as independent structures serving the whole cemetery, were built platforms. On these, rituals were performed which apparently included drinking and the smashing of the vessels used. The evidence for ceremonies associated with the dead suggests that ancestors were important in contemporary religion. Other ways of disposal of the dead (cremation, burial in jars) are known at various times in the Neolithic and Early Bronze Age. Finds from mainland Greece are scanty, suggesting different practices, and perhaps different beliefs.

Information about religious activities unconnected with funerary practice is less easy to come by. The hill-top Peak Sanctuaries of later Crete probably began to be used in the Early Bronze Age, and Mikri Vigla on Naxos seems to have been a focus of Early Cycladic cult. Figurines found in settlements hint at the existence of domestic shrines.

There has been speculation that the Early Cycladic marble figures (see plate 2.4) were first displayed in private (or public) shrines and only later deposited with the dead (with the individuals who had originally dedicated them at crucial points in their lives – childbirth, war, rites of passage), also that the island of Keros, where larger quantities of marble objects have been found than can be explained as the contents of looted graves, was some kind of a pan-Cycladic sanctuary. Offerings (e.g. figurines of animals, nursing mothers) suggest concerns with human and animal life and fertility and that of crops. If some are deities, their function was to please and propitiate.

## ARTS AND CRAFTS

In this sphere pottery is very prominent (see above). Although there are many coarse domestic vessels, which usually lack surface finish, most shapes are, from the beginning, well balanced. Decoration is achieved by varying the surface-finish with coating, burnishing etc. and/or by incising or painting patterns. In the Cyclades these may be filled with a white substance to bring out the motifs. Designs are mostly geometric, at first rectilinear but later relaxing into the use of curved elements. But there are also a few pictorial

**Plate 2.5**  Early Cycladic II clay frying pan, from Chalandriani on Syros, *c*.2500 BC

motifs (see plate 2.5). In the Cyclades again, the fact that many of these are derived from shipping or the female body is surely symbolic of the importance of the former to material prosperity and the latter to the survival and physical well-being of the community. In Crete and the Cyclades vessels were also made of marble and, to a lesser extent, other stones. Cycladic pieces tend to be of white marble, whereas the Cretan are often variegated. Shapes follow those of pottery. The lines are often simple and very appealing. Figures were also made in marble, mainly in the Cyclades. The folded-arm form is the most common, but there are others, including the 'hunter-warrior'. The small terracotta votive figurines which were common dedications, mainly in Crete, are mostly important for what they tell us about the interests and concerns of their dedicators (as discussed above) than any artistic quality. Metalwork is mostly functional (bronze cauldrons, swords and daggers), but there are some vessels of gold and silver and occasional pieces of jewellery with repoussé decoration. Seals, at first of soft stone and other malleable materials (ivory), are particularly common in Crete, some with the body of the object in animal form. They were the precursors of one of the most accomplished art-forms of the Minoan palaces, where a wider range of materials, shapes and motifs was employed and techniques became highly sophisticated. There are also some seals and impressions from the Neolithic and from the mainland Early Bronze Age. Their function was to provide marks of personal ownership, perhaps also amuletic.

## LIFE IN THE CYCLADES IN THE EARLY BRONZE AGE

What sort of a picture can be built up of life in a settlement of the Early Bronze Age? Let us focus on the Cyclades. Early villages were small, usually not more than a few families, perhaps like some modern farmsteads, each with its own threshing floor. Island landscapes seem superficially bare but often have surprising green pockets near a water source. Settlement gravitated to these and particularly to the larger coastal plains, where proximity to agricultural land was combined with access to the sea. Hill and promontory sites as Ayia Irini on Kea were popular. Hillsides may have been terraced, as in later times when Pholegandros provides a spectacular example.

Into such physical surroundings were ancient islanders born. The concern for pregnant women, not entirely disinterested since healthy children would secure the future both of the family and the community, is shown by the swollen bellies of some of the marble figurines and with the rearing of small children by crude clay figurines apparently of nursing mothers. Their houses were small but not necessarily primitive, kept tidy by conscious domestic effort. Wooden furniture and fresco decoration are attested by the Late Bronze Age, but there may have been simpler equivalents in the earlier period. We can imagine children playing outside, or in the narrow alleys of larger sites, developing attachments to domestic animals which are reflected in some of the figurines, if these are toys. As soon as old enough, they would have been pressed into service to help with agricultural activities, perhaps too with the domestic production of pottery or textiles. Growing strength and maturity brought greater possibilities of contribution to family and community, recognized certainly in rites of passage for which some of the figurines (warriors, mature women) may have been manufactured. Each house probably had its devotional objects and there were presumably centres of public ritual, though, apart from the Cretan and Cycladic cemeteries, there is little evidence for either of these. In the community at large, rituals and festivals connected with the land would have been paramount and carefully observed, partly indeed for bringing relief from the hard grind of everyday life. Again we can look to Greece in more recent times when religious festivals can encompass trading and the marketing of livestock, as well as providing an occasion for intercommunal negotiation. Recreation in general was probably based on what was readily available – conversation, sitting in the cool of the summer evening or huddling round the winter hearth; swimming; perhaps board games. Travel would have been very limited – walking to the fields, perhaps to neighbouring settlements. Sea transport may have been in specialized hands, and the arrival and departure of vessels, especially on longer trading voyages, an excitement, especially if visitors spoke strange languages, as the Cretans did. Visitors might be hostile, sometimes surely pirates.

Warfare is rather a grand term for the local skirmishes over land or trading rights which were probably the main causes of conflict, but they would have been nonetheless critical and frightening events. Fear of them led to the building of defences – a major public project. In the last phase of the Early Bronze Age, there is evidence of international conflict. But here, as in the description of so many aspects of prehistoric life, we must take care not to give those terms a modern interpretation. There was no warfare involving vast nations and elaborate organization. Rather we should see small groups of people being forced (by famine or some other cause?) to move individually although as part of a larger wave of which they were not necessarily aware, bringing with them customs and artefacts which are then introduced with varying degrees of permanence to those communities which they manage to dominate. These conflicts were international, not in scale, but because they involved people from outside the Aegean area.

Administration in the smallest settlements was most likely based on the structure of the family. Few were large enough for us to think in terms of organizational bodies. It is depressing, though perhaps unsurprising, that we know relatively so much about death. Life expectancy was limited: twenty-six has been suggested as an average expectation at birth, for the Late Bronze Age. The dead had a contact with another world denied to the living and were of potential benefit to them. Thus they were provided with elaborate graves and equipment. Funerals would inevitably have been a time of personal sorrow and reflection on the human condition. We can visualize grave construction, a sad procession of participants approaching the cemetery of Ayioi Anargyroi on Naxos, laying their dead in the grave together with belongings, performing the appropriate rituals with food and wine and returning to the settlement to get on with their lives. Anniversaries would have been conscientiously observed.

FURTHER READING

Barber, R. L. N., 1987: *The Cyclades in the Bronze Age.* London: Duckworth/ Iowa City: University of Iowa Press.

Dickinson, O. T. P. K., 1994: *The Aegean Bronze Age.* Cambridge: Cambridge University Press.

Fitton, J. L., 1989: *Cycladic Art.* London: British Museum.

Higgins, R., 1981: *Minoan and Mycenaean Art* (2nd edn). London: Thames and Hudson.

Hood, M. S. F., 1967: *The Home of the Heroes: The Aegean before the Greeks.* London: Thames and Hudson.

Hood, M. S. F., 1971: *The Minoans.* London: Thames and Hudson.

Hood, M. S. F., 1978: *The Arts in Prehistoric Greece.* Harmondsworth: Penguin/New Haven: Yale University Press.

MacDonald, W. A. and Thomas, C. G., 1990: *Progress into the Past: The Rediscovery of Mycenaean Civilization* (2nd edn). Bloomington and Indianapolis: Indiana University Press.

Treuil, R., Darcque, P., Poursat, J.-C. and Touchais, G., 1989: *Les Civilisations égéennes du néolithique et de l'âge du bronze.* Paris: Presses Universitaires de France.

Vermeule, E. T., 1972: *Greece in the Bronze Age* (2nd edn with new introduction). Chicago: University of Chicago Press.

Warren, P. M., 1989: *The Aegean Civilizations* (2nd edn). Oxford: Phaidon.

Warren, P. M. and Hankey, V., 1989: *Aegean Bronze Age Chronology.* Bristol: Bristol Classical Press.

# 3 / THE BRONZE AGE
PALACE SOCIETIES

## *Oliver Dickinson*

### EARLY DEVELOPMENTS

The Greeks had a tradition of a 'heroic age' of greatness in their past, but this preserved little information about the Bronze Age apart from the names of some of the great sites. For instance, the legends contain no suggestion that the civilization of Crete was not originally 'Greek', and many features of the 'heroic age', as vividly presented in the Homeric poems, find their best parallels in the 'Dark Age' that followed the collapse of the Bronze Age civilizations. Equally, in placing the establishment of the first settled communities only a few generations before the 'heroic age', Greek tradition preserved no hint of the length of human history in Greece. Archaeology provides a much longer perspective, stretching back many millennia, and important developments towards civilization were already taking place in the third millennium BC, when an interconnected group of complex societies became established in the south Aegean. The continuous history of many major settlements (e.g. Mycenae, Tiryns, Thebes, Mallia, Akrotiri) goes back to this time if not before. But for reasons that are still obscure the societies of the Greek mainland and the Cyclades effectively collapsed late in the third millennium, although there are few signs of trouble in Crete. There was recovery later in the Cyclades, but on the mainland society reverted to a village level and remained there for several centuries, during which it is hard to detect significant change, although population and prosperity may have slowly increased.

One very significant development in Crete and several south Aegean islands is the establishment of townlike settlements. Although often small (they can be 10,000 square metres or less in extent and few exceed 200,000 square metres), and hard to investigate in their earlier phases because of later overbuilding, they were clearly the largest concentrations of population in their territories, and possessed a street layout, onto which relatively complex building blocks fronted (see figure 3.1), and sometimes a fortification wall. These settlements would have acted as central

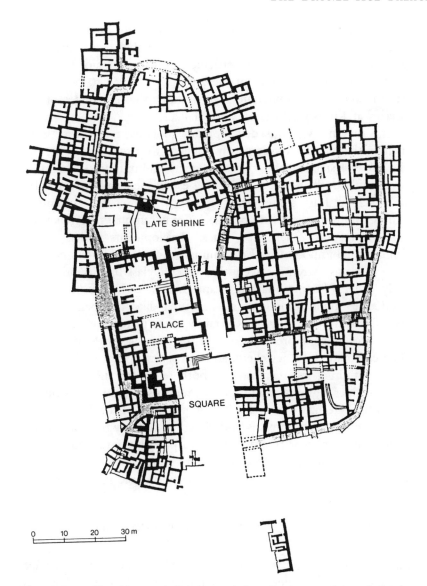

**Figure 3.1** The centre of the town of Gournia in east Crete. Second Palace Period

places, providing bases for the practice of crafts, overseas trade, large-scale storage, administration and probably communal religion. In the most important settlements on Crete major buildings which served one or more of these purposes began to be erected early in the second millennium BC, notably the first stages of the palaces at Knossos, Phaistos, and Mallia.

The reasons why this development took place in Crete must include the island's fertility, early contacts with the Near East, and the notable stability and cohesion of its communities, which are perceptible both in the already long-established collective tombs, of which at least some were apparently focuses for communal rituals, and in the growing popularity of communal religious sites, particularly peak sanctuaries. These developments underline the fundamental importance of communal religion to Minoan civilization: it seems extremely likely that its elite class had its origins in early leaders of communal ritual, and that the labour and resources needed to build monumental structures like the palaces were mobilized through religion. Certainly, once pictorial evidence becomes common, representations of the elite class, identifiable by their elaborate dress, jewellery, and hair styles, appear exclusively in scenes of ritual and ceremonial; both sexes are shown, but no obvious ruler figures stand out, and it remains questionable whether Minoan Crete had monarchs. The importance of the Minoan palaces as ceremonial centres is underlined by the way that their plans include not only courtyards that were probably intended for important assemblies, but special suites of rooms that are best interpreted as for ritual and ceremonial purposes (see figure 3.2).

## PALACE FUNCTIONS AND ECONOMY

Although the written material of the earlier stages of the palace societies remains undeciphered, it must seem likely that they had considerable structural similarities, especially in their economic organization, throughout their history, and that activities for which there is clear evidence in the Linear B tablets of the fourteenth and thirteenth centuries BC were already conducted in some form in the earlier palaces. From the start they apparently acted as centres of large-scale storage and focuses of important ceremonial/ritual activity, and patronized high-quality craftwork in metal, pottery (the famous 'Kamares' ware) and other materials. But it cannot

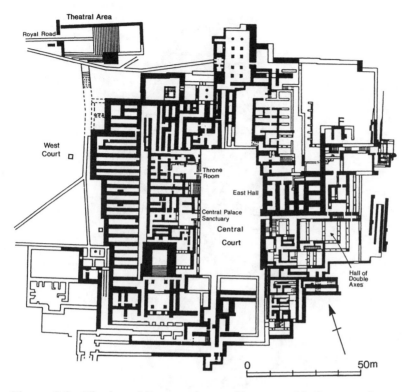

**Figure 3.2** The later Minoan palace at Knossos, with features of more than one period

be shown that they originally dominated society. It is reasonable to assume that the group or class which managed them expanded its power in the course of the First Palace Period, as the palaces themselves were expanded and incorporated features inspired by Near Eastern palatial architecture, such as fine stone masonry façades and columned entrances, to symbolize the status of their users. The 'palace class' also seems to have progressively adopted some arts of administration from the Near East. Most significant are the practice of using seals of stone and other materials to stamp clay sealings (see figure 3.3) that could be applied to containers and storeroom doors, thus controlling access to stored goods, and the use of written scripts to record and monitor the quantities and movements of such goods on rectangular tablets and other items of clay. Both sealings and inscribed items have been found collected in deliberate deposits, which suggests that they could serve as administrative tokens.

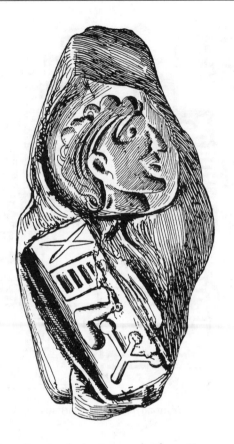

**Figure 3.3** A sealing made by two seals, from Knossos: one with a man's face, the other inscribed in the 'hieroglyphic' script. Early Second Palace Period

Whether the goods received in the palaces represent some form of general taxation, or simply the produce of palace-controlled land, this system indicates that civilization in Crete, as in the Near East, depended upon intensive exploitation of the land. The most recent analyses of the material replace the traditional view that a palace controlled all agricultural activity in its territory by a picture of parallel interacting economies, in which that of ordinary communities remained largely unspecialized and was not palace-directed, while that in territories under direct palatial control specialized in a few staples like wheat, olive oil, and wool. These would have been used to feed, provide materials for, and 'pay' those who managed or worked for the palace, including a large dependent workforce that produced highly specialized goods, particularly elaborate textiles. These could be used as prestigious gifts and religious offerings, but were more important for trade, which was absolutely necessary to obtain materials like metals that Crete did not have.

## THE DEVELOPMENT OF MINOAN CIVILIZATION

Although many features of Minoan civilization have Near Eastern analogues, it is distinctive for its unfortified major settlements (although a system of forts and guard posts, linked by roads, has been plausibly identified in eastern Crete) and for many features of its religion, especially the importance of rural sites such as peak sanctuaries and caves, and the perceived emphasis on epiphany rituals in which a god was summoned to a ritual and often impersonated by a human being. However, there is no good reason to believe either that this religion focused on a single, universal goddess, or the linked hypothesis that Minoan society was 'matriarchal', although women clearly played an important role in religion and hence in the elite class. Links with the Near East are clearest in the fields of craftwork and trade: a rather thin distribution of First Palace Period Minoan artefacts, mostly fine quality pots, in the Near East must reflect trading activity in some way and can be filled out by textual references to Kaptara, widely believed to signify Crete, in the archives of Mari on the Euphrates. These references indicate that Cretan merchants were present at the Syrian coastal city of Ugarit and received a quantity of tin, and that Cretan manufactured goods, including textiles and metalwork, reached Mari as royal gifts from Ugarit. By the seventeenth century, Crete may have been returning influences and even craftsmen to the Near East, to judge from the discovery of wall and floor paintings that have strong Minoan links at various sites, especially Tell ed-Dab'a (Avaris) in the Egyptian Delta, where the exceptionally rich material has now been dated to the beginning of the New Kingdom.

Although Kythera had effectively become part of the Minoan sphere by the beginning of the First Palace Period, in general Cretan influence expanded only slowly in the Aegean during this time. It may principally reflect an interest in trade for metals: copper, silver and lead from Cycladic islands were already reaching Crete in pre-palatial times, and were now being produced in quantity from the Laurion sources in south Attica (they may also have come from Lakonia). The distribution of finds suggests widespread Cretan activity in the Aegean as far north as Samothrace, as indicated by remarkable recent discoveries at Mikro Vouni, including sealings. Although this evidence becomes much more copious in the final stages of the First Palace Period, it is questionable whether it indicates Cretan colonization or take-over of the old settlements in most cases; but the most recent excavations do suggest that Miletos was a purely Minoan foundation, dating to the beginning of the Second Palace Period.

As the First Palace Period progressed there may have been increasing competition and conflict between the developing states of Crete, from which Knossos emerged the ultimate victor. Certainly, it is the leading site of Crete in the Second Palace Period and can plausibly be seen as the capital of a state that reduced most other major centres in Crete to dependent status. Various indications suggest the development of a more homogeneous society: the major palaces have notably uniform plans, of which many features such as the central court and ceremonial complexes may be reproduced in smaller buildings; documents sealed with special types of sealing were apparently dispatched between Knossos and other important centres, including Ayia Triadha, Gournia, and Zakro; the Linear A script was in universal use; and identical types of offering, including stone vessels inscribed in this script, are found at religious sites of different kinds throughout the island. Communal religion may increasingly have come under central control: many local peak sanctuaries seem to have gone out of use, and those that survived show evidence of 'palatial' interest. The appearance of a class of buildings often called 'villas', that have many of the features of palaces, including ceremonial complexes and substantial storage facilities, and sometimes produce administrative documents, suggests an intensification of the elite's control outside the palaces' immediate environs. This may reflect a drive for more intensive exploitation of the land, detectable in a general expansion of settlement; for example, the islet of Pseira, site of a thriving town, was apparently totally terraced for agriculture.

## A NOTE ON CHRONOLOGY

There are two major disputed areas in the chronology of the Aegean Late Bronze Age at present. One centres around the dating of the eruption of Thera, variously placed between *c.*1628 and *c.*1525 BC; the higher date would force raising the conventional dating of the Second Palace Period (*c.*1700–*c.*1450 BC) by 50 to 100 years. There are telling arguments on both sides and this is not likely to be resolved quickly. The second concerns the date of the destruction of the final phase at Knossos. It is variously placed in the early or middle fourteenth century or in the thirteenth century BC; the consequence of accepting the last would, in the author's view, raise more problems than it would solve, and here a fourteenth-century dating is followed.

## THE SECOND PALACE PERIOD

In the Second Palace Period Minoan civilization undoubtedly reached its height: the towns were most extensive, the palaces and other buildings were most elaborate, the major peak sanctuaries were adorned with structures, and wealth was further displayed in the lavish use of metal, especially for religious offerings, and the production of extremely fine artwork, intended, it seems, largely if not entirely for use in ritual contexts (see plate 3.1). Supplies of the materials used to demonstrate this wealth largely depended on trade relations with the Near East, which were probably intensifying: pottery from Cypriot and Syro-Palestinian centres began to appear at Cretan coastal sites, especially Kommos, the port of Phaistos, and paintings from the tombs of high-ranking Egyptian officials of the earlier fifteenth century BC document contacts that may well have been diplomatic as well as commercial.

At the same time Minoan influence in the Aegean reached a peak. The evidence is especially strong at the large and important settlement of Akrotiri on Thera, but occurs in various forms, including the use of Linear A, at all the major island centres. While it remains questionable whether anything like a 'Minoan empire' was established in the south Aegean, the hypothesized Knossos-dominated state would surely have been the great power of the region, the centre of a network of allies and dependants.

Centres of power now began to arise in the southern mainland, the heartland of the developing Mycenaean culture. They were clearly in contact with and considerably influenced by Minoan civilization, but display a different social development, in which increasingly elaborate modes of burial were the focus for displays

**Plate 3.1** A faience figure representing a goddess or a priestess, from the 'Temple Repositories' at Knossos. Early Second Palace Period

of status and assertions of cultural identity. The leading settlements did not become towns, nor were Minoan methods of administration adopted. The popularity of weapons as grave-goods suggests a more marked emphasis on leading males' prowess as warriors than is found elsewhere in the Aegean. Warfare may have been a principal means by which the early Mycenaean principalities were created, but the great wealth evident in the lavish grave-goods (see plate 3.2) probably derived more from involvement in the increasingly intensive and long-distance trading activity in the Mediterranean than from looting. It is hardly coincidental that at this very time Aegean contacts with the central Mediterranean can be documented by finds of mainland types of pottery on the Lipari islands and Vivara, off the coast of Italy, and great quantities of amber

**Plate 3.2**  The finest of the gold burial-masks found in the Shaft Grave Circle A at Mycenae. Early Second Palace Period

which must originate in continental Europe arrived at several mainland centres, including Mycenae itself.

The appearance of stability created by the monumental buildings and extensive settlements of this period in the Aegean may be deceptive. The political situation could have been unstable, complicated by the rise of new powers on the mainland; certainly, several island towns were extensively fortified. The eruption of Thera which destroyed Akrotiri must have been a major disaster; important sites in north and east Crete seem to have been seriously damaged. Yet the collapse of Minoan civilization at the end of the Second Palace Period is separated from the eruption by a considerable period and remains hard to explain, although better attributed to social breakdown under internal strains than to an implausibly wide distribution of contemporaneous earthquakes or of invading Mycenaean armies.

Nevertheless, in the turmoil the mainlanders came to the fore, not only extending Mycenaean influence into the islands, but apparently providing the dominant element in the ruling class of a revived Knossos state, which remained significant into the fourteenth century BC and preserved in its culture much of the old Minoan tradition. Most probably the needs of the new rulers stimulated the development of the Linear B script and much can be learned from the tablets preserved at Knossos about the state's extent and activities. It evidently controlled most of central and western Crete and had a particular interest in sheep-ranching for wool, on a scale that could have required a quarter to a third of all the pasture in Crete. The archaeological evidence suggests very close links between Knossos and leading centres of the mainland, through which knowledge of the arts of administration was surely transmitted. When the palace of Knossos was finally destroyed, the major Mycenaean centres and the west Cretan settlement of Kydonia (modern Khania) continued the traditions of palace society.

## THE MYCENAEAN PALACE CIVILIZATION

The great centres of the mainland, principally Mycenae, Thebes, and Pylos, now presided over an increasingly homogeneous civilization spread through the whole south Aegean (though Crete retained many specifically Minoan characteristics), which extended its influence into the north Aegean, Balkans and central Mediterranean. There is no good reason to believe that this civilization formed a unified political system under Mycenae's control; more probably the greater centres each had spheres of influence and formed alliances with and against each other. Arguments that the state Ahhiyawa named in Hittite documents from this period was a Mycenaean state, based primarily on the resemblance between this name and the commonest name applied to the Greeks in the Homeric poems, Achai(w)oi, remain inconclusive. Rather, the Mycenaeans seem to have remained politically on the fringe of the heavily interconnected world of the Near Eastern civilizations; but they were increasingly tied into its trade networks, which now extended into the central Mediterranean and the Black Sea, as the discovery of typically Near Eastern 'oxhide' copper ingots in Sardinia and Bulgaria shows. The contents of the Cape Gelidonya and Ulu Burun wrecks off the south coast of Turkey, most probably Cypriot or Syrian to judge from their anchor-type and the great majority of their contents, provide a striking demonstration of the significance of bulk trade in commodities, particularly metal, at this time. A newly found shipwreck off Iria, down the coast of the Argolid from Asine, contained big Cypriot *pithoi* (storage jars), of a type found as far west as Sardinia, with smaller Aegean storage jars. The much more conspicuous Mycenaean pottery, distributed very widely around the Mediterranean, documents less significant but still substantial trading activity by the Mycenaean palace societies; much of it consists of likely containers for scented olive oil, the ancient equivalent of perfume, which was evidently an important product of the palaces.

There are several indications of a wide spread of prosperity during this period, especially on the mainland, where the number of identifiable settlements is greater than at any time until the Classical period. Fine mass-produced pottery was distributed universally, and there are numerous cemeteries of well-constructed 'family tombs', mostly of the rock-cut chamber-tomb type, which must have been used by a considerable proportion of the population at the larger settlements. The rulers built themselves impressive tombs and palaces, smaller and less complex than those of Minoan Crete but still elaborate (see figure 3.4), and might fortify their citadels in the 'Cyclopean' style, whose monumentality is far greater than required by the needs of defence and is best interpreted as a form of display. Fewer resources were expended on religious structures, and, in general, religion, though important, seems to have played a less central role than in Minoan civilization. But the palaces probably acted as ceremonial centres, among their other functions, as is suggested by their large courtyards and the common occurrence of procession frescoes in significant positions; the typical 'megaron' suite of rooms probably had a primarily ceremonial purpose.

Although the production of good quality weapons continued, there is no reason to suppose that Mycenaean civilization was particularly warlike, a misconception closely linked with the belief that it is depicted in the Homeric poems. On the contrary, the general impression is of a relatively peaceful and stable society. In some respects Mycenaean civilization was not the equal of Minoan: the major centres are less townlike, and the craftworkers were less

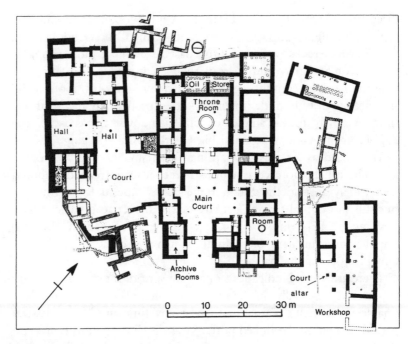

**Figure 3.4** The palace at Epano Englianos (Pylos) in its final form. Late thirteenth century BC

innovative; but more was achieved in terms of practical engineering, including the construction of fortifications, dykes, dams and roads.

But the cost of all this construction may in the end have become too great, and the conditions of trade, on which the Mycenaean palace societies ultimately relied to support themselves, may have become less favourable. There are signs of deterioration and likely internal conflict during the thirteenth century BC and by *c*.1200 BC or not much later there had been a general collapse, signalled by the destruction of many major sites. Many factors may have contributed to this – disastrous earthquakes seem to have afflicted Tiryns and Midea, perhaps also Mycenae, in the Argolid – but there is no good reason to attribute it to hordes of invaders who destroyed all in their path, whether Dorians (a tenacious view largely based on tendentious interpretations of Greek traditions), central Europeans, or the so-called 'Sea Peoples' (whose significance has been vastly overrated in this writer's opinion).

But the system that had sustained the Aegean Bronze Age civilizations had been destroyed and could not be re-created, for it depended ultimately on stable conditions in the Near East and here the political systems had thoroughly broken down by the mid-twelfth century BC, though many cities survived. It has been argued that this resulted in a period of innovation and new opportunities, but while the cities of Cyprus and Phoenicia may have thrived, in the Aegean all the indicators suggest decline. The previous cultures essentially continued, with some innovations; many major settlements survived the collapse and recovered to limited prosperity for a while. But this could not be sustained: by 1000 BC communities throughout the Aegean had become little more than villages and contact between the various regions of the Aegean, let alone with the wider world, had become intermittent. Nevertheless, they transmitted elements of the Bronze Age past to their successors.

## THE ESTABLISHMENT OF THE GREEK LANGUAGE

The Greeks believed that they had always lived in Greece, but the recognition that Greek was an Indo-European language led to the supposition that the first Greek-speakers must have entered Greece from elsewhere, the favoured direction being the north, because of the theory that the Indo-European 'homeland' was located in the great steppe region stretching from central Europe to central Asia. This produced the classic article by Blegen and Haley, published in the *American Journal of Archaeology* 1928, which argued for an 'arrival of the Greeks' in the southern mainland around 2000 BC, on archaeological and linguistic grounds. Cultural continuity from then to the Mycenaean civilization was considered assured, so that the Mycenaeans were Greeks and could be identified with Homer's heroes. But many still followed Evans's view that the Mycenaean civilization was simply a provincial branch of Minoan, therefore non-Greek, and that the Greeks arrived at the end of the Bronze Age as the destroyers of this civilization.

The argument over when, or whether, the Greeks 'arrived' has continued, but the fact that Greek-speakers were present in Greece during the Late Bronze Age is demonstrated by Ventris's brilliant decipherment of the Linear B script as Greek in 1952, confirmed by his collaborative work with Chadwick and that of a host of other scholars since; the intelligibility of virtually all material discovered since the decipherment constitutes the strongest proof

**Plate 3.3** A Linear B tablet from Knossos, listing (left to right) a man's name, and ideograms for a corselet, chariot and horse that either belong or are assigned to him. Fourteenth century BC

that it is correct. The type of Greek represented is recognizably 'east Greek', particularly close to the semi-isolated dialects of later times, Arcadian and Cypriot. The oldest Linear B texts in Greece are widely believed to be those of Knossos (see plate 3.3), where the script was probably developed (see pp. 40–1). No inscribed material on the mainland can be dated much before the thirteenth century, by which time the script was well established: it was certainly in use at Mycenae, Tiryns, Thebes, Pylos, Khania and a central Cretan site (not necessarily Knossos), and inscribed items, mainly originating from western Crete, have been found at several other sites. All of this tends to indicate that Greek had become the dominant language of the Aegean.

The script includes symbols for vowels and open syllables only, with some sets doing double or treble duty to represent similar sounds; thus, *ka* could also stand for *ga* or *kha*. Complicated rules were devised for handling the clusters of consonants that are common in Greek, involving the insertion of extra vowels or, more frequently, omission of the first of two consonants, also dropped at the ends of words; thus, *spermon*, 'seed', was written *pe-mo*. Interpretation was aided by the use of ideograms, signs that indicate commodities, artefacts, types of livestock, etc. (see plate 3.3), helping the reader to know what was meant, but the system could hardly have been used for long passages of continuous prose or verse, when such aids could rarely be deployed. It must remain extremely doubtful that writing was used for more than the terse lists on tablets, and statements of origin on storage vessels, that have survived, or that it was used at all outside the small administrative class. It is therefore not surprising that it disappeared with the collapse of the palace societies that used it.

Thereafter, with the exception of a bronze spit from a tomb at Old Paphos in Cyprus dated in the eleventh century BC, which is inscribed in the local syllabary with a Greek name, no examples of written Greek can be identified before the eighth century BC, when a completely different, alphabetic, script was adopted.

FURTHER READING

Barber, R. L. N., 1987: *The Cyclades in the Bronze Age*. London: Duckworth/University of Iowa Press.

Cadogan, G., 1976: *Palaces of Minoan Crete*. London: Barrie and Jenkins.

Chadwick, J., 1976: *The Mycenaean World*. Cambridge: Cambridge University Press.

Dickinson, O., 1994: *The Aegean Bronze Age*. Cambridge: Cambridge University Press.

Doumas, C., 1983: *Thera: Pompeii of the Ancient Aegean*. London: Thames and Hudson.

Hood, M. S. F., 1971: *The Minoans*. London: Thames and Hudson.

Hood, M. S. F., 1978: *The Arts in Prehistoric Greece*. Harmondsworth: Penguin/Yale University Press.

MacDonald, W. A. and Thomas, C. G., 1990: *Progress into the Past: The Rediscovery of Mycenaean Civilization* (2nd edn). Bloomington and Indianapolis: Indiana University Press.

Treuil, R., Darcque, P., Poursat, J.-C. and Touchais, G., 1989: *Les Civilisations égéennes du néolithique et de l'âge du bronze*. Paris: Presses Universitaires de France.

Ventris, M. and Chadwick, J., 1973: *Documents in Mycenaean Greek* (2nd edn). Cambridge: Cambridge University Press.

Vermeule, E., 1972: *Greece in the Bronze Age* (2nd edn with new introduction). Chicago: University of Chicago Press.

Wardle, K., 1994: 'The Palace Civilisations of Minoan Crete and Mycenaean Greece, 2000–1200 BC', chapter 6 in B. Cunliffe (ed.), *The Oxford Illustrated Prehistory of Europe*. Oxford: Oxford University Press.

Warren, P. M., 1989: *The Aegean Civilisations* (2nd edn). Oxford: Phaidon.

# 4 / ARCHAIC INTO CLASSICAL

## *Graham Shipley*

### THE DARK AGE

After the breakdown of the Mycenaean palace-states system, Greece entered the so-called Dark Age (conventionally defined as 1100–900 BC). The Linear B script was abandoned and there are no written sources from this period; were it not for archaeology, we would be entirely reliant on inferences from early post-Dark Age sources such as the epic poems of Homer and on classical and later writers such as Thucydides, who devotes several pages of remarkably intelligent guesswork to early Greek history. However, the archaeological record, though fragmentary, shows that many of the characteristic features of the palace age disappeared: overseas trade generally ceased, the administration of the countryside from ruling centres ended, and Mycenaean society dissolved into isolated small towns and villages. The painted pottery styles of the late Bronze Age were replaced by a simple 'protogeometric' decoration.

One of the few beacons shining out of this Dark Age is the settlement of Lefkandi (its ancient name is unknown) on the island of Euboia (see plate 4.1). Here a 'princely' burial complex has been excavated containing gold and bronze artefacts, rare for this period. Evidently Lefkandi had not lost touch with the technologically more advanced Near East, though there was a decline in overseas links in the middle of the Dark Age, as elsewhere in central Greece. While the wealth of its elite may have been remarkable for this period, there is no precise evidence for the size of its population, and we cannot be certain how typical or untypical this settlement was.

The fall of the Mycenaean palace system, however, did not leave utter chaos in its wake; despite the paucity of archaeological remains it would be unwise to assume a devastating drop in population. Basic forms of organization were recreated at a local level, and so long as the Greek peninsula escaped natural or man-made catastrophes such as had destroyed the palace system, its natural resources would ensure that a complex society developed again, in time.

**Plate 4.1** View of Lefkandi on the island of Euboia

## THE RISE OF THE *POLIS*

By the ninth century BC, archaeology testifies to a revival of material exchanges with eastern lands and to increasing social differentiation. Protogeometric pottery develops into the 'geometric' that gives the next period (*c.*900–700 BC) its modern name; its most elaborate forms suggest a prosperous elite, anxious to embody their power in public symbols such as the giant vases that were used as grave-markers. The story of the following centuries is to a large extent that of changes in this elite and in its relationship with the rest of the population.

The Geometric period saw the rise of the *polis* or 'city' – the term is usually translated as 'city-state', or better 'citizen-state' – the characteristic social, religious and political institution of Greece down to the Roman period. Archaeological discoveries suggest that during the eighth century many communities decided to express their sense of identity through permanent monuments, principally in the form of stone temples. The first of these may have been on the island of Samos in the eastern Aegean, a region where Greeks from the mainland had settled during the late Dark Age. Here, soon after 800 BC (if the early date proposed is correct), a hundred-foot-long temple was built for the community's patron goddess, Hera. Such edifices imply a collective effort and the ability to mobilize resources and labour on a large scale over a period of years, and some have taken them as indicating the growth of a collective mentality which may be characteristic of a new kind of community. It is also likely that by now (if not earlier) public decision-making and ceremonies were chiefly the preserve of males, as they would remain for centuries.

Another possible sign of a structural leap in Greek society comes from the 'colonies' (the word 'colony' is an imprecise translation of the Greek *apoikia*, which means roughly a 'home away from home') founded by many Greek states from the eighth century onwards. Their precursors, such as at Pithekoussai on the island of Ischia in the bay of Naples, or at Al Mina in Syria, may not have been fully-fledged *poleis*, but from about 740 BC we see the foundation of new cities that became independent states – unlike the 'colonies' of modern imperial powers. They were usually founded outside the Aegean by an existing *polis*. Syracuse in Sicily, like a number of colonies, was founded by men from Corinth; many others were built on the coasts of Italy, southern Asia Minor, and the Black Sea, with a few more in North Africa (such as at Cyrene), southern France (notably Marseilles) and Spain. The motives for these ventures probably included a desire for land and a desire for profit; in some cases poverty or civil strife was a spur to emigration, suggesting a society undergoing traumatic change, perhaps because of a rapidly increasing population (see figure 4.1).

In the west at least, the Greeks were competing for space with the Phoenicians, a Semitic people from the Levant, who were actively trading there before them and had founded Carthage in North Africa (on traditional dating) before 800. Traders at this early date, however, can scarcely be distinguished from pirates. Where they did not simply seize wealth, they sought to make favourable exchanges in kind (coinage was not invented until about 600 BC) with peoples who could give them commodities and luxuries – such as slaves, metals, textiles, leather, or timber – that were in short supply in Greece and were in demand among Greek elites. Cities such as Corinth on the Isthmus, which Thucydides especially picks out, grew rich on middleman trade and the levying of harbour tolls. Corinthian pottery was also exported widely, but was probably valued more for its contents (such as oil-based perfumes) than for its decoration, the point we emphasize today.

It is striking how often a colonial site, within a generation or two of its foundation, shows evidence of 'rational' planning: straight

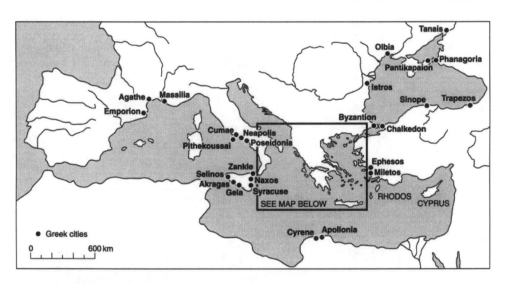

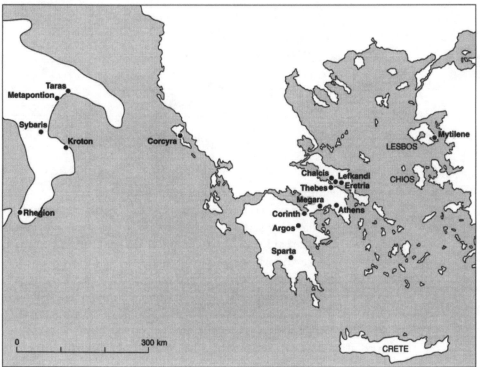

**Figure 4.1** A selection of major Greek cities in the Mediterranean and beyond

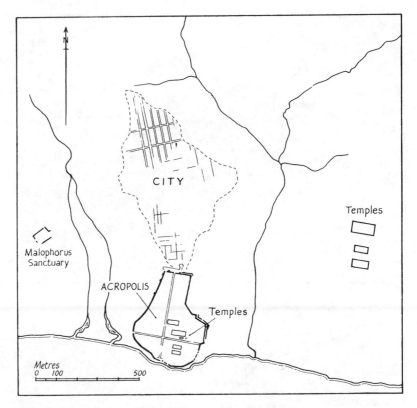

**Figure 4.2**  Plan of the Greek 'colony' of Selinos in Sicily

streets meeting at right angles, house blocks of uniform size, open central spaces for public buildings, and so on (see figure 4.2). This may imply that the settlers in these new foundations, or their leaders, had a clear idea of what kind of settlement was appropriate to their view of themselves as a particular kind of community, the *polis*. Equal house blocks do not, of course, make a society egalitarian, but they do suggest that – at least among the landowners of the new societies – a relatively open system of decision-making prevailed. Not for nothing is the word *polis* the direct root of the word for 'citizen', *polites*; the idea that the city consisted of its members – typically not the whole adult population, of course, but a select group of them – was intrinsic to the *polis* from an early date. It can be seen, perhaps, in the assemblies portrayed in Homer's *Iliad* and *Odyssey*, before which the leading men debate issues and whose support they seek.

Colonization was facilitated by a change in military technology. Armour had been improving throughout the Geometric period, and bronze swords and spears meant that Greeks could easily overcome less well-armed natives. Now a total 'package' was developed that required a large number of citizens to combine in military activity – another reflection of an 'open' male society. By the seventh century most Greek states had adopted the 'hoplite' style of fighting, in which opposing rectangular formations of heavy-armed soldiers fought head-to-head in a ritualized push-and-shove combat.

In Greece itself, the world of the *poleis* developed quickly in the late Geometric period and the Archaic period that followed (another name taken from art history). An alphabet similar to the Phoenician, but with certain important innovations, was adopted, perhaps by traders; it was soon being used for ceremonial purposes such as inscriptions on religious offerings. Until about 700 BC singers like Homer had performed their long oral poems from memory, recreating them orally for each occasion with the help of rules that gave structure and consistency to their improvisations. The poems will thus have developed continuously, and Homer stands at the end of a centuries-old tradition of oral epic. Now his narratives of the Trojan war, expanded to such vast proportions that only a part can have been recited at any one sitting, were written down and made permanent (see chapter 9).

Shorter poems such as those of Hesiod, who lived at roughly the same time as Homer, were performed at inter-state religious festivals which brought together the elite males of different cities to compete in athletic and artistic performance. The oldest games, the four-yearly Olympics, were inaugurated (according to tradition in 776 BC) at Zeus and Hera's sanctuary at Olympia in the north-west Peloponnese. Others included the Pythian games in Apollo's shrine at Delphi. The architecture of sanctuaries also reflects inter-state rivalry: cities sought to outdo each other by the generosity of their gifts to the gods, including permanent buildings.

## FROM ARISTOCRACY TO DEMOCRACY

All this took place within the framework of an aristocracy whose increasing wealth came chiefly from large landholdings. Probably they alone could build the seagoing vessels in which the produce of their estates could be taken for exchange abroad, or in which armed citizens went on piratical adventures in the hope of gain. The cultivation of wealth and the good life became their ideal, and at both public festivals and private *symposia* (drinking-parties) the expressive songs of the lyric and elegiac poets were sung, many of which give an insight into the individual and collective mentality of aristocrats of the time.

Since aristocrats depended for their wealth and status on the allegiance of relatives and a retinue of other free, or semi-free, men, they could, if they chose, mobilize armed men in support of violent political change. A Greek aristocrat was fiercely competitive, yet egalitarian: he desired to outshine others, yet no one man must be allowed to outdo them all. If that happened, the result was tyranny, as happened often in the seventh and sixth centuries. The 'tyrant' (*tyrannos*) was not a brutal dictator in modern terms, more likely an aggrieved aristocrat who appealed over the heads of his rivals to their followers, the people (*demos*) as a whole, to help him take sole power: in short, the most aristocratic of aristocrats.

Paradoxical as it may seem, the tyrants, while destroying the competitive balance of aristocratic society, gave a boost to the cultural and political development of their cities in their pursuit of popularity. In Corinth, Kypselos, one of the first tyrants (*c*.657–625 BC) may have promoted the foundation of Corinth's Adriatic colonies. In Samos, Polykrates (*c*.550–522 BC) used warships doubling as cargo vessels to exact wealth from other cities and created a cosmopolitan court where gifted artists and poets came to perform. He probably commissioned such monuments as the spectacular city walls, a mighty harbour mole to shelter warships and trading vessels, and a new temple of Hera. The wealthiest tyrannies, however, were in the cities of the west, particularly at Syracuse in the fifth and fourth centuries.

Until now Athens had been a rather minor *polis*, but political change created the conditions for a rapid growth of wealth and power. To defuse aristocratic faction-fighting (*stasis*) and alleviate the grievances of a demos increasingly oppressed by large landowners, the leaders appointed in 594 BC an arbitrator, Solon. Their main aim in so doing was to prevent tyranny, which could easily result from a combination of elite and popular grievances. Accordingly Solon curbed aristocratic luxury, defined the privileges of different wealth-grades of citizens, outlawed enslavement for debt and gave back to small farmers control of their land. Though these reforms increased freedom for citizens, one long-term result was probably that Athens became one of the main slave-owning states, as landowners replaced semi-free labour with the captive variety.

But aristocratic rivalry could not be legislated away, and tyranny came anyway. Peisistratos and his sons (546–510 BC) organized public works including a new temple to the city's patron goddess, Athena. They respected the laws, allowing other aristocrats to be appointed *archon* of the city (ceremonial chief magistrate), and fostered the unification of Attica by instituting circuit judges and developing existing religious rituals that integrated the town with the rural settlements. The Peisistratids have a surprisingly good reputation in the accounts of ancient authors.

It is no surprise that tyranny gave way to more faction-fighting, nor that the man who won, Kleisthenes, did so by the tyrants' own device of appealing to the people for support. The roots of the famed Athenian democracy (*demo-kratia*, 'people-power') lie in the politicking of the rich: in pursuit of aristocratic goals, Kleisthenes and his supporters brought the *demos* into politics more than ever before. His reforms segmented the countryside into groups of villages, each represented on a central council. All Athenian citizens, wherever in Attica they lived, were enrolled into ten new 'tribes' which made up the citizen army. The device of 'ostracism' was introduced, whereby the people could expel a leading politician for ten years to defuse the rivalry that could generate tyranny. Kleisthenes successfully prevented tyranny – every aristocrat's nightmare – but also undermined the old politics: aristocrats had to learn new rules.

## ALTERNATIVE POLITICAL SYSTEMS

A very different society existed in Athens' main military rival, Sparta in Lakedaimon (Lakonia) in the south-east Peloponnese (see plate 4.2). Unusual in having two kings and two royal houses, Sparta did not colonize overseas on any large scale: its only substantial colony was at Taras (modern Taranto in Italy). Instead it seized the territory of neighbouring Messenia (*c*.720 BC) and turned its people into serfs, known as Helots, who farmed the land as before but gave up much of their produce to the Spartans. Perhaps around 675 BC, disputes among Spartans about land and privileges led to the formalization (attributed to a lawgiver called Lykourgos) of

**Plate 4.2**   The modern town of Sparta with Mount Taygetos behind

equal rights for full citizens; but this, combined with the existence
of a large serf population, produced a rigidly divided society.

To keep control of the Helots the Spartans devoted themselves
exclusively to military training and the pursuit of civic virtue; trade
and crafts were left to the free village peoples of rural Lakonia, the
Perioikoi ('dwellers-around'). Despite their military excellence, the
Spartans depended heavily on their subjects: not only for food,
utensils and weapons, but even for military manpower, for the
loyal Helots and Perioikoi made up the majority of the famed
Spartan army.

This hierarchical society gave rise to an entirely different town–
country relationship from that in Attica. No political structure
integrated centre and hinterland; the rural people had no stake in
the city, where a few thousand Spartans took all major decisions.
Whereas in Attica city and country folk took part in processions
linking rural cult sites to the town, Sparta was 'ring-fenced' by
sanctuaries that were apparently exclusively Spartan. As far as we
know, Spartan religious ceremonies, far from tying town to country as in Attica, seem to have expressed the unbridgeable gap
between Spartans and their subjects.

Different political landscapes can be observed in other parts of
Greece. In the north and west, areas such as Macedonia were not
extensively urbanized, and whole territories were ruled by Greek-

speaking kings who cultivated links with their more sophisticated southern cousins. In parts of central Greece and the Peloponnese the city-states were too small to dominate large areas, and more collective arrangements applied. The Aitolians north of the gulf of Corinth, for example, lived in towns but co-operated in a quasi-federal union centred upon a cult site at Thermon. At times their collective army was a major force in Greek politics, and while small *poleis* like these were often satellites of the major city-states of eastern Greece, we should not forget that they were just as Greek as the others and probably more typical of the Greek landscape.

## Greeks and the 'other'

In the east a new power had arisen. Under Cyrus I (560–529 bc) the Persian empire expanded as far as the Greek cities of the Ionian coast, which were captured in 546 (they had previously been under the domination of the kings of Lydia in western Asia Minor). Persian rule meant paying tribute to the king's local delegate, the 'satrap' (provincial governor), but otherwise was not oppressive: the king's interest was chiefly in the tribute and in levying military contingents from the myriad peoples he ruled. To do so, he had his friends among the aristocrats in each city; and, Greek aristocracy being the competitive thing it was, it was inevitable that these men would have their opponents, who would portray Persian domination as an abrogation of freedom.

A revolt by the Greeks of Asia Minor broke out in 499 bc and was quelled in 494. Athens helped the Ionian rebels despite having earlier appeared to acknowledge the king's suzerainty, and in due course King Darius dispatched an invasion force to Greece. In 490 it was heroically attacked and comprehensively defeated on the shore at Marathon in eastern Attica by an army from Athens and the small town of Plataia (see plate 4.3).

Ten years later King Xerxes' much larger army and fleet at first defeated an alliance of most of the Greek cities at the battles of Thermopylai and Artemision and burned the temples of Athens. It was at Thermopylai that king Leonidas and three hundred Spartans, together with the men of Thespiai, sacrificed themselves to allow the greater part of the Greek army to escape; Thermopylai, like Marathon, thus created heroes and legends. Later in the same year, however, Xerxes' fleet was devastated at Salamis by a navy in which

**Plate 4.3**   The Athenian Treasury at Delphi erected to celebrate the victory at Marathon in 490 BC

the Athenians and Corinthians played the major role. The following year saw Xerxes' land army defeated at Plataia by a combined Greek force under the Spartans, while the Athenians and other allies again overcame his fleet at Mykale in Asia Minor, liberating the Ionian cities from Persia. In 479 BC, as a thank-offering for their victory over the Persians, the Greeks erected in the Apollo sanctuary at Delphi a bronze serpent-column topped by a golden tripod, the coils of the three serpents engraved with the names of those states who fought in the war (see plate 4.4).

Some cities where pro-Persian aristocrats were dominant and Persian supremacy had been acknowledged, including Argos and Thebes, were notable by their absence from the Greek alliance; they were said to have medized, or 'gone Median' (to the Greeks 'Median' was synonymous with 'Persian').

To the Greeks the wealthy cities of Sicily and Italy were just as much within their horizons as those of the homeland. In Greece in 480–479 BC there may have been almost as much rejoicing at the Syracusan victory over Carthage in the battle of Himera as at the victories over Xerxes. Both events seem to have occasioned a redefinition of Greek identity which was henceforth generally seen as implacably opposed to that of 'barbarians' (*barbaroi*, those who burbled – 'bar-bar' – in foreign tongues). The new 'other' of the Greeks is well illustrated in Aeschylus' tragedy *The Persians*, performed in Athens in 472, in which Persianness is presented as an inversion of Greek 'normality': Persian women are strong, their elders weep on learning of Xerxes' defeat, and their army and navy are weakly and womanish, everything that Greek men were supposed not to be.

Greek society is presented to us largely through the writings of free males and the works of art produced for them. Though citizen status varied, a practice common to every community was – as in most historical societies – the tendency to reinforce the community's identity negatively, by excluding other groups both in practice and through ideological constructs. Greeks had always, or at least since the late Dark Age, interacted with other peoples, and the early poets do not emphasize the differences; Homer's Trojans are indistinguishable from Achaians. From the colonizing period on, Greeks expected to overcome foreign nations easily, but after the Persian wars 'barbarians' became a source of fascination and fear (see plate 4.5). Even the historian Herodotos from Halikarnassos in Asia Minor, who must have seen foreigners in the marketplace

**Plate 4.4**  The Serpent Column originally erected *c*.479 BC in the sanctuary of Apollo at Delphi; this remaining section now stands in the Hippodrome in Istanbul

**Plate 4.5**    A foreign invader in the Persian Wars as visualized by an Athenian vase-painter, *c*.470 BC

every day, believed foreign races were strange and different; for example, while admiring Egypt as more ancient and in many ways superior to Greece, he could still assert that everything there was done back-to-front.

The pamphlet *On airs, waters, and places* attributed to the fifth-century medical writer Hippokrates embodies a stronger prejudice: Greece has a central, ideal location, neither so hot as to enervate (like Asia) nor too cold for intelligence (like Europe). The same rationalization of military superiority is expressed by Aristotle in his *Politics* (or, more accurately perhaps, *Civics*). Noticing that barbarians are often ruled by Greeks or by kings, he theorizes that they are innately slave-like, as are women. The marriage of two barbarians, indeed, is for him indistinguishable from that of two slaves.

Slaves, who were often themselves non-Greek, represented another 'other' for the Greeks. They appear already in Homer, usually as war-captives. Besides chattel slaves, however, many states possessed what may for convenience be called serfs: semi-free Greek-speaking populations tied to working the land for citizens; the Helots of Sparta, mentioned earlier, were such a class. Greeks could also make chattel slaves of Greeks, for instance after capturing a city; but slaves tended to come from peripheral regions of the Greek world, brought back by traders. In many Greek city-states, particularly in prosperous slave-owning states like Athens, unfree labour funded the freedom and privileges of citizens. In Attica large gangs of male slaves worked in wretched conditions in the silver-mines; luckier ones were bought in twos and threes by farmers to be house-slaves and labourers. In towns Greek-speaking males could hold responsible positions, but – in contrast to Roman society later – it was not the normal expectation that a slave would eventually be freed.

## THE WORKINGS OF ATHENIAN POWER

After the battle of Mykale in 479 BC the Aegean allies, displeased with Sparta's overbearing leadership, asked the Athenians to lead an anti-Persian alliance. Because its treasury was on the sacred island of Delos, modern historians call it the 'Delian league' (see figure 4.3). Campaigns against Persia were pursued for a generation, until peace was (probably) concluded around 450 BC. Persia's influence on Greek affairs would remain important, however.

By the time of the peace treaty the Delian league had become the Athenian empire in all but name. Predominant in naval strength from the start, Athens – helped by its staunchest allies, the large island *poleis* of Mytilene (in Lesbos), Chios and Samos and their large fleets – began to coerce the weaker allies and granted itself rewards for defending Hellenism: symbolic, in the shape of temples to replace those burnt by Xerxes (notably the Parthenon; see chapter 12); economic, in forms such as *klerouchiai* ('cleruchies'), quasi-colonial landholdings established for Athenian citizens in the farmland of recalcitrant allied cities.

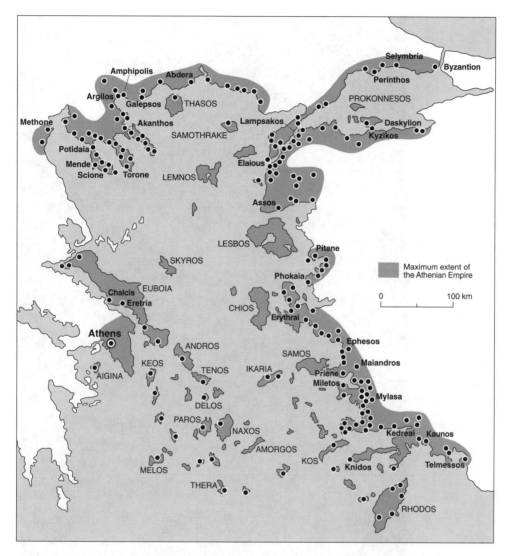

**Figure 4.3** The allies of Athens during the fifth century (the shaded area shows the maximum extent of the Athenian Empire)

The allies' subscriptions to the common fund were increasingly thought of as tribute to Athens itself (see plate 4.6). More and more Aegean trade was attracted into the Piraeus, the constitutions of allied states were increasingly determined by Athens, and military and naval campaigns brought tangible rewards to Athens. Athenian citizens began to enjoy unheard-of privileges: public pay

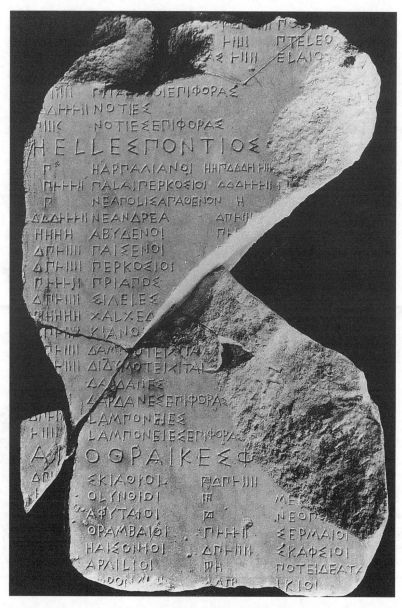

**Plate 4.6** A fragment of the Athenian quota-lists showing the tithe of tribute devoted to Athena (440/439 BC)

for jury service, pay for rowing in the navy (where the poorer majority performed their military service), lavish public festivals, and dramatic competitions, funded by rich citizens, between the best comic or tragic poets. Not surprisingly, Athens was now the cultural hub of Greece. Sculptors and architects, thinkers and poets, all flocked to Athens to meet each other – and to win lucrative rewards. Philosophy developed rapidly under the stimulus of the Presocratics and the so-called Sophists (*sophistai*) – professional purveyors of wisdom, *sophia* – who taught, for a fee, skills such as rhetoric, the art of winning in debate, an appropriate technique for a city ruled by debates (see chapter 10).

Despite the prejudice of ancient upper-class writers, Athens was no dictatorship of the proletariat but a co-operative venture between the rich and the not-so-rich. Aristocrats still dominated politics and were elected to military commands, and political leadership remained an elite preserve, though the rules had changed. As had always been the case, most speeches in the assembly were by the rich and powerful; but they could now be prosecuted if their promises were not redeemed. Thus a coincidence of interest grew up between elite and ordinary citizens in the form of an uncompromising imperialism. The connections between democracy, 'high' culture, and a successful empire are not to be glossed over. Furthermore, for all its reputation Athens was an extremely unusual Greek state.

The great enemy was no longer Persia. Sparta, the leading hoplite state, dominated the Peloponnese through alliances; the most important of these was with Corinth, which had a fleet nearly as powerful as that of Athens. The Spartans and Corinthians feared and resented Athens' dominance of the Aegean. As early as the 450s jealousy turned to open, though intermittent, hostility. Athenian–Spartan enmity went back to the sixth century, and the so-called Peloponnesian War of 431–404 was in a sense only the high point of a long antagonism.

In Thucydides' analysis the main cause of the war was Spartan fear of Athens' growing power, though arguably there was fear on both sides, especially the fear of losing allies to one's enemy together with their military and naval resources. The first phase of the conflict saw Spartan invasions of Attica and Athenian raids on the coasts of the southern Peloponnese; the latter led eventually to the capture of 292 Spartans – a significant percentage of the Spartiate warrior class – at Sphakteria in 425 BC. By now, however,

Athenian manpower may have suffered long-term damage from the plague of 430–429. Further campaigns took place in the northern Aegean. In 421 Athens negotiated an advantageous peace treaty, but conflict erupted again in the Peloponnese. The course of the war was changed by Athens' disastrous Sicilian expedition of 415–413, the failure of which led to the desertion of some of Athens' major allies, prolonged naval warfare in the Aegean, and eventually the loss of all the allies except Samos. Even so, the Peloponnesians could not have won without an inpouring of Persian gold to pay for their armies and navies.

After the Sicilian catastrophe the growing fear in Athens and the frequency of military setbacks accelerated the formulation by disgruntled aristocrats of alternative political theories. Those cities where landowners determined policy – where oligarchy, the rule of the few (*oligoi*), prevailed – seemed more 'rational'. Athens' military decline was further hastened by short-lived but violent oligarchic coups in 411 and 404, the second of which was actually put down by the victorious Spartans in 403.

## GREECE IN THE FOURTH CENTURY

The Spartans resisted calls to destroy Athens, and there is no sharp break in history at 404 BC: it is business as usual, with city-states vying to gain the upper hand during the first half of the fourth century. In fact, defeated Athens fared better than victorious Sparta: within a generation there was a new Athenian-led alliance (less imperialistic than the first, at least in intention), and the thoroughgoing democracy enjoyed, if anything, even more of a heyday than before. This is the period from which we have the greatest number of Athenian public documents inscribed on stone, as the complexity of administration and the wealth of the city continue to increase.

It is unclear how the economy of Greece in general fared after the Peloponnesian war. There is evidence that trade with the Near East was on the increase and that the population of Greece had reached a peak, suggesting a flourishing agricultural economy. It is, indeed, arguable that the fourth century was the golden age of the *polis*: more cities were free of outside domination than at any time since the early archaic period, and the urban amenities and monuments of many cities owed more to the fourth century than to the fifth. One example is Priene in Asia Minor, refounded on

**Plate 4.7**   The temple of Athena and the plain below the town of Priene in Ionia (Western Asia Minor)

a new site and endowed with paved streets on a rectangular grid and public buildings built in marble (see plate 4.7).

In 371 Sparta was humbled at Leuktra in Boiotia by the new model army of the Thebans, who were for a time the dominant power in southern Greece. Sparta never recovered from this, its first outright defeat for three hundred years. Messenia was lost, and with it most of the Helots; Sparta became a relatively second-rank player in Greek politics. This, however, did not leave Athens a clear field. Not only were Greek states increasingly dependent on Persian kings and satraps for favours and cash, but a new power arose in the shape of Macedonia, where King Philip II introduced new military techniques and built Greek-style cities. In the 340s he loomed large in Greek politics: the chief concern of Athenian politicians like Demosthenes was how to deal with Macedonia. In 338 Philip defeated the southern states in battle, but his ultimate aim seems to have been conquest and glory rather than consolidation, for he sought to unite them in a crusade against Persia, the final revenge for Xerxes' invasion.

Philip was murdered, however, before his expedition was properly under way, and it was left to his son Alexander the Great to carry out his intentions. Alexander, even more than his father, was thoroughly imbued with Hellenic culture: he carried Homer's *Iliad* with him, and seems to have identified strongly with the youthful warrior of that poem, Achilles, destined for eternal glory but an early grave. Consciously imitating the Greeks' legendary war against Troy, in seven short years (334–327 BC) Alexander overthrew the Persian empire, first taking Asia Minor, then the Levant, Egypt, the Fertile Crescent, Iran and Afghanistan, and even penetrating north-west India only to be turned back by the reluctance of his Greek and Macedonian troops to venture any further from home.

Briefly united under one ruler, Greece and the eastern Mediterranean lands potentially represented a single culture-sphere. New Greek emigrations took place, Greek cities were founded in new lands, and naturally the old political order, based on the narrow confines of the autonomous *polis*, had to change. Even so, in Greece the city remained the focus of public life: the military freedom to act that had made it wealthy was taken away, but the ideological bond between Greekness and membership of a city was too well entrenched to be set aside for any king.

### FURTHER READING

Andrewes, A., 1955: *The Greek Tyrants.* London: Hutchinson.

Cartledge, P., 1993: *The Greeks: A Portrait of Self and Others.* Oxford: Oxford University Press.

Davies, J. K., 1993: *Democracy and Classical Greece* (2nd edn). London: Fontana.

Forrest, W. G., 1995: *A History of Sparta* (3rd edn). London: Bristol Classical Press.

Hornblower, S., 1991: *The Greek World 479–323 BC* (2nd edn). London: Routledge.

Murray, O., 1993: *Early Greece* (2nd edn). London: Fontana.

Snodgrass, A., 1980: *Archaic Greece: The Age of Experiment.* London: Dent.


### CLASSICAL SOURCES

Crawford, M. and Whitehead, D., 1983: *Archaic and Classical Greece: A Selection of Ancient Sources in Translation.* Cambridge: Cambridge University Press.

Herodotus, *The Histories*, trans. A. de Sélincourt (Penguin Classics). Harmondsworth: Penguin.

Hesiod, *Theogony and Works and Days*, trans. M. L. West (World's Classics). Oxford: Oxford University Press.

Hippocrates, 'On airs, waters, and places', in G. E. R. Lloyd (ed.), *Hippocratic Writings* (Penguin Classics). Harmondsworth: Penguin.

Homer, *The Iliad*, trans. M. Hammond (Penguin Classics). Harmonds-
    worth: Penguin.

Homer, *The Odyssey*, trans. E. V. Rieu; revised D. C. H. Rieu (Penguin
    Classics). Harmondsworth: Penguin.

Thucydides, *History of the Peloponnesian War*, trans. R. Warner (Penguin
    Classics). Harmondsworth: Penguin.

Xenophon, *History of My Times*, trans. G. L. Cawkwell (Penguin Classics).
    Harmondsworth: Penguin.

# 5 / GREEK KINGS AND ROMAN EMPERORS

## Helen Parkins and Graham Shipley

When Alexander the Great, the Greek-speaking ruler of Macedonia, died at the age of 33 at Ekbatana in Media, he had conquered the Persian empire, but he had not reigned long enough to establish the structures to hold it together. He hoped to create a Greco-Persian ruling elite bound by marriage ties, but after his death the kingdom broke apart. Improvidently for so great a commander, he had not designated a preferred heir. The two official successors, a brother considered weak-minded (possibly epileptic) and a son born posthumously to the Baktrian princess Roxane, never commanded the same devotion as their father.

The Macedonian generals – the Diadochoi ('Inheritors') or Successors – parcelled out the kingdom along the lines of the old Persian satrapies (provinces). Rivalry and jealousies led to wars and shifting alliances. In 301 BC a key battle involving all the main contenders was fought at Ipsos in Phrygia; the aged Antigonos Monophthalmos ('the One-eyed'), who had held the generalship of Asia, was killed, and his son Demetrios Poliorketes ('the Besieger') put to flight. The event is held to mark the end of any hope that Alexander's empire could be reunited. The last two of the original Successors, Lysimachos and Seleukos, died violent deaths as late as 281 BC, over forty years after Alexander's death.

Even by the time of Ipsos, however, Alexander's sons were long dead. From 306 BC and shortly afterwards the various Diadochoi and their sons now called themselves kings (*basileis*), each claiming to be the legitimate inheritor of Alexander's kingdom. The era of these dynasties is called the Hellenistic period, though scholars no longer take it for granted that any thoroughgoing Hellenization ('Greekification') of Near Eastern society took place.

Egypt was the first satrapy to gain a lasting ruler: Ptolemy, the governor since 322 BC. His descendants mostly bore the same name. Asia was governed from 311 BC by Seleukos, father of the Seleukid dynasty. Macedonia at first remained under regents such as Antigonos, but was later ruled by claimants to the throne such as his son Demetrios. Only in 276 BC did the third member of the dynasty, Antigonos II, establish permanent rule.

The Antigonids never controlled the whole Aegean, nor even the whole of the Greek mainland: parts of the Peloponnese remained independent for a century. But the Macedonian garrisons at Corinth, Piraeus, Chalkis, and Demetrias in Thessaly – fortresses one king called the Fetters of Greece – represented a frame of control that was hard to break. The southern Greeks did revolt soon after Alexander's death and in the 260s, but Macedonia was too powerful for them and the freedom of the city-states was gradually eroded. Troops were billeted on them, troops were probably levied for the royal army, and contributions to the king's treasury were expected. Macedonian power was consummated in 222 BC, when Sparta was defeated by a coalition of various Peloponnesian cities and Antigonos III.

In Egypt the effects of Greco-Macedonian power upon the political landscape were much less marked. This already ancient kingdom had a unified core in the Nile valley. As under the earlier independent pharaohs or Persian satraps, society was largely conditioned by the annual Nile flood. The natives were mostly peasants with legal but not political rights; above them a priestly class, guardians of tradition and of the people's freedom, remained an important rival to the king's power. Agriculture was tightly controlled by a bureaucracy that owed more to earlier rulers than to the Ptolemies. Taxation was complex and closely monitored, but Greeks were exempt; many received plots of land, which Egyptians farmed for them. Little Hellenization of society or the landscape took place, and apart from the new capital at Alexandria there were almost no new cities. Throughout the history of Ptolemaic Egypt there was a fundamental opposition between the interests of a privileged Greek-speaking elite and the native population which vastly outnumbered them – though in time there was intermarriage and more opportunity for non-Greeks to rise in society.

In the east the Seleukid kings inherited most of the former Persian empire conquered by Alexander, which stretched from the Aegean to Afghanistan, and took over the Persian administrative system that had held together a diverse range of cultures and landscapes. Like Alexander, the Seleukids founded Greek towns in which to settle their veterans, often alongside older settlements; but in general the impact of Greek culture was limited, and many native priests and nobles retained their social position even as they gradually adopted Greek ways or intermarried with settlers. In Asia Minor, where the coasts were dotted with old Greek towns, some inland satrapies remained semi-independent; in the mid-third century Pergamon broke from Seleukid control and grew to rival the main Hellenistic kingdoms in power and wealth.

The heartland of Greek culture remained the Aegean, but the new diaspora of Greek-speakers was probably more numerous than that of the earlier colonizing movements. It was no longer limited to coastlands, but spread widely across north-east Africa and western Asia.

## KINGSHIP

The fourth century was the golden age of the Athenian democracy, though Athens no longer had an empire; indeed, more Greek city-states were free than at any time since the sixth century. Many cities adopted the institutions and terminology of democracy, or at least combined a citizen assembly with an oligarchic council.

Alongside city autonomy, however, there had been a resurgence of monarchy not seen since the days of the tyrants. Rulers like Jason of Pherai (Thessaly) and the Hellenizer Maussollos (Mausolus) of Karia (Asia Minor) played a major part in Greek affairs, and helped create the political and visual codes of kingship that later rulers adopted. Philip and Alexander, by the very scale of their actions, had expanded the role of kings as protectors of Hellenism and disseminators of Greek culture through city foundations.

Alexander's personal charisma was a new aspect of kingship, one that his successors had to work hard to match. They had to tread carefully – were they his heirs, or the underminers of his legacy? – but political realities dictated that they adopt the royal title. For Ptolemy and Seleukos this was not a large step: when they took over their provinces they stepped into the shoes of the pharaoh and the Persian king respectively. Their non-Greek subjects may have noticed little change. From that time or even earlier we see characteristic developments in the representation of monarchs, whether through written accounts like the story, told by the first-century BC historian Appian, of Seleukos I fighting a bull bare-handed, or through visual images such as coins or statues. It is unlikely that the features of any king or queen are portrayed truly:

**Plate 5.1** Roman copy of a portrait bust of Demetrios I Poliorketes (336–283 BC), with small bull's horns in his hair, recalling the god Dionysos, third century BC

their official image was conditioned by the virtues they wished to embody, such as courage, justice, and benevolence, or was embellished with specific signifiers, for example to give a king a military aura or link him with a specific deity (see plate 5.1). Many portraits reflect the supposed features of Alexander: his luxuriant hair and his gaze upturned to heaven are very characteristic, and were often imitated in later royal portraits (see plate 5.2).

**Plate 5.2**  A head of Alexander, from Egypt, third century BC

Alexander believed that he was descended from a god, and was said to have been recognized as the son of Ammon (Amûn) when he was in Egypt. Greeks had often paid religious honours to dead heroes, mythical or historical, and even to victorious generals, so it needed no revolution in religious practice for them to honour Alexander as a divinity. The Successor dynasties continued the trend, gradually moving from divine honours to actual deification: first after death, then during their lifetime. Ptolemy II set up a cult of his late father Ptolemy I and his last queen, later adding himself and his wife and sister Arsinoe (brother–sister marriage was not unknown among earlier Egyptian rulers), to make a quartet of sibling gods. In many Greek cities, cults of the Successors and their families were set up prominently beside those of Olympian deities.

Various non-Greek cults were also brought into Greek cities. One was Serapis, a conflation of the Egyptian Osiris and Apis, which the Ptolemies hoped to make a focus of devotion for their subjects, both Greek and Egyptian, but which became more popular outside Egypt. The spread of new cults is an indication of increased communication between different parts of the world, and suggests that people's horizons were expanding beyond the confines of a single *polis*.

To understand these religious changes we do not have to believe in either a collapse of traditional, 'true' Greek religion or the gullibility (or cynicism) of rulers and ruled. Greeks had often adopted foreign cults, and did not view other nations' gods as false. As for ruler-worship, kings had such vast power that it made sense to credit them with divine power and divine ancestors. Ruler-cult did not undermine or replace the old gods. While few temples of Olympians were now built, the same went for other deities, and antique temples began to acquire the respect enjoyed by medieval cathedrals today. They continued to host festivals and receive lavish dedications, not least from kings. The reality of religious change cannot be disputed; but all religion develops continually, especially when society itself is changing quickly.

## CITY AND KING

After the unsuccessful revolt of 322–321 BC, Athenian democracy was tightly circumscribed by pro-Macedonian governors. Elsewhere, the Successors favoured compliant tyrants operating within the forms of democracy. In practice, political activity ceased to be open to all citizens, and town councils were drawn from a narrow propertied elite. For the third century the evidence of archaeological field survey points tentatively to an increase in the size of upper-class landholdings and a fall in the numbers of smallholders, some of whom may have migrated into cities.

Those cities, however, no longer enjoyed the freedom of action they had had before the Macedonian take-over. Most obviously, they no longer fought wars with their neighbours, and service in a citizen militia was replaced by mercenary service for a king. As well as garrisons, kings set up naval bases in coastal and island towns, such as the Ptolemaic fleet stations on Thera and Samos. New political realities meant that city politics was mainly restricted to administrative and diplomatic matters; indeed, a whole new diplomatic culture arose, as embassies plied between cities.

For a *polis*, its most important relationship was now with the king who exercised domination over it. Often his power was not expressed formally but embodied in a treaty made as if between equals. The reality was of course otherwise, but cities exploited this relationship to extract concessions and benefactions, even playing one king off against another. Cities could also play on the glories of their past history. Like Philip and Alexander, kings wanted to be seen as the guardians of Greek liberty, so there were opportunities for putting pressure on them.

The increasing polarization of wealth, combined with the delicacy of the king–city relationship, ensured that rich citizens and powerful kings conferred material benefits upon the people. Attalos II of Pergamon (159–138 BC) donated funds for a massive colonnaded stoa (see plate 5.3) in the *agora* (marketplace) of the Athenians (did they have the option of not accepting?). Kings paid for wheat shipments during shortages, when the townsfolk would otherwise have been thrown back on the old staples of oats and barley, and gave lavish gifts to city cults and to international sanctuaries like Olympia and Delphi. Not all of the city elite were public-spirited: kings sometimes had to act as chief magistrate or priest, meeting the expenses of the job when no citizen was willing to do so.

The massive resources available to kings, as well as the mushrooming wealth of some members of the elite, are reflected in the scale and quality of new public buildings. Theatres became larger and had stage-buildings of stone. The well-off citizen's house,

**Plate 5.3**   Reconstruction of the Stoa of Attalos in the Athenian *agora*, originally built in the second century BC

formerly a modest dwelling, became a place for private ostentation with mosaics and colonnaded courts (see plate 5.4). New towns were laid out on geometric lines, indicating that plentiful resources – and labour, free or slave – were available. Priene's new layout was described in chapter 4. Elsewhere we have new towns like Ai Khanoum in Baktria (north-east Afghanistan), where Greek buildings (cult complex, gymnasium, theatre and fine houses perhaps for the garrison) are set in a standard 'Hippodamian' grid-plan of straight streets (see figure 5.1). The most spectacular example of the new monumentality is the citadel of Pergamon (see pp. 84–7).

Alongside these developments went changes in the formal relationships between communities. Areas of Greece previously on the margin of politics moved into the limelight by adopting 'federal' structures, though this term suggests more integration than actually existed. The *poleis* of Achaia in the northern Peloponnese revived their old 'league' (*koinon*, strictly 'community', 'commune'), originally a religious association, which became a major power block dominated, ironically, by a *Dorian* town, Sikyon, whose leader Aratos imposed his formidable personality in the 240s, coercing many towns into joining. Each Achaian city largely retained

**Plate 5.4** Hellenistic house ('The House of Cleopatra') on Delos, second to first century BC

its old laws, but united political action was achieved by pooling citizenship, and major decisions were taken by a group of representatives of member states. The main aim of the league was to keep Macedonia out of the Peloponnese while preventing Sparta's resurgence. Eventually, however, those aims proved incompatible and Aratos brought in the Macedonians to defeat Sparta (see p. 77).

An equally powerful *koinon* arose in Aitolia, which from the 210s was an ally of Rome in its wars against Macedonia. Constitutional innovation was not limited to 'leagues'. Other cities – often at considerable distances from one another – agreed to share citizenship or made treaties of friendship. Piratical peoples like the Aitolians welcomed deputations from towns or sanctuaries seeking *asylia*, 'immunity from plunder'. All these are expressions of the increasing integration and harmonization of the Greek world, something that perhaps could only be achieved by dissolving the old ideal of complete autonomy for each *polis*.

## PERGAMON

A good example of a Hellenistic city whose relationship with a king was of paramount importance is Pergamon in north-western

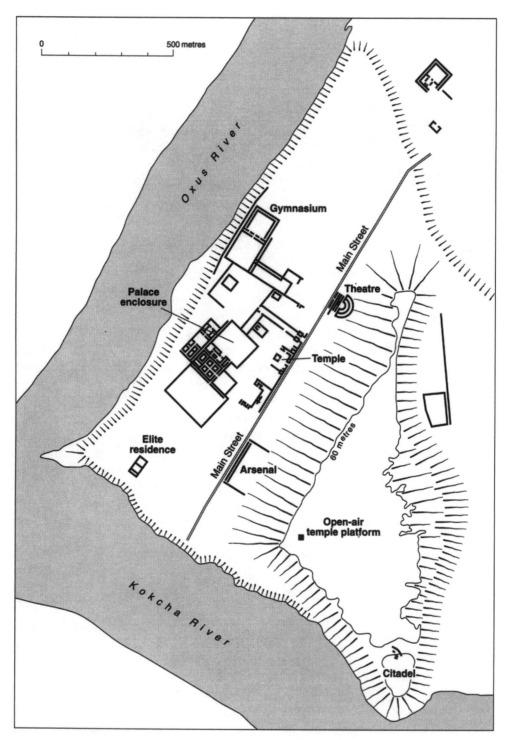

**Figure 5.1** Plan of the Hellenistic city at Ai Khanoum (Afghanistan)

**Figure 5.2** Drawn reconstruction of Pergamon (Asia Minor), showing the upper acropolis

Asia Minor. This obscure inland town was made famous by the Attalid dynasty founded by Philetairos, treasurer to king Lysimachos. The first titular king, Attalos I (241–197 BC), and his successors Eumenes II and Attalos II, made Pergamon a major power, an ally of Rome and a great centre of Greek culture. It remained important even after the last king, Attalos III, bequeathed it to the Roman people in 133 BC.

The *polis* of Pergamon remained nominally independent, however. It was partly with democratic Athens in mind that the natural acropolis (396 metres high) was remodelled in stages to accommodate the public buildings appropriate for a cultural capital (see figure 5.2). Under Eumenes II the city was fortified with a wall, and expanded down from the top of the citadel with the aid of artificial terracing. The new city was laid out so as to dominate the plain to the west.

Ancient visitors would take a paved road winding up from the south, past the lower *agora* of Eumenes II with its large colonnades and ranges of shops, to the great gymnasium on three terraces, where not only athletic training and contests but also philosophical education, public lectures, and other public ceremonies took place. Further up they would see a sanctuary of Demeter built in the early third century BC and enlarged by Attalos I. Coming to the upper town they would find a second, earlier *agora*, and above it Eumenes II's great altar of Zeus (see plate 5.5), built to commemorate the victories of Attalos I over the Gauls of Asia Minor, with its sculptures representing the battle of the gods and giants and the adventures of the Homeric hero Telephos, mythical

**Plate 5.5** Reconstruction of the altar of Zeus, Pergamon (*c*.190–150 BC)

ancestor of the kings. The Attalids also commissioned the finest sculptors of the day to depict the defeated Gauls in statues which were dedicated in Pergamon and Athens.

At the top of the hill were a large colonnaded enclosure sacred to Athena, a huge open theatre of Greek style with a promenade terrace and *stoa* below, and the royal palaces of Eumenes II and Attalos I. Behind the Athena precinct was Eumenes II's library, housing the largest collection of manuscripts outside Alexandria. Under Eumenes Pergamon became home to many of the most famous writers and thinkers of the day, rivalling Alexandria as a cultural centre. The large enclosure to its north contains a temple of Trajan, and the topmost part of the acropolis is occupied by military houses, barracks, and arsenals. Other buildings in the plain below the town included a vast Asklepios sanctuary, originally built in the fourth century BC, which attained its greatest importance in the Roman period, and a Roman amphitheatre.

This monumental complex has been described as 'unrelentingly monumental' and 'chilly', and its buildings are sometimes regarded as memorials to secular power; but most of them had a cultic function and are just as much a claim of continuity – a claim to have inherited the mantle of Greek culture – as a symbol of a new political order.

## CHANGES IN HIGH CULTURE

The most splendid city of the Hellenistic world, however, was Alexander's capital, Alexandria 'by Egypt', where his body lay embalmed in a mausoleum built by Ptolemy, an emblem of universal rule appropriate for a cosmopolitan city where native culture was not predominant. Little of Alexandria survives, though its street-plan has been traced and we know from ancient descriptions that it had a spectacular monumental centre with a lighthouse, two harbours, a palace, and other royal buildings (see figure 5.3). Among the projects of the first two Ptolemies were a library and the Mouseion ('sanctuary of the Muses' rather than 'museum'), where scholars and thinkers from across the Greek world enjoyed royal patronage. The Ptolemies devoted enormous wealth to making Alexandria a cultural capital to outshine Athens.

Literature, like other aspects of Alexandrian culture, did not break with the past, but built upon earlier forms (see chapter 9). Most characteristic, to modern eyes, is the poetry, mostly by men like Kallimachos who were not only poets but also scholars and librarians. The nostalgic genre of pastoral poetry, idealizing the old rural life, was developed by Theokritos, while short, pithy epigrams flourished alongside conceits such as 'pattern poems' forming the shape of the object they described. Such self-referential, 'literary' creations were no less Greek than the plays of classical Athens, but were made for a society where educated citizens no longer debated political issues but wished to dabble in theoretical speculation and looked back to an idealized *polis*. It is no coincidence that the main elite philosophies, Zeno's Stoicism and the quietism of Epicurus, took the gods for distant observers of humankind and offered happiness through individual worth: Stoicism through reasoned action for the public good, Epicureanism through 'hedonism' – not indulgence but the true pleasures of a virtuous, quiet life (see chapter 10).

Ptolemaic patronage also extended to science, where permanent additions to knowledge were made in mathematics, geometry, physics and astronomy. Eratosthenes, for example, calculated the earth's circumference from observed data. The hypothesis of a heliocentric, rather than geocentric, universe was tested but put aside – reasonably enough, because of its inherent improbability and its incompatibility with religion. Much was learnt about geometry and the properties of numbers. Some of the new investigation

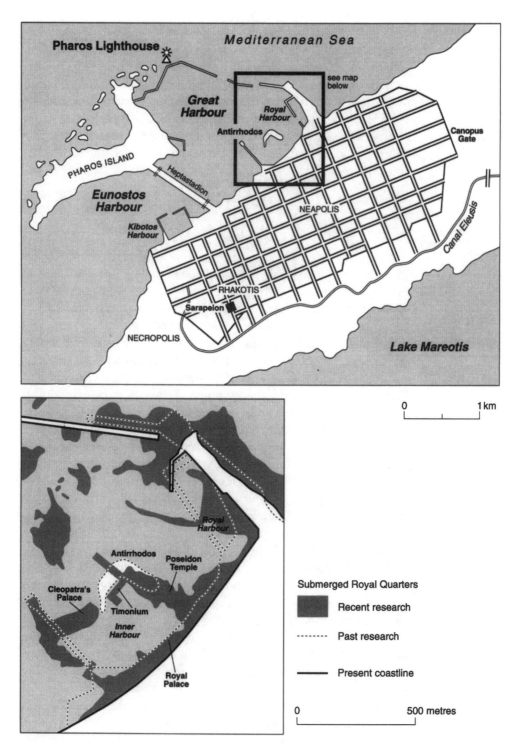

**Figure 5.3** A street plan of Alexandria, showing its principal monuments

had practical ends in view: better physics led to better artillery, while astronomical data helped achieve more accurate astrological predictions, the two subjects not yet being separate (see chapter 10). At the same time, much theoretical work represents an elite at play. The 'scientists' were not dispassionate explorers aiming to improve the lot of mankind, but leisured aristocrats, literary artists and public figures.

## THE RISE OF ROME, 229–146 BC

Into this world of kings and cities a new power intruded. As the Macedonian phalanx with its long spear, the *sarissa*, had irresistibly overwhelmed the southern Greek city-states, so in turn the Roman legions and the enormous manpower of Italy foretold the suppression of the Hellenistic kingdoms. From the late third century onwards the Romans lost no opportunity to further their interests and subvert the existing order. Macedonia, the Seleukids and Pergamon were either actual or potential threats to be neutralized; the Romans mistrusted kings, having cast off monarchy long since. Upper-class careers were geared to military success, giving Roman aristocrats every incentive to find excuses to cross the Adriatic.

Rome's early relations with Greece, in fact, were interventionist without necessarily being aggressive. Although the Romans acted, for example, against the piratical kingdom of Illyria in 229 BC – their first military involvement in Greece – they did not subsequently annex the kingdom when, arguably, they could have chosen to do so. Similarly, when they had defeated Philip V in 197 BC and his successor, Perseus, in 168 BC, Greece was theirs for the taking; yet in the event, although Macedonia became a Roman province, southern Greece was effectively annexed only in 146 BC, and did not formally become a province until another century and more had gone by. The Romans' apparent hesitance raises the question of whether they acted only in self-defence or out of self-interest. Certain incidents within the same period seem to be more strongly suggestive of aggression; without doubt, by the mid-second century BC there seems to have been a distinct change in Roman behaviour towards Greece and the East.

The second Macedonian war is generally agreed to be a turning-point. In 200 BC the Romans could no longer bear the presence of Philip V in Greece, and decided to lead a force against him, probably because they perceived the alliance reportedly concluded between Macedonia and Syria as posing a threat to themselves. After they emerged victorious in 196 BC, their general Flamininus declared Greece to be free; in fact, this freedom was somewhat notional. Greece became a client state, and effectively acted as a protective zone between Italy and the remaining Hellenistic kingdoms.

Between 196 and 62 BC, when the Roman general Pompey succeeded in subduing another significant threat in the Greek east, in the person of Mithridates VI Eupator, king of Pontos, Rome's dealings with Greece seem gradually to have become harsher. The apparent change in tone is paralleled elsewhere, lending credence to the idea that Rome increasingly acted from self-interest, and that its leaders and generals became increasingly greedy for land and loot. Indeed, it could be argued that Italy suffered as badly, if not worse, over the same period. In Italy until about 200 BC, Rome had been keen to make cities allied or friendly and to plant Roman colonies in areas where it was less sure of loyalty, whereas from 200 BC onwards alliance and friendship were much less freely granted, and the more ominous presence of governors and standing armies superseded the creation of colonies.

The difference in Roman attitude is immediately observable in its actions following the end of the third Macedonian war. In 168 BC, under the leadership of L. Aemilius Paullus, the Romans defeated Perseus. Macedonia and Illyria, now its ally, were subsequently declared free but were in fact made to pay tribute. Moreover, in an act that foreshadowed the fate of southern Greece and of Rome's later enemies, part of Epirus was sacked as punishment for having turned against Rome.

Twenty years later the shadow of Macedonia once again loomed. This time revolt was led by Andriskos, who posed as a son of Perseus. Once again the Romans sent out a force to deal with the problem, and once again the Romans emerged successful. Macedonia was immediately annexed and was split into four republics.

Trouble in Greece continued, however, in the form of uprisings organized by the Achaian league. Events came to a head in 147–146 BC while Rome was preoccupied elsewhere with Jugurtha and Hannibal, in Spain and Africa respectively. L. Mummius was sent east with two Roman legions to quell the Achaians. Achaian resistance finally came to an end at Corinth, where in 146 BC Mummius and his soldiers triumphed. The Roman senate wreaked its revenge by ordering the city to be destroyed. Corinth was plundered and razed to the ground, and its people either enslaved or massacred – a treatment also meted out by the Romans to Carthage in the same year, and later to Numantia in Spain in 133 BC. All three actions served to demonstrate Rome's irresistible power. In effect, Achaia was now a Roman province; Greece was no longer free.

In the east, the unity of the Seleukid kingdom had begun to fracture in the mid-third century, with areas like Pergamon in the west and Baktria (*c.* modern Afghanistan) in the east asserting their autonomy. Antiochos III (the Great) briefly restored Seleukid rule in the far east, but he was defeated by the Romans and their new ally Pergamon in 188 BC, and his territories in Asia Minor were shared out between Pergamon and the Rhodians. In the succeeding generations the Syrian remnant of the kingdom was eroded by attacks from eastern peoples. Meanwhile Pergamon, like so many of Rome's allies, came to be mistrusted and, as was noted earlier, the kingdom ceased to exist in 133 BC. In the first century BC Pompey, like a second Alexander the Great, redrew the map of the Levant, creating several new provinces. The last Hellenistic monarch was Queen Kleopatra, lover of Caesar and of Antony, who took her life in 30 BC, leaving Egypt to become a Roman province as well.

## GREECE IN THE ROMAN EMPIRE

As the Roman poet Horace said, 'captive Greece captured its violent conqueror and instilled the arts into rustic Latium.' Roman art, architecture, literature, and philosophy were to a large extent founded upon Greek, and while aristocrats might scorn the military weakness that had made Greece easy prey, they mostly admired the Greek cultural heritage. Not that the adoption of Greek ways did not provoke passionate opposition; most famously, Cato the Elder in the early second century BC sought to curb Hellenistic influence in Rome. The combination of Roman sensitivity about the basis of their identity with their admiration for many things Greek allowed Greek cities, now within Roman provinces, to harp once more upon their historic past and demand the respect due to venerable institutions. Roman governors, answerable to the Senate in Rome, intervened in inter-city disputes, kept the peace, and created memorials to their achievements.

One Roman commander (possibly Sulla) transported a classical temple of Ares from the Attic countryside and rebuilt it in the middle of the Athenian marketplace, a clear indication of the ability of the new imperial power to make the urban landscape deliver its own propaganda. Both Julius Caesar and his heir Octavian (Augustus) added a new marketplace further east, while Hadrian in the second century AD built a library to rival that of Alexandria, completed the temple of Olympian Zeus begun by the Athenian tyrants seven centuries before, and extended the city south-eastwards. The passage from the old to the new was marked by a ceremonial archway that left no one in doubt as to the benefactor's identity (see plate 5.6).

The rich, who under Macedonian monarchies had glorified themselves and their cities through monuments, continued to book their passage to posterity. Herodes Atticus, an Athenian who became consul at Rome in AD 143, was responsible for many civic monuments, among them the Odeion on the south side of the Athenian Acropolis and the open-ended stadium on the side of Ardettos hill, restored in the 1890s for the first modern Olympics.

More curious to our eyes, but no less revealing of the changed city, is Gaius Julius Philopappos, grandson of the last Greek king of Kommagene in Asia Minor and consul at Rome in AD 109. He honorifically held the chief magistracy of Athens, commemorating it with a marble memorial on a hill facing the Acropolis. Monuments like these symbolize the breaking down of old boundaries and the inevitable cosmopolitanism of a civilized, peaceful and above all powerless province of the Roman empire.

For the leisured Roman, Greece became a kind of heritage site in which the past was overvalued to the detriment of the present. The Greek writer Pausanias (second century AD) has left a detailed guidebook to many sites, but his interest is mostly in monuments to Olympian gods and local heroes erected in an earlier age. Roman visitors to Sparta watched supposedly ancient rituals, such as Spartan youths undergoing tests of endurance in the form of prolonged flogging; yet at the same time Sparta was becoming a normal Roman provincial town.

Archaeological field survey is starting to reveal wider changes outside the urban areas. As in the Hellenistic period, the intervention of an outside power seems to have led to the rich getting richer while the rest were left behind and lost control of their land. Villa estates of rich men (often possessing Roman citizenship) such

**Plate 5.6** Hadrian's Arch, Athens, which divided the old city from a new suburb created by Hadrian, completed AD 131/132

as Herodes Atticus may reflect an interest in estate-based farming for profit, rather than long-term self-sufficiency as before. Ordinary farmers may again have sought security in the town, or stayed on the land as tenants or wage-labourers. The *pax Romana* brought new amenities to Greek towns, but undermined the symbiotic relationship between the town and country populations that constituted the classical *polis*.

FURTHER READING

Alcock, S. E., 1993: *Graecia Capta: The Landscapes of Roman Greece.* Cambridge: Cambridge University Press.

Ferguson, J., 1973: *The Heritage of Hellenism* (Library of European Civilization). London: Thames and Hudson.

Green, P., 1990: *Alexander to Actium: The Hellenistic Age.* London: Thames and Hudson.

Hammond, N. G. L., 1989: *The Macedonian State: Origins, Institutions, and History.* Oxford: Clarendon Press.

Lloyd, G. E. R., 1973: *Greek Science after Aristotle* (Ancient Culture and Society). London: Chatto and Windus.

Long, A. A., 1974: *Hellenistic Philosophy: Stoics, Epicureans, Sceptics* (Classical Life and Letters). London: Duckworth.

Momigliano, A., 1975: *Alien Wisdom: The Limits of Hellenization.* Cambridge: Cambridge University Press.

Mossé, C., 1973: *Athens in Decline 404–86 BC*, trans. J. Stewart. London and Boston: Routledge and Kegan Paul.

Sherwin-White, S. and Kuhrt, A., 1993: *From Samarkhand to Sardis: A New Approach to the Seleucid Empire.* London: Duckworth.

Shipley, G., forthcoming: *The Greek World after Alexander* (Routledge History of the Ancient World). London: Routledge.

Smith, R. R. R. 1991: *Hellenistic Sculpture: A Handbook* (World of Art). London: Thames and Hudson.

Tarn, W. W. and Griffith, G. T., 1952: *Hellenistic Civilisation* (3rd edn). London: Arnold.

Walbank, F. W., 1992: *The Hellenistic World* (Fontana History of the Ancient World). London: Fontana.


CLASSICAL SOURCES

Austin, M. M., 1981: *The Hellenistic World from Alexander to the Roman Conquest: A Selection of Ancient Sources in Translation.* Cambridge: Cambridge University Press.

Plutarch, *The Age of Alexander: Nine Greek Lives by Plutarch*, trans. I. Scott-Kilvert. Harmondsworth: Penguin. (Includes Alexander, Demetrius I, Pyrrhus, etc.)

Polybius, *Rise of the Roman Empire*, trans. I. Scott-Kilvert. Harmondsworth: Penguin.

# PART 3

## Classical Mosaic

# 6 / THE GREEK COUNTRYSIDE

## Lin Foxhall

### INTRODUCTION

The Greek countryside has been a humanly managed landscape for at least 8,000 years, when the crops and techniques of farming first appear. Since then it has been used and modified in many different ways, often depending as much on political, social and economic factors as natural, ecological ones. Greece is a patchwork of terrains and environments, so it is difficult to generalize about land use from one region to another – even within a small area the potential for human exploitation of the landscape varies tremendously.

During the archaic and classical periods of Greek history, when the *polis* (city-state) was the dominant form of political organization in most places, there was a fascinating interplay between different ways of conceptualizing the countryside. Though we normally think of cities as urban centres, the *polis* also incorporated the surrounding rural territory as an essential component. This was not empty space. On the contrary, the evidence of both documentary sources and archaeological survey suggests that it was full of villages, farmsteads, permanent and seasonal agricultural and industrial installations, sheepfolds, shrines and even fortifications. Though the *polis* defined its boundaries in relation to other city-states, most of that space was owned and exploited by private households, not by the community as a whole. This picture of a city's territory, on closer inspection, turns out to be a mosaic. The image we see was created by the cumulative effect of many small decisions, invisible to us, made by individual households.

### OWNERS AND WORKERS

In most city-states, land ownership and citizenship went hand in hand, and only landholders were citizens. Athens was exceptional in this: Athenian citizens did not *have* to own land, but only citizens *could* own land. Who precisely owned land, and how much, is debated. Many scholars consider the *polis* (especially democratic

Athens) to have been dominated by small-scale, 'peasant' citizen farmers, typified by characters like Dikaiopolis in Aristophanes' comic play, *Acharnians*, who tries to stop the Peloponnesian War single-handed so that he can make a living from the land in peace. This may be an illusion. Analysis of what little data we have for the landholdings of the wealthy elite suggests that even in democratic Athens a small number of rich landowners held a much larger proportion of the total cultivable land than the large number of small-scale landowners. The disparity between the amount of land in the hands of the rich and the poor is likely to have been greater in city-states without democratic governments. On the other hand, the size of landholdings and scale of farming operations even among the rich in Greece was small compared to the size of the property holdings of wealthy Romans.

In Athens, the best documented *polis*, most land in the city's territory (known as Attica) was in the control of men. This is largely because of inheritance customs. At least in rich families, land was usually divided equally among the sons. Daughters received their share (usually a smaller share than sons) of the patrimony as dowry on marriage in the form of money or moveable property. Clearly Athenians felt this was important: Aristotle expressed worry and disapproval that in Sparta women owned a considerable proportion of the land (*Politics* 1270a23). However, elsewhere in Greece it is likely that men possessed more land than women. The fifth-century BC Law Code from Gortyn, Crete, suggests that similar inheritance customs, which devolved more land to men, were in force at that time (though women did own some land).

Land was frequently divided into smaller parcels on inheritance, though it might sometimes be amalgamated by purchase, the strategic marriage of a girl with no brothers, or by other means. In consequence the patchwork of ownership across the countryside changed dynamically every generation. Even the parcels of land owned by the wealthy were frequently very small. Holdings were usually fragmented, with one landowner possessing plots scattered over a great distance (see plate 6.1). This is clearly witnessed in the few extant records of the property of wealthy men in Athens, notably in the so-called 'Attic Stelai' and other records inscribed in stone of the magistrates called the *poletai*, who were responsible for auctioning off the property confiscated by the state as punishment from citizens who had committed a legal offence. In these

**Plate 6.1** Individual families ploughing smallholdings of vines, Methana

documents, landholdings belonging to a single owner appear in the neighbourhoods of several different Attic deme villages, and sometimes in several different parts of the Athenian empire, spread across the Aegean. In part because of the predominance of scattered, constantly reconfigured, landholdings, settlements were nucleated. In other words it was simpler to exploit an estate which consisted of a number of small plots (which might be different ones over two or three generations) from a central place like a village or town than from an isolated farmstead.

But this is not the whole story. Some remote plots might be worked from temporary accommodation, occupied seasonally for only a short time, or even from more permanently occupied farmsteads. Archaeological survey has revealed large numbers of small, isolated rural sites with evidence of occupation between the sixth and fourth centuries BC in many parts of Greece, many more than appear in some other periods. It is difficult, however, given the imprecise nature of such evidence, to be certain whether these were inhabited seasonally or permanently. It is even hard to judge exactly how long any particular site might have been in use during the classical period: it is possible, even likely, that not all were occupied simultaneously for the whole period.

Who worked the land varied greatly by region and with the class of the landowner. The role of agricultural slavery in Athens has been much debated in recent years. We know that slaves were important, but it is difficult to ascertain how far down the socio-economic scale their use went: how poor could a household be and still afford a slave to help them farm? Although scholars have speculated about the use of hired wage labour, tenants, and the extent of land-leasing, it is impossible to reach firm conclusions given the scarcity of the historical sources. Certainly there is no positive evidence for the private rental of land on a substantial scale, however convenient it might have been as a means of circumventing the problem of working widely scattered holdings.

In other areas of Greece different sources of agricultural labour emerged. In Sparta a class of non-free labourers (rather like mediaeval European serfs) existed, known as Helots. Early in the archaic period, the Spartan *polis* had annexed a large area of the western Peloponnese called Messenia. Both in the countryside of Lakonia (the territory of Sparta) and in Messenia the indigenous peasant farmers were enslaved to the Spartan state as a class, originally perhaps around the eighth to seventh centuries BC. Later in the classical period, the state assigned each Helot household to a Spartan citizen's estate. The Helot household then worked for the Spartan as sharecroppers, paying over a proportion of the crop grown each year. Though Spartan citizens seem to have been able to pass on these Helot-worked holdings to their heirs, the state reserved the right to reassign them to other Spartiates, especially in the absence of direct descendants. Spartan citizens (especially wealthy ones) probably owned other, private land in addition to these Helot-worked allotments. Similar systems are well documented in Gortyn, Crete, and are known, though not in detail, from other parts of Greece as well.

## CROPPING REGIMES

The cropping regimes in most of southern Greece at lower altitudes have been focused for millennia on the 'Mediterranean triad': cereals, olives and vines. Cereals were unquestionably the basic staple food, and thus the most important crop. Many species and varieties were grown. In the dry and unreliable climate of southern Greece, notably Attica, barley was more reliable than wheat, though the latter was preferred for food, since it makes more palatable bread. Wheat performed better in cooler and wetter areas like Thessaly and the western Peloponnese. Cereals, especially barley, could be grown almost anywhere, if necessary, even between fruit trees as small-scale farmers do in Greece today. In ancient times it is likely that such polycropping was mostly practised by peasant farmers rather than by big landowners. Some summer-planted cereals such as millet were also grown. Though millet was probably more productive in northern Greece, it was cultivated even in Attica, perhaps as a standby in case the main cereal crop failed. Shortfalls of grain occurred frequently, especially in the driest parts of Greece, perhaps as often as one year out of five.

Vines thrived on well-drained soils on gentle slopes. Although even poorer farmers probably had some vines, wealthy farmers might specialize in producing high-quality vintage wine on their estates. Wine production for the market was a risky enterprise. If successful, the profits could be very high, but the risk of failure (especially under pre-industrial processing conditions) was also very high – it was all too easy to end up with vats full of vinegar. Vines were often grown as low cordons and propped on stakes, though a vine for table grapes or raisins near a house or in a courtyard could be grown high up a trellis or portico. Sometimes in intensively worked ornamental orchards, vines were grown up other fruit or timber trees. Ancient installations for treading grapes are sometimes found in the countryside in vine-growing areas of Greece. This suggests that it might have been easier to extract the juice out in the fields and bring it back to the town or the village in skins or jars on the back of a donkey.

It is hard to imagine the Greek landscape without the immortal olive tree. Olives are well adapted to the climate, though the yield is erratic and they only produce fruit every other year. Though important, olive oil must always have been something of a luxury, especially for the poorest people. The oil had many uses in the ancient world: for food, lighting, perfume, medicine, manufacturing and as a soap substitute and skin treatment. To produce olive oil, a considerable amount of specialized crushing and pressing equipment was needed which probably would have been too expensive for peasant farmers to afford, even though the pressing equipment of the classical period was very basic (see plate 6.5) compared to that of the later Hellenistic or Roman periods. Very little pressing equipment which can be securely dated to the classical period has been found by archaeologists, though finds of later wine and oil presses are relatively common. It is possible that small-scale cultivators paid the wealthy owners of oil presses to process their olives. Table olives, however, are very easily made: the most basic recipe consists of placing alternate layers of salt and olives in a jar. Olives are nourishing and full of calories. They seem to have been an important staple food, especially for poorer people.

It is wrong, however, to think that Greek farming was limited to the Mediterranean triad. Other important crops were also grown. A number of legumes were sown in rotation with cereals, especially broad beans (*Vicia faba*), lentils, chickpeas, lathyrus peas and several kinds of vetch. Some might serve alternately as animal fodder or human food, depending on the available supply of grain. The most significant of the other fruit trees was the fig. Figs provided sweetening in the absence of other available sugar sources, and choice fresh figs were considered a treat even by the elite classes. Dried figs were a very important staple food in times of grain shortage or war: they produce more calories per unit area than any other crop (about 15,000,000 kilocalories per hectare). However, to judge from the complaints in the ancient sources, people clearly became very tired of eating them as emergency rations.

Greeks also had a wide range of other tree crops such as the almond, pomegranate, plum, apple, pear, medlar, mulberry and quince. By the classical period they had developed sophisticated techniques for cultivating and propagating all these tree crops, including grafting, layering and training them in special restricted forms of growth where appropriate. Greeks also enlivened their diet with a number of garden vegetables and herbs. These included several kinds of greens such as celery, parsley, coriander, chicory, black nightshade (*Salonum nigrum*), and an *Amaranthus* species. Also grown were haricot (navy) beans (eaten green and dried), beets, onions, leeks, garlic and various plants related to cabbages. Most of these seem to have been much tougher and more strongly flavoured than the varieties we grow today, and some which we now grow for their fleshy roots (such as beets and turnips) the Greeks grew for their tasty leaves. Ancient Greeks did not grow potatoes, tomatoes, peppers or aubergines (eggplant). Although citrus was known by the later fourth century, it seems to have been grown as an ornamental plant in Greece at first: only later was its culinary potential realized. Flax, for linen, was also an important crop, but the Greeks of the classical period did not have cotton or silk.

## ANIMAL HUSBANDRY

Animal husbandry was an essential element in ancient farming systems. One of the most important animal by-products was manure, the best readily available fertilizer for crops. Cattle, donkeys, mules and, to a lesser extent, horses were the primary sources of traction and transport. Both oxen and cows were regularly used for ploughing. Mules were expensive because, as a sterile hybrid of donkeys and horses, they do not reproduce naturally (see plate 6.2). Horses were the prerogative of the rich since they were expensive to feed and not well suited to much of the Greek terrain. The humble but sure-footed donkey was probably the most ubiquitous beast of burden, especially where there were no roads and wheeled vehicles could not be used.

Cattle, sheep, goats and pigs were raised for meat, though it was generally a luxury in ancient times. Cow's milk was almost never used, but milk from sheep and goats was important for cheese and other dairy products. One of the most interesting, still made today in rural Greece, is called *trachanas* or *chondros*. Coarsely milled grain boiled with milk is dried in the sun. Stored in tightly sealed jars, it preserves milk for a long time. Some sheep were raised specifically for their fine wool, and sheep's wool and goats' hair of all qualities were necessary for producing assorted textiles, from clothes to tents and sleeping mats.

The advantage of keeping sheep and goats is that they utilize parts of the Greek countryside which humans cannot exploit directly. Many Greek hillsides are covered in *maquis* growth: low, dense shrubby vegetation which sheep and goats will happily graze. They can also eat leaves gathered from trees or pruned branches, stubble or stalks of arable crops, or the weed growth under trees and in fallow fields.

Pigs, too, are renowned for their ability to subsist on waste products (see plate 6.3). In parts of Greece with large expanses of oak forest, pigs were fed on acorns. Pigs, sheep and goats all allowed the Greek farmer to make economical use of every bit of the landscape in which he lived. Even the wildest mountainsides were used by ancient Greeks to provide timber, firewood, charcoal, lime, basketry materials, dyestuffs, nuts, mushrooms and wild herbs for medicinal and culinary use (see plate 6.4).

Though many features of life in the Greek countryside have changed since classical antiquity, there are still some recognizable

a

b

**Plates 6.2 a–d** Transporting by mule-cart, ploughing and sowing, Athenian black-figure cup-painting, *c.*540 BC

c

d

**Plate 6.3**  Taking pigs to market, Athenian red-figure vase-painting, *c.*470 BC

**Plate 6.4**   Charcoal burner at work, South Argolid

elements. The basic food staples have not changed, though they are integrated into quite different agro-economic regimes, especially since Greece came under the European Union in 1981. In common with their classical predecessors, modern Greek farmers still engage in the 'life and death' game of winning a livelihood in an environment governed by that most fickle of all goddesses: *Tyche*, capricious Chance.

## THE GREEK AGRICULTURAL YEAR

The Greek agricultural cycle (see table 6.1) begins in the autumn, with the onset of the winter rains. Until sufficient rain has fallen to moisten the earth, sowing is futile, and the ants and mice will consume the seed before it germinates. It was apparently normal practice in classical times to plough in the seed as it was sown (see plate 6.2). The main season for sowing the most important arable crops extended from about October until mid-December. Barley

| Modern month<br>*Attic month* | Sept.–Oct.<br>*Boedromion* | Oct.–Nov.<br>*Pyanopsion* | Nov.–Dec.<br>*Maimakterion* | Dec.–Jan.<br>*Posideon* |
|---|---|---|---|---|
| Agricultural jobs | manuring and field clearing | | | |
| | | ploughing and sowing cereals and legumes | | |
| | vintage and pressing | trenching, manuring, pruning vines | | |
| | | | trenching, manuring, pruning other fruit trees: planting new trees | |
| | fig harvest | | | |
| | | olive picking and pressing (every other year) trenching, manuring, pruning olive trees | | |
| | watering | | | |
| | | | lambing and kidding | |

**Key**

| | |
|---|---|
| —————— | Duration of task |
| ▨▨▨▨▨▨ | Moderately intense work required |
| ▧▧▧▧▧▧ | More intense work required |

**Table 6.1**  A plan of the Greek agricultural year

was sown first, then wheat, along with winter-sown legumes. Sowings were made starting with plots at the highest altitudes, working downward to lower ones.

Just before the sowing season, a number of important festivals of Demeter occurred. These included the Thesmophoria, an exclusively women's festival celebrated universally throughout Greece, and the famous Eleusinian Mysteries, held at the sanctuary of Demeter in Eleusis, north-west of Athens (see chapter 8).

But sowing was not the only job for autumn. Under the farming regimes of the classical period, most of the pruning of fruit trees and vines was done at this time, along with the essential but back-breaking work of digging the soil around them into trenches. This was done in order to direct water from the winter rains towards their roots. The technique also helped minimize water run-off and soil erosion. And in the years when the olive fruited, the bulk of the olive harvest (and the associated pressing and processing) occurred between late October and late December (see plate 6.5). This was undoubtedly the busiest time of the agricultural year. It

| Jan.–Feb. Gamelion | Feb.–Mar. Anthesterion | Mar.–Apr. Elaphebolion | Apr.–May Mounichion | May–June Thargelion | June–July Skirophorion | July–Aug. Hekatombaion | Aug.–Sept. Metageitnion |
|---|---|---|---|---|---|---|---|
| fallow ploughing | | | | | fallow ploughing | | |
| | | | | cereal and winter legume harvest | | | |
| | weeding cereals | | earthing up trees | barley wheat earthing up tree and vine trenches | threshing and crop processing for storage | | |
| vine and tree digging and pruning | | | | | | | |
| | | grafting | | fig fertilizing | | | fig harvest |
| | | | | | | fresh | dried |
| | | | watering young trees | | watering young trees and vines | | |
| lambing and kidding | | | | | | | |
| sheep and goat milking and processing | | | | milk and milk processing | | | |

**Plate 6.5**  A lever press weighted with boulders, Athenian black-figure cup-painting, late sixth century BC

is unlikely to be accidental that during the Athenian month Maimakterion (which usually fell between mid-November and mid-December in our calendar) there are no major religious festivals and not a single recorded instance of a meeting of the assembly: almost everyone must have been busy out in the fields. The religious festival called the Haloa, celebrated in honour of Demeter and Dionysos with mid-winter bonfires, was celebrated, probably with great relief, at the termination of this busy time.

From about February onward the countryside came to life again, as the last of the vine-pruning, missed in the autumn, was rapidly completed before bud burst. Spring-sown cereals, legumes and vegetables could be sown from about March onward until after the rains ceased around April. Spring is also the time when the flowers appear and the Greek countryside is at its most beautiful. This was celebrated, along with the opening of the new wine from the last vintage, at an Attic festival called the Anthesteria, the 'Flower Festival'. During the spring cereal growth takes off, but so do the weeds. Hand-weeding cereals must have been essential for obtaining a decent yield.

The cereal harvest, like the sowing, was spread out over many weeks between late May and early July. Generally barley ripens before wheat, and crops at lower altitudes and in warmer, drier, more sheltered situations are ready to harvest before those which are higher, wetter or more exposed. Threshing and winnowing generally took place, as they have until recently, on packed earth or stone-paved threshing floors set on windy hillsides (see plate 6.6). These are well removed from settlements so that the dusty chaff does not invade houses and washing lines. Unlike the cereal or hay harvest in northern Europe and North America, this is not a particularly rushed period, as by now there is little danger that rain will spoil the stacked sheaves.

The summer is comparatively slack: the time, as Hesiod said 'when I may lie in the shade facing the West Wind, drinking the shining wine and eating my fill' (*Works and Days* 592–4). The trenches dug around trees would have been smoothed flat around May, and the top layer of soil dug to a fine texture and heaped up around the trunk to keep in the moisture. If there was time and labour available, it might be dug once more in the height of summer to aid in moisture retention. Otherwise, most of the summertime jobs are pleasant ones, picking almonds, figs, and processing the fruits of the year.

**Plate 6.6**  Threshing, Methana

The end of summer comes in September with the best job of all: the grape harvest and the wine-treading. Even the wasps join in the celebrations. And though the work is arduous, it is fun, a pleasant respite before the hard toil of the busy autumn rolls round again.

### FURTHER READING

Amouretti, M.-C., 1986: *Le Pain et l'huile dans la Grèce antique* (Annales Littéraires de l'Université de Besançon 328). Paris: Société d'Edition 'Les Belles Lettres'.

Burford, A., 1993: *Land and Labour in the Greek World*. Baltimore and London: The Johns Hopkins University Press.

Cherry, J. F., Davis, J. L. and Mantzourani, E., 1991: *Landscape Archaeology as Long Term History: Northern Keos in the Cycladic Islands from Earliest Settlement until Modern Times* (*Monumenta Archaeologica* 16). Los Angeles: University of California, Institute of Archaeology.

Foxhall, L., 1997: *Olive Cultivation in Ancient Greece: Seeking the Ancient Economy* (*BICS Supplementary Monograph Series*). London: The Institute of Classical Studies.

Hanson, V. D., 1995: *The Other Greeks: The Family Farm and the Agrarian Roots of Western Civilization*. New York: The Free Press.

Isager, S. and Skydsgaard, J.-E., 1992: *Ancient Greek Agriculture: An Introduction*. London: Routledge.

Jameson, M. H., Runnels, C. N. and van Andel, T. H., 1994: *A Greek Countryside: The Southern Argolid from Prehistory to the Present Day*, Stanford (California): Stanford University Press.

Osborne, R., 1985: *Demos: The Discovery of Classical Attica*. Cambridge: Cambridge University Press.

Osborne, R., 1987: *Classical Landscape with Figures: The ancient Greek city and its countryside*. London: George Philip.

Wells, B. (ed.), 1992: *Agriculture in Ancient Greece* (*Proceedings of the 7th International Symposium at the Swedish Institute in Athens*). Stockholm: Swedish Institute at Athens.

White, K. D., 1977: *Country Life in Classical Times*. London: Paul Elek.

# 7 / POLITICS AND PUBLIC LIFE: THE URBAN SCENE

## Nick Fisher

### INTRODUCTION

Two thousand five hundred years ago decisive steps towards the most influential form of direct democracy of the ancient world were taken in Athens, with the reforms of Kleisthenes in 508/7 BC. We know far more about political and social life in Athens in the classical period than in any other of the numerous, notionally independent, small city-states (*poleis*), for a number of reasons. First, Athens rapidly became one of the two most powerful Greek states, along with Sparta, and made some efforts to 'export' its innovative and controversial system of government as one means of increasing support for its fifth-century empire. Hence both the city and its democracy commanded the greatest historiographical attention, then and since. Second, in this period it produced a remarkable number of great playwrights, historians and philosophers, many of whose works have survived. Third, unlike its great rival Sparta, it sought deliberately to be an 'open society'; as a result a good many non-Athenian writers and thinkers settled, permanently or temporarily, in the city and reflect it in their writings (often very critically). Fourth, the Athenian system published in profusion, and in the permanent form of the stone inscription, many records of its decisions and accounts of the work of its magistrates. Many more public inscriptions have been found from Attica than from any other state in this period, though this 'epigraphic habit' was to spread throughout the Greek world and lasted well into the Hellenistic and Roman periods as a distinctive and major cultural phenomenon. Finally, a century's detailed archaeological investigation, above all in the *agora* (city centre), continues to reveal much about Athenian public life. Hence this chapter necessarily focuses on Athens, untypically large and developed though it probably was. Some attention, however, will be paid to the even more untypical Sparta and to some other cities for which useful evidence exists.

**Plate 7.1** An Athenian inscription making provision against tyranny, topped by a relief carving showing Democracy crowning Demos ('The People') (337/336 BC)

## ATHENIAN DEMOCRATIC LIFE

Athenian democracy (plate 7.1), like all political systems in the Greek world, was restricted to the descent group of adult male citizens (on average perhaps 30,000 or so; probably more, perhaps over 50,000, in the mid-fifth century). They thus formed an elite 'club', in contrast to the different types of inferiors with fewer or almost no rights: non-Athenians living in Athens (*metoikoi*), women, and slaves. What distinguished Athens, and presumably other 'democratic' *poleis*, were the related principles that the laws gave equal protection and rights to all citizens, with no restriction in terms of wealth or ownership of land, that all citizens had reasonable access to office-holding (whether through election or the use of the lot) and that a relatively large proportion of the citizens regularly participated, and were rewarded (to a relatively small degree) for doing so, in the varied governmental bodies which made and administered the city's decisions through the processes of ordered, rational and open discussions, followed by the taking of votes. But general principles, their ideological justifications and actual practices can often diverge: one needs to ask how, and how effectively, in classical Athens, did the system deliver efficient government, the widespread participation of many citizens, and stability and cohesion rather than hostility and conflict between the different social classes.

## THE URBAN SETTINGS OF ATHENIAN PUBLIC LIFE

After Kleisthenes' reorganization, all citizens were members, firstly, of the 139 demes where their direct male ancestors had registered in 508/7 BC, and where many of them, in fact, still lived throughout the period of the democracy. Most of these demes were in the Attic countryside, rather than in the linked urban areas of Athens and the port of Piraeus, and many citizens may have first gained experience of public meetings, elections and office-holding in their own self-governing demes. All demesmen were also members of the linked larger bodies of *trittyes* ('ridings') and *phylai* ('tribes'), which also held their meetings and rituals, and played significant parts in the organization of the land army. Representation for the all-important Council of 500 (50 from each tribe) and for the 6,000 jurors manning the law courts was also organized through the demes and tribes: councillors and jurors were chosen by lot from lists prepared in the demes of those willing each year to stand. Many athletic or musical competitions at state festivals such as the Panathenaia and City Dionysia were also organized on a tribal basis. Finally, all citizens could attend the mass meetings of the assembly (*ekklesia*), held on the Pnyx at Athens (see figure 7.1), which took the most important decisions of the state.

Thus, while the majority of Athenians remained landowners (small or large), and significant minorities earned a living as craftsmen, sea-traders, retailers and so on, those who participated in the central religious, social or political life of the *polis* had usually to take the walk into the heart of the city. Though some major festivals, for example the Eleusinian mysteries, involved other centres in the territory of the *polis*, the centrality of Athens itself was emphasized even then by a procession to or from the centre of Athens. The civic and political heart of the city was constituted by, first, the Acropolis, in the classical period essentially home to the city's chief

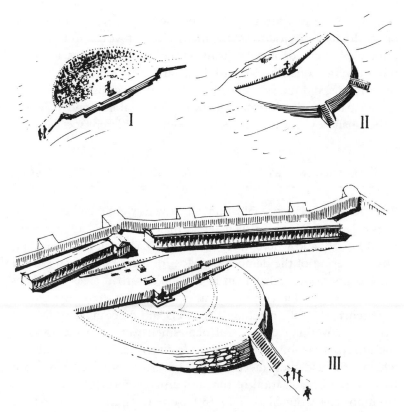

**Figure 7.1** The Pnyx of Athens where the assembly met; the three phases show the enlargement from the fifth to the fourth centuries BC

gods and religious activities focused on altars and temples such as the Parthenon and the Erechtheion; second, the smaller Areopagus hill, where the ancient and originally much more aristocratic Council still met to hear homicide and some other cases; third, the Pnyx hill, where the assembly met (see figure 7.1); fourth, the open areas below the Acropolis, notably the main *agora*, where the Council of 500 (*Boule*) met in the Bouleuterion, its standing Committee of 50 met in the round Tholos, the public records were kept, the courts met, and other magistrates dispensed their business. In the *agora* too, citizens could consult public notices on stone or wooden boards, shop from innumerable small stalls and shops, negotiate deals in trade or politics, or hear the news or the gossip in the colonnades (*stoai*), laundries and wine shops. Beyond the *agora* lay the Kerameikos area, where there were the potters' quarters, many bars and brothels, and outside the city wall, the public burial grounds and grave monuments. Magistrates and councillors ate, fairly frugally and mostly at public expense, in dining areas attached to their buildings; more lavish civic entertainment was provided at the Prytaneion (north-east of the Acropolis), for visiting dignitaries, returning ambassadors and those very few Athenians to whom the city wished to give the signal honour of 'free meals for life at the Prytaneion': the granting of this honour to the aggressively democratic politician Kleon in the 420s BC caused offence, and the ludicrous suggestion of Sokrates at his trial for impiety and corruption of the young, that this should be his 'penalty', ensured his condemnation to death by hemlock.

## PARTICIPATION IN THE ORGANS OF GOVERNMENT

The assembly, open to all citizens over 20, took place in an area (the Pnyx hill) where archaeological investigation has revealed that, in the fifth century, little more than *c*.6,000 could be seated on the hillside (more perhaps may have stood at the sides or back on occasions). After the restoration of the democracy in 404 BC, the orientation of the space was reversed, and the whole area more clearly enclosed; it may perhaps have been able to accommodate rather closer to 7,000, now all seated on benches (see figure 7.1). From the late 390s assembly-goers (probably the first 6,000 to arrive) were paid, and attendance perhaps more regularly met the target of over 6,000. Thus the democracy felt satisfied that no more than one-fifth or so of the total number of citizens constituted an adequate number to make the vital decisions of the state, and democratic discourse equated the assembly with 'the people' without question. It is no coincidence that 6,000 was also the number of votes cast necessary for a valid ostracism, in the period (*c*.508–415 BC) when this was a common way of relieving political tensions, by expelling a powerful politician for ten years; it was also the number of jurors appointed each year (see plate 7.2 and figure 7.2). In the later fourth century there were four regular assembly meetings a civic month (forty a year), but numbers of meetings at earlier stages are obscure, though there was at least one statutory meeting a month from the fifth century on. Such evidence as we

**Plate 7.2** An Athenian juror's ticket (*pinakion*), mid-fourth century BC

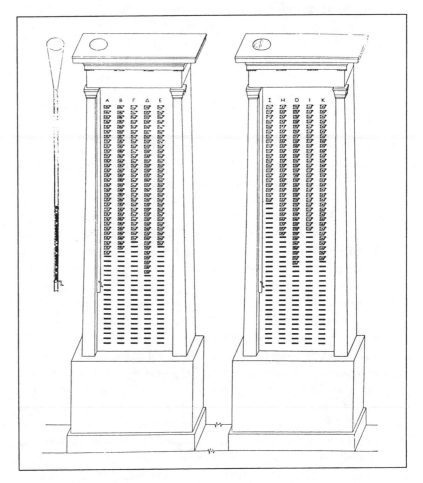

**Figure 7.2** An Athenian allotment machine for the law courts, fourth century BC

have – often biased and contradictory – is perhaps most compatible with the view that the assembly did indeed attract a reasonable cross-section of citizens, and a largely unpredictable mixture on each occasion. It is likely enough that those who lived in or near the city (which would include many farmers as well as those who worked in the city or in the port of Piraeus) would tend to turn up rather more often, and the politically keen and active would attend more vigorously than the more apathetic; but overall the majority of poorer citizens was certainly well represented.

Members of the Council of 500, like all Athenian magistrates and jurors, had to be at least 30 years old; one could serve no more than two terms on the Council in a lifetime, and not in successive years. Given these facts, and also the probability that the average age of councillors was about 40, it seems likely that at least a third, perhaps as many as a half, of all citizens would have to serve at least once for the system to work as it did. The responsibilities were heavy (preparing business for the assembly, controlling it, managing many other aspects of administration and finance), and all councillors, like all other magistrates, were subject to the all-important procedures of the scrutiny before holding office (*dokimasia*) and the investigation of one's conduct in office afterwards (*euthuna*).

Power at least equal to that of the assembly was exercised by the 6,000 jurors, who were also conceived as 'the people' *tout court*. The courts tried many patently 'political' cases as well as private disputes; in fact a great many of the cases before the popular juries combined inextricably personal and political disagreements, often part of a sequence of legal 'feudings' between leading Athenians. Through the process whereby those who had proposed successful motions in the assembly could be prosecuted for having done so illegally (*graphe paranomon*), the people's court was in fact the only body that could check what the assembly did, and the jurors were themselves not subject to account or scrutiny for their decisions (as was pointed out at the climax of the critique of the courts in Aristophanes' comedy *Wasps*). Like the councillors and the magistrates, jurors had to be at least 30 years old. On balance they seem probably to have been a fair representation of social classes, though traditional beliefs in the value of the experience of age, and the greater free time available to the elderly, may well have made it especially attractive to such citizens, as their portrait in Aristophanes' play strongly suggests.

## POLITICIANS AND THE PEOPLE

Overall, then, the political system achieved an astonishingly high degree of interest and personal commitment: very many ordinary, hard-working citizens spent much of their time sharing in the decision-making and administration of their city. Citizens who kept themselves apart from all such activities could find themselves criticized, as in Perikles' funeral speech reported by Thucydides (*Histories* 2.34–46), for being 'useless'. Throughout the period, there was also, of course, a leisured elite of the rich, whose composition in fact was subject to considerable change; their personal and financial contributions were crucial to the working of the system. 'Generals' (*strategoi*), ten elected each year, provided military and political leadership (and there were other elected military officers); a continuous series of generalships held between 443 and 429 was the institutional base of Perikles' personal dominance in Athenian politics in that period. Ambassadors, elected *ad hoc*, represented the city; from the mid-fourth century elected boards of officials advised on financial distributions, and their chairmen became extremely influential (these leading figures were, successively, Euboulos, Demosthenes and Lykourgos). Most importantly, the major roles in the public debates, and in the more important legal trials, were played by self-selecting, mostly rich, individuals known as orators or politicians, for whom public life was virtually a career. In the fifth century, men like Kimon, Perikles, Kleon and Alkibiades regularly combined the roles of general and orator, speaking and proposing motions in the assembly, often pleading in the courts; in the fourth century there was more frequently a differentiation between the rhetorical and financial experts such as Euboulos, Demosthenes and Lykourgos and military men such as Iphikrates, Chabrias and Chares. In the financial sphere, most Athenians paid no tax on their capital wealth or income, while the wealthiest (perhaps as many as 2,000–3,000) were liable to an irregular property-tax (*eisphora*), and the 1,200 or so richest were also liable to involvement in the complex system of public 'liturgies'. Such men were required to contribute, in cash and personal commitment, to the running of a warship or to the management of the many state festivals such as the Dionysia (see plate 7.3). Such financial contributions to community activities could involve severe, at times unpredictable, strains on rich men, and may have contributed to impoverishment and changes in elite membership. Yet

**Plate 7.3**  The choregic monument of Lysikrates, Athens (335/334 BC), celebrating his victory after paying for a boys' chorus at the City Dionysia

many elite Athenians chose to do more than was strictly required and claimed credit, as election candidates or in law suits, for their expenditure and efforts. The system in fact maintained a complex negotiation of interests and benefits between the people and the rich. All the rich were under some pressure to contribute to a system where final power was exercised by the majority of poorer citizens in the assembly and the courts; but the more ambitious and politically active of them were encouraged to contribute more with the prospects of a return in the form of 'honours' – prizes, crowns, statues and honorific decrees – and chances of more successful public careers. To a considerable extent this seems to have worked; not only were many rich men persuaded to contribute money and efforts more generously, in the hope of a return, but also a greater class cohesion and community spirit was fostered, as the richest Athenians became involved in leadership roles in competitive areas of military and civic service where ordinary citizens were also deeply involved, as rowers, participants in festival games and contests, or as spectators. These complex exchanges will also have forced the rich to develop their farms or other assets to generate cash sales, and accompanied an increased monetarization and development of the Athenian economy, for the benefit of many, especially those living in the city. On the other hand, of course, resentment at these and other aspects of the democratic system is also amply attested, by critics such as the author of the oligarchic pamphlet written in the 420s BC known as the Pseudo-Xenophon, or the 'Old Oligarch', who grumbled that the rich had to pay for the fleet and festivals, while the poor took the pay and the rich got poorer (1.13); or Xenophon himself, who could represent the life of a rich man as heavily burdened by these taxes and liturgies, as well as by the obligations to entertain friends and gatherings of citizens (*Household Management* 2.5–7). This material suggests that many rich, especially the less politically minded or the unsuccessful, still felt harshly treated by their deprivation from the types of power exercised by elites in other less democratic cities and by the social pressures imposed by the tax and liturgy system, and by the courts. On balance, though, the system worked well in Athens. We are unfortunately not at all well informed how comparable mechanisms worked in other democratic cities in Greece, though a number of comments in Aristotle's *Politics* suggests that they were widely employed.

## URBAN SOCIAL LIFE

The combination of intense competition and a spirit of consensus and cohesion can be seen to permeate the two main forms of leisure activities which dominated the social life of most men in Greek cities: gymnastic, athletic and musical games during the day; and the shared, ritualized eating, drinking and other forms of play in the evenings. Originally perhaps felt rather to be the preserve of aristocratic elites, all these activities can be seen to have undergone processes of expanded participation, to varying degrees in different cities.

### COMPETING IN GAMES AND WAR

The divisions in the Greek world, together with their prevailing systems of values, helped to create a culture in which constant warfare, over land, resources or glory, and intense competition for prizes and honour in athletic and other contests, acquired mutually reinforcing significances which it would be difficult to exaggerate. Greek cities recognized the need to prepare their citizens to fight, according to their means, on horseback, on foot, or at sea, and the desirability of honouring those who excelled in war or died for their cities. They also gave great encouragement to their citizens' involvement in gymnastic and athletic training and competition, partly as military preparation and partly for the enjoyment of the spectacle of sporting competitions between naked young men (from the sixth century, at least, open homosexual attachments between young men and adolescents flourished, especially among the elite classes; see chapter 15). The importance given to the games in the four-year circuit (created in the early sixth century BC) of 'Panhellenic' or 'Crown' Games, at Olympia, Delphi, the Isthmus at Corinth and Nemea, is indicated by the regular proclamation of a truce throughout the Greek world for the duration, to allow access for athletes and spectators, and by the public honours and wealth showered on the winners (for example at Athens, Olympic victors received free meals at the Prytaneion for life). Many successful athletes developed political careers or ambitions. While the 'Crown' Games provided only prizes of crowns of olive or bay, valuable prizes were available at other games (such as the prestigious Panathenaic games at Athens, where large jars of expensive olive oil were the prizes), and top-level athletics became in time less an aristocratic preserve than at first. Certain cities too (notably the Greek city of Kroton in South Italy in the sixth century) put more effort and subsidies into producing champions and gaining prestige.

In the classical period, Sparta based her educational system and the remarkably uniform and regimented social life of her citizens on the need to maintain constant military preparedness and terror against their Helot ('serf') population and to hold her position as the strongest land-power in Greece. Hence from the age of 7 until 60 male Spartan citizens (*Spartiatai*) spent more of their time than other Greeks in connected and well-organized programmes of gymnastic and athletic activity, ritual contests in running and endurance, as well as singing and dancing at festivals, and rigorous hoplite training. At Athens, many other festivals besides the great Panathenaia involved athletic competitions in running, jumping, discus-throwing, boxing and wrestling, and equestrian events. At various levels, a great many Athenians must have been involved in preparing for such contests, often in 'tribal' teams, and generally in training in the *gymnasia*. These *gymnasia* were the major social settings in ancient cities, and the location also for meetings and for political or philosophical discussions. Major schools of philosophy, such as Plato's Academy and Aristotle's Lyceum, grew around such *gymnasia*, and they were also the place where friendships or homosexual love-affairs developed (women and slaves were not permitted to participate in gymnastic life).

Connections between military and athletic training were recognized, though doubts came to be expressed about the suitability for fighting of advanced athletic training. While the poorer majority of citizens did their military service as rowers in the fleet, which was the main basis of Athenian power and hence a significant justification for full-scale democracy, or as light-armed troops, paradoxically the heavy-armed infantryman ('hoplite') who owned his own small farm, remained ideologically the ideal paradigm of the citizen. Young men about to be citizens (known as *epheboi*) appear to have engaged in an initiatory process for two years in which they had their own contests in the Panathenaia and other festivals, and also some elements of military training and garrison duties. For these *epheboi*, the military aspects of their training were considerably tightened up and the religious activities extended in the 330s BC as a response to the Athenian defeat at the hands of Philip of Macedon in 338. The hoplites, cavalry and rowers must have been

**Plate 7.4**  Bronze figurine of a Spartan hoplite, sixth century BC

put through basic training from time to time in their tribal units, but military training was at a markedly lower key in Athens, and in most other cities, than in Sparta (see plate 7.4). Efforts to catch up were made in the fourth century, above all at Thebes, which steadily increased her place among the Greek powers in large part through greater concentration on training, strategy and tactics, and also on the development of a crack corps, the Sacred Band, made up of 150 pairs of devoted homosexual lovers.

### DRINKING PARTIES AND MALE SOCIAL GROUPS

A significant contribution to the complexity and openness of Athenian politics and society was made by the lively functioning of a variety of all-male small groups or associations to which citizens belonged, necessarily or from choice. To what extent such groups should be seen as operating in the public or the private sphere can be hard to determine. The traditional *symposion*, with its formalized

**Plate 7.5** Drinking, playing and singing at an Athenian symposion, Athenian red-figure cup-painting, *c.*470 BC

structure of drinking procedures (reclining on couches, drinking wine mixed with water from a shared mixing-bowl, and so on) and the music, conversation or sexual entertainments, was the characteristic evening activity of the elites throughout Greece, and provided the pattern, in various degrees of excess or restraint, for a wide variety of group-meetings, as well as for the basic 'party' of casual friends, held in the smartest 'men's rooms' of their private houses (see plate 7.5). Potentially subversive were groups of friends (*hetaireiai*), who co-operated together in politics or legal disputes, as well as regularly drinking together; the predominantly elitist or ostentatiously extravagant and offensive tone of many such groups often appeared contrary to democratic values, or even – especially at times of high political tension, such as in the period between 415 and 404 BC – a focus of oligarchic plots. All Athenians, however, belonged, in addition to the demes and tribes established by the Kleisthenic reforms, to older pseudo-kinship organizations called *phratriai* ('brotherhoods'), which also held regular festivals, and produced further sub-divisions (bands of *orgeones*, or *thiasoi*). They might also join voluntary groups, also often called *thiasoi* or *orgeones*; these typically took the form of cult-groups dedicated to an individual god or hero. Many of them were composed of both citizens and non-citizens, and often helped to foster the introduction of foreign cults into Attica. All such groups operated along the same democratic procedures and values as the city organizations, and their social activities focused on common meetings, sacrifices and conviviality, along the model of the 'private' *symposion*. This range of social gatherings and associations, open to most, perhaps all, citizens, at least on rare occasions, enabled them to form new friendships and to gain supporters and new social identities; they were able to demand that their life-styles could, at times at least, include some pleasures previously felt to be the preserve of the aristocracy, such as fresh fish, entertainers such as female musicians and dancers, or a flutter over dice or a cock-fight.

In Sparta, on the other hand, in theory all citizens belonged solely to the official organizations of common 'messes' (*syssitia*), which shared uniform and strictly limited patterns of activities, promoted approved values and strongly discouraged drunkenness or dissenting voices. The food was normally austere (the famous 'black broth'), though solidarity could also be enhanced when the richer members of the messes contributed extra food, especially hunted meats, for their mess-mates. However, no matter what the reality of this picture, at least from the mid-fourth century onwards, the growing tensions in Spartan society clearly led to more open divisions and disunities in the messes, as in the educational and social structures more generally.

We can say even less about the functions of the similar groups and associations in other cities, many of which suffered many more attacks of disunity or civil war (collectively known as *stasis*) than did either Athens or Sparta. In such cases more important and disruptive roles were evidently played by committed groups (*hetaireiai*) of politically ambitious men seeking personal power, while claiming to represent the principles of democracy or oligarchy. The classic analysis of this during the Peloponnesian War is found in Thucydides' account of civil war on the island of Corcyra (*Histories* 3.80–5), and in many places conditions did not improve through the fourth century BC.

### FURTHER READING

Bérard, C. et al., 1989: *City of Images: Iconography and Society in Ancient Greece*. New Jersey: Princeton University Press.

Camp, J. M., 1986: *The Athenian Agora: Excavations in the Heart of Classical Athens*. London: Thames and Hudson.

Cartledge, P. A., 1978: *Sparta and Lakonia: A Regional History 1300–362 BC.* London: Routledge and Kegan Paul.

Davies, J. K., 1981: *Wealth and the Power of Wealth in Classical Athens.* Salem, New Hampshire: The Ayer Company.

Finley, M. I., 1985: *Democracy Ancient and Modern* (new edn). London: Chatto and Windus.

Hansen, M. H., 1991: *The Athenian Democracy in the Age of Demosthenes.* Oxford: Blackwell Publishers.

Hunter, V., 1994: *Policing Athens: Social Control in the Attic Lawsuits, 420–320 BC.* New Jersey: Princeton University Press.

Kyle, D. G., 1987: *Athletics in Ancient Athens.* Leiden: Brill.

Murray, O., 1990: *Sympotica: A Symposium on the Symposion.* Oxford: Clarendon Press.

Murray, O. and Price, S. (eds), 1990: *The Greek City from Homer to Alexander.* Oxford: Oxford University Press.

Ober, J., 1989: *Mass and Elite in Democratic Athens: Rhetoric, Ideology and the Power of the People.* New Jersey: Princeton University Press.

Ober, J. and Hedrick, C. W. (eds), 1994: *The Birth of Democracy: Catalogue of an Exhibition Celebrating the 2500th Anniversary of Democracy, at the National Archives, Washington DC.* Athens: American School of Classical Studies.

Powell, A., 1988: *Athens and Sparta: Constructing Greek Political and Social History from 478 BC.* London: Routledge.

Sinclair, R. K., 1988: *Democracy and Participation in Athens.* Cambridge: Cambridge University Press.

Whitehead, D., 1986: *The Demes of Attica, 508/7 – ca. 250 BC.* New Jersey: Princeton University Press.

# 8 / GREEK RELIGIOUS PRACTICES

## *Robert Parker*

### INTRODUCTION

Greek religion first becomes observable for us around 700 BC, the approximate date of the first two surviving Greek poets, Homer and Hesiod. It was not, of course, invented from nothing at that date. The chief god Zeus, often called Zeus *Pater* (Zeus 'the father'), is a descendant of the Indo-European sky god: the proof is the near identity of his name with those of his Indian and Roman equivalents *Dyaus pitar* and *Diespiter* (Jupiter). The Linear B tablets, found in Mycenaean palaces from the period 1400–1200 BC and written in an early form of Greek, show that a good number of the gods of classical Greece were already known then, along with other figures who disappeared. Within the historical period, beginning *c*.700 BC, some gods and goddesses entered Greece from outside – Bendis from Thrace in the fifth century, for instance, or much later Isis from Egypt – and others such as the healer Asklepios developed from minor into major figures. But by and large the similarities between the gods of Homer and those mentioned by Pausanias, who wrote a *Guide to Greece* in the second century AD, are much more striking than the differences. Interpretations changed, no doubt; from about the sixth century BC philosophers began to understand traditional gods in new ways, or to allegorize away the more outrageous doings ascribed to them in myths. But they continued to worship at the old altars. What will be described in these pages remained in essence the religion of the Greeks from the Homeric age (and no doubt long before) right until the rise of Christianity.

### MYTH

Early Greeks believed that the world was surrounded by a great river, Ocean, from which all other rivers took their origin. Myth, in the great Swiss historian Jacob Burckhardt's formulation, was the 'spiritual Ocean of the Greek world'. Its importance is by no means confined to the religious sphere, but it did affect religion in various ways. The most familiar myths, it is true, usually recounted the doings of men; but a significant few told of the wars and marriages and offspring of the gods early in the history of the world. They thus explained the present organization of the pantheon and indeed of the universe. The first ruler was Heaven, *Ouranos*; he was castrated and overthrown by his son *Kronos* (castration here representing mythically the primal separation of Earth from Heaven); Kronos sought to devour his children but was bound and overthrown by the youngest of them, the present ruler Zeus. The kingship of Zeus, the third ruler, is thus seen as a kind of endpoint towards which history was moving, a culmination; and Zeus is associated both with justice, since he was right to overthrow so unnatural a father, and with power, since he had the strength to do so. The division of meat between gods and men at sacrifice was very unequal: men consumed all the good meat, and assigned to the gods only bones and fat. Another 'archmyth' traced this fundamental feature of sacrificial practice back to a trick played on Zeus by a god friendly to man, Prometheus, on the occasion of the first sacrifice. Another prime point of contact between religion and myth is the cult of 'heroes', lesser powers of more local scope whom the Greeks worshipped alongside the gods. These heroes of cult are not identical with those of myth and legend, but the two groups do overlap; to take three of the best-known mythological heroes, while any cult received by Oedipus was very obscure, Orestes was a figure of some importance at Sparta (his father Agamemnon and his aunt Helen still more so), and Herakles was worshipped as virtually a god throughout Greece.

More broadly, the heroes of myth belonged to a special age, lasting only a few generations, of superhuman achievement; but it was in just this special age that according to legend almost all the institutions of Greek religion had their origin. So the myths and their cults had their roots in the same soil. Myth was also fundamental in shaping the Greeks' sense of their own identity. The three chief linguistic groups into which the Greeks of the historical period were divided, for instance, were 'Ionian', 'Dorian' and 'Aiolian'; they had their origins, according to myth, in Doros and Aiolos, sons of Hellen, whose name means 'Greek', and their nephew Ion. Individual Greeks had begun by the fifth century to become cautious about claiming direct descent from gods or heroes; but the Athenians collectively remained 'descendants of

**Plate 8.1** Bronze figurine from Thebes, dedicated to Apollo by Mantiklos, early seventh century BC

Theseus' or 'descendants of Erechtheus', inhabitants of the land for possession of which the gods Athena and Poseidon had once fought. More fundamental still was the way in which myth remained the central vehicle for Greek art and poetry and thus for Greek imaginative experience. The tragedians dramatized the myths, myths were the main theme of the sculptures that adorned the temples, and as one drained one's wine at a *symposion* one was likely to be confronted by a mythological scene at the bottom of the cup. This is why the question 'is it true?' was much less often posed than we might feel it should have been. Myths were indispensable as a vehicle not just of thought but also of imagination and feeling.

## CULT

From myths we turn to practices. A little bronze figurine of a warrior (see plate 8.1) made around 650 BC bears on one of its thighs the verse inscription 'Mantiklos dedicated me out of his tithe to far-shooting Apollo of the silver bow; grant him a fine return, Phoibos.' A vast divide separated mortals from the deathless gods in power and strength and honour; nonetheless, as this tiny example shows, classical Greeks believed or hoped that the relation between them could be one of reciprocity, an exchange of goods and services. The gods had in their gift such basic goods as health, wealth, success, and victory in war. Mortals for their part were bound, not to 'believe' or 'have faith', as in Christianity, but to grant the gods certain honours, gifts, and services.

The Greater Panathenaia, the most splendid festival of Athens, nicely illustrates what these gifts and honours could be. It was celebrated every four years, and the central ritual act was the presentation to Athena on each occasion of a new robe which a group of aristocratic maidens had, as a special privilege, long laboured to prepare. The same mythological scene was always depicted on the robe, the battle of the gods and giants, and Athena was always shown in the forefront of the fight. This cunningly woven scene of warfare honoured the goddess in two fundamental aspects, as patroness of the 'works of women', including weaving above all, but also as a warrior herself and a sturdy supporter of male warriors. The robe was brought to Athena in a magnificent procession, which the Parthenon frieze depicts or at least alludes to; it moved up through the business and commercial centre of the city, the *agora*, to the goddess's temple on the Acropolis, and select representatives of most sections of Athenian society took part, again of course as a high honour. On one level what was happening was the presentation of a gift to the goddess; on another, Athens was putting herself on display and making a statement about what and whom she held in honour. The procession was a 'show' (*thea*, cf. theatre), a word that is applied with revealing frequency to Greek festivals. A show of another type was provided by an extensive programme of athletic and musical competitions, including for instance recitations of the poems of Homer, that also formed part of the Greater Panathenaia. It is highly characteristic that elements which we would classify as entertainment belonged to the festival; almost without exception both 'sport' and 'art' took place only in religious contexts. Festivals, including the Panathenaia, also regularly contained performances that we have less difficulty in recognizing as religious. The singing by choirs of songs of various types in honour of the gods was a basic form of worship; such choirs, which had to perform intricate dance movements as they sang, normally consisted of the young, and learning to take part in them was an important part of the education of well-born youths and, particularly, maidens. But the choral performance even of a hymn was also a 'show', and the distinction which comes so easily to us between 'religious' and 'secular' or 'entertainment' aspects of festivals is one that the Greeks did not make. A most important final aspect of the Panathenaia was sacrifice. Large numbers of cattle were slain, and in the classical period the whole citizen population of Attica feasted at public expense in honour of the goddess.

Innumerable Greek festivals are known, and we cannot begin to survey them all. But selection poses its own acute problems. One festival at Athens contained a rite that dramatized the moral dilemmas associated with killing and eating animals. An ox was slain; the killer immediately turned and fled, as if he had killed a human. A trial was then held to establish who was guilty of the crime, and 'the water-bearers blame those who whetted the axe, the whetters the man who passed it on, this man the one who slew the ox, and the slayer the knife: and the knife, being unable to speak, they condemn for the murder' (Porphyry *On Abstinence* 2.30). According to another text (Pausanias *Guide to Greece* 1.24.4 and 28.10), it is the axe that is condemned and thrown into the sea. This rite already seemed quaintly old-fashioned to Aristophanes in the fifth century. Still more startling is the practice attested for several cities, including Athens, of driving out (but not, it now seems, actually killing) two human 'medicines' (*pharmakoi*), who were apparently meant to take the ills of the community with them, like the 'scapegoats' of the Old Testament. An account of Greek festivals that stresses instances such as these will look very different from one that takes the Panathenaia, as we have done, as typical. The best remedy for the hazards of selectivity is probably to look at the most popular festivals of a single city; and this on grounds of evidence will have to be Athens.

## ATHENIAN FESTIVALS

Athens was famed for the abundance of her festivals, but five stand out which must have been highlights of the year for almost every Athenian.

1   The *Greater Panathenaia* we have met already; it also had a scaled down form, the Lesser Panathenaia, for the intervening years.

2   The *City Dionysia* was the most important occasion on which new tragedies, comedies and satyr-plays were performed. This festival too, like the Panathenaia, was a pre-eminently civic event; honours for meritorious citizens and foreigners, for instance, were often 'proclaimed' before the assembled citizenry in the theatre. But we should not forget that on the day before the tragedies began an image of Dionysos had been escorted into the city in procession and ritually 'received'; so the civic arts festival was also the celebration of the advent of a god. Such ritual 'arrivals' are particularly characteristic of the cult of Dionysos. According to myth, as seen most vividly in Euripides' play *Bacchae*, Dionysos met fierce resistance when he first arrived in Greece from the east, a new god, and it was partly in punishment for this rejection that he established his outrageous rites in which women went out to dance wildly on the mountains (see plate 8.2). In reality, very few Athenian women probably had the chance to tread the mountains, but the perception of the god expressed in the myth as one who arrives, dramatically and perhaps disruptively, is certainly present in his rituals.

3   The *Anthesteria*, another festival of Dionysos, is another of the Athenian big five, and was perhaps the most popular of all, the closest Greek equivalent in emotional terms to Christmas. Its occasion was the first broaching, in February, of the autumn's vintage, and at its centre were singular drinking parties which included a competition in draining a large jug of wine at speed. The participants then tumbled cheerfully down to the old shrine of 'Dionysos in the Marshes', open on this day alone, to dedicate the garlands they had worn when drinking. But it was almost certainly also on this occasion that, in the cryptic words of our sources, the wife of the *archon basileus*, one of the most prestigious annual magistrates, 'was given to Dionysos' as a bride. About the mechanics of this transaction we can only guess (was 'Dionysos' a statue? or did the *archon* impersonate the god?). But clearly the symbolic aim was to link the god with the city, at his periodic advent, in the closest possible way. It is quite plausible that events of the festival are also reflected on a series of vases that show women dancing, sometimes wildly, in the presence of a mask of Dionysos on a pillar, and/or a large jug of wine. If that is so, Dionysiac dancing (even if not on a mountain) could form part of the normal

**Plate 8.2** Ecstatic dancing in honour of Dionysos-Sabazios and Cybele, Athenian red-figure vase-painting, *c*.440–430 BC

experience of an Athenian woman. Certainly there was more to this complicated festival than cosy drunkenness at all-male parties in celebration of the new wine. One day of the festival counted as ill-omened or polluted; there is some late evidence that the souls of the dead were felt to be at large; status distinctions too were to some degree relaxed, masters being obliged to give their slaves a share in the festivities.

4   A fourth major Athenian festival (major in fact in almost all Greek cities) was the *Thesmophoria*. 'Women's festivals' are an important category, and within it the Thesmophoria is much the most important. It lasted for three days, during which the married women of Athens, very remarkably, camped out *en masse* in specially erected huts. Demeter, goddess of corn, and her daughter Persephone were its honorands, and at one level the festival was evidently concerned with the fertility both of fields and of women (which were closely connected in Greek thought, the standard

formula for instance whereby a man betrothed his daughter being 'I give you this woman for the ploughing of legitimate children' (Menander fragment 720K)). A central rite was the fetching up from underground chambers of the rotten remains of piglets and cakes which had been deposited there earlier (the first day was called *Anodos* or 'Ascent'). This sludge was then placed on certain altars, and farmers who took a little and mixed it with their seed-corn (this being autumn, the season of sowing) were, it was said, assured of a good crop. But it was scarcely necessary for all the citizen wives of Attica to displace themselves from their homes for three days if the whole purpose of the festival was to perform this elementary agricultural magic. At a different level the Athenians were well aware that it related just as much to gender roles. Aristophanes' play *Women at the Thesmophoria* shows the women holding an assembly and passing decrees (including a death sentence on misogynist Euripides) during the festival; this is, of course, comic fantasy, but inscriptions reveal that the festival was organized by female 'magistrates' and thus that it was indeed an occasion when women could be felt, very unusually, to regulate their own affairs as if they were men. This time of symbolic self-determination was not, however, one of liberation. Only respectable matrons were admitted; they spent most of the second day sitting on the ground, fasting (hence called *Nesteia*); and during the festival they were known as 'bees', an emblem for the ancients of sexual continence. The third day was called 'Fair Birth' (*Kalligeneia*), and the message of the festival seems to be that respectable women, those fit to perform their proper function of bearing citizen children, must be restrained and chaste. Such women then receive honour, being judged fit to participate in the rites of the two august goddesses.

5   The final great Attic festival is most unusual. Candidates for initiation in the *Eleusinian Mysteries* spent a week or so in preliminaries; they then marched the roughly fourteen miles to Eleusis in a loosely structured, merry, even ribald procession; after further preparations, at the climax of a long torchlit night ritual, a revelation was made to them (we do not know of what) in the great initiation hall by the 'shower of sacred things'. This final revelation had two grades, so that to become a full initiate one had to return for a second year. Those who duly did so were encouraged to hope for a better lot in the afterlife (*Homeric Hymn to Demeter*, 480–2):

**Plate 8.3** Attic marble votive relief showing worshippers approaching Artemis, found at Brauron (Attica), *c.*330 BC

> Blessed is that mortal who has seen these things.
> But he who is uninitiated in the rites
> and has no share in them
> fares worse even after death in the dank darkness.

The Mysteries were an Athenian state cult (though open to Greeks at large) of the highest prestige, and are the most important exception to the generally true claim that the concerns of mainstream Greek religion were resolutely of this world. But even initiates of Eleusis did no more than nurture 'hopes' about what was to come.

## FORMS OF RELIGIOUS ACTION

From festivals we can turn back to the forms of action in Greek religion. In discussing the Panathenaia we have already met the four most important: processions (see plate 8.3), choral singing and dancing, gifts and sacrifices. Gifts in the form of votive offerings were extremely important in the individual's commerce with the gods; Greek temples were full of them, ranging from expensive works of art to humble lead figurines worth a few pence. Still more important was sacrifice. It too was interpreted as a form of gift to

**Plate 8.4** Preparations for the sacrifice of a ram at a stone-built altar, Athenian red-figure vase-painting, *c.*420 BC

the god, and was in fact much the commonest form of such giving, occurring in almost every conceivable context. The procedure at a typical sacrifice can be divided very roughly into three stages.

(1) *Preliminaries.* An animal is brought to the altar, usually in procession; a group of worshippers assembles around it (see plate 8.4), and lustral water and barley grains are passed around the circle. A little water may be splashed on the animal's head to

make it 'nod' assent to what is to come. The main sacrificer cuts hair from the victim's head and utters a prayer, and the other participants throw forward a handful of the barley grains. Note that sacrifice is invariably accompanied by prayer, though often of a very simple type ('grant us health and wealth'); conversely, sacrifice is much the most important context in which prayers are uttered.

(2)  *The kill.* Small animals are held directly over the altar and have their throats cut there, so that their blood falls on to it. Larger animals are stunned with a blow from an axe; the neck is then drawn back so that the throat can be cut and the blood caught in a bowl for transfer to the altar. We can note in passing that small animals such as sheep and goats were much the commonest victims for private and often even public sacrifice, though epic poetry tends to show the heroes bringing expensive and prestigious offerings such as bulls.

(3)  *Division of the meat.* The thigh bones and some pieces of fat are burnt on the altar for the gods; libations of wine are poured over them as they burn. The entrails are put on spits, roasted on the altar fire, and distributed among the participants to be eaten immediately. The rest of the meat is then boiled, divided out, and normally consumed on the spot (though 'takeaways' were sometimes permitted). At this stage omens were often taken, from the burning of the gods' portion on the altar and from the condition of the entrails.

There were numerous variations on the standard pattern of sacrifice described so far, and small details evidently bore a large charge of meaning for participants immersed in the sacrificial code. Some sacrifices were burnt whole, some were 'wineless', some were performed not on altars but in pits or hearths in the ground. There were also a series of practices that might be called 'quasi-sacrifices': to ratify oaths or perform certain purifications, for instance, animals were killed according to several of the procedures listed under stages one and two above, but the carcase was then simply disposed of, offered neither to god nor man.

What is the point of sacrifice? Why do men kill to worship? There are few more puzzling questions. Even if we consider Greek sacrifice alone, it is hard to find a unitary explanation. One school of interpreters sees the rite as a dramatization of violence, a set of procedures serving to evoke and exorcize the guilt of killing. For another the point is, precisely, to prevent such guilt from arising, to insist that sacrificial killing is not murder, to sanitize the necessary act of killing by setting it in a sacral, licensed framework. On the first view the heart of the matter is the kill, on the other the feast that follows. Against the former it must be objected that innumerable sacrifices were performed by Greeks, as a preparation for dinner parties for instance, in contexts where we can be sure that the participants were far from being preoccupied with the evil allure of violence. The other view feels much truer to the everyday reality of Greek sacrifice, but it fails to explain the various cases where the meat of the animal was not eaten, where therefore a religious value seems to be assigned to the actual killing.

Divination we have so far mentioned only in passing. But it was of the greatest importance, in two ways. On the one hand, one of the chief comforts of religion in most Greeks' view was the 'advice' given by the gods to mortals faced by a crisis, such as plague or crop-failure, or a difficult decision (for one consulted an oracle with a view to action, not out of idle curiosity). On the other, divination filled a gap of a quite different type: the Greeks had no sacred texts, no charismatic religious leaders, no church hierarchy with authoritative figures at the top; if a change in religious practice was to be made, the only authority that could be appealed to in justification was that of the gods themselves, as mediated through an oracle. So whether a city was thinking of going to war or introducing a new cult, founding a colony or re-siting a temple, it would probably ask a god whether to do so would prove 'beneficial and advantageous'. And individuals regularly posed questions about their private affairs: about their health, their business prospects, their plans for travel or for marriage, their childlessness or their nagging anxieties about the legitimacy of the children they did have.

The techniques of divination were very various. The most prestigious was 'inspired' prophecy – what anthropologists call 'trance-mediumship' – as purveyed for instance by the Pythia, mouthpiece of the god Apollo at the oracle of Delphi (see plate 8.5). But there was also much drawing of lots, observation of the flight of birds and interpretation of the omens derived from sacrifice; this last technique was particularly important, being the stock-in-trade of the professional seers who accompanied armies on campaign. And at many oracles, healing oracles such as that of Asklepios in particular, the patient performed 'incubation' by sleeping in a special chamber in the god or hero's shrine. He or she

**Plate 8.5**   The sanctuary of Apollo at Delphi

then, it was hoped, received instructions direct from the god in a prophetic dream (see plate 8.6).

How can an account of Greek religious practices be drawing to a close without having mentioned priests and priestesses? The truth is that their functions and powers were extremely limited. Sacrifice, for instance, was often performed by a priest or priestess; but there was no need for this to be so, and the job could be done just as legitimately by a private individual or, on a public occasion, by a magistrate of the state. Above all, ultimate authority in religious affairs lay not with a priesthood but with whatever body made secular decisions (whether a king, an oligarchic council, or a democratic assembly). So at Athens it was the citizen assembly which decided (in consultation with the gods themselves, via oracles) what gods were to be worshipped on what occasions by what rites. A tiny illustration: we happen to learn from an inscription that it was a duty of the 'council' on the little island of Mykonos to select 'the loveliest sow' for sacrifice to Demeter at a particular festival. There could be no better emblem of the relation between 'church' and 'state' in Greece – or rather of the absorption of church within

**Plate 8.6** Attic marble votive relief to the healing hero Amphiaraos at Oropos (Attica), showing a patient simultaneously asleep and being cured by the hero, fourth century BC

state – than this pig beauty-contest, duly judged by the good councillors of Mykonos.

### FURTHER READING

Bremmer, J. N., 1994: *Greek Religion* (*Greece and Rome*, New Surveys in the Classics 24). Oxford: Oxford University Press.

Burkert, W., 1977: *Griechische Religion der archaischen und klassischen Epoche*. Stuttgart: Kohlhammer (*Greek Religion*, trans. J. Raffan. Oxford: Blackwell Publishers, 1985).

Buxton, R., 1994: *Imaginary Greece: The Contexts of Mythology*. Cambridge: Cambridge University Press.

Dowden, K., 1992: *The Uses of Greek Mythology*. London and New York: Routledge.

Graf, F., 1987: *Griechische Mythologie*. Munich and Zürich: Artemis (*Greek Mythology: An Introduction*, trans. T. Marier. Baltimore and London: The Johns Hopkins University Press, 1993).

Parke, H. W., 1977: *Festivals of the Athenians*. London: Thames and Hudson.

Parker, R., 1995: *Athenian Religion*. Oxford: Clarendon Press.

Sourvinou-Inwood, C., 1991: *'Reading' Greek Culture: Texts and Images, Rituals and Myths*. Oxford: Clarendon Press.

Vernant, J.-P., 1992: *Mortals and Immortals*, ed. F. I. Zeitlin. New Jersey: Princeton University Press.

Zaidman, L. B. and Schmitt Pantel, P., 1989: *La Religion grecque*. Paris: Armand Colin (*Religion in the Ancient Greek City*, trans. P. Cartledge. Cambridge: Cambridge University Press, 1992).

# 9 / THE SPOKEN AND THE WRITTEN WORD

## *Kenneth Dover*

### INTRODUCTION

The transmission of Greek literature in writing began about 700 BC, when the Greeks adapted to their own language a simple script evolved in Lebanon, and it has continued from that day to this. *Ancient* Greek literature is usually, and reasonably, regarded as ending by AD 500, when pagan culture, after mixing with Christian in a surprising variety of ways, was finally submerged.

Despite the popular saying 'The Greeks had a word for it', they did not have a word equivalent to our 'literature'. In early times they distinguished between 'song' and 'speech'. Later, to compose poetry was to 'make' it, and a poet (as at one time in Scots) was a 'maker' (*poietes*). For the composition of prose their least ambiguous term was one analysable as 'put together in writing', but this was applied indiscriminately to reports, contracts, technical instructions, philosophical arguments, historical narratives, orations and stories. They were thus spared the need to ask the question which preoccupies many modern critics, 'What is literature?'

Only a small fraction of ancient Greek literature survived into the Middle Ages and so to our own day. For instance, we know the names of more than 370 Greek playwrights and the titles of some 1,670 of their plays, but we have the complete text of only 44 of those plays, plus half a dozen incomplete; for what we know of the rest we are dependent on passages from them quoted by scholarly works during the period when the Greek world had become part of the Roman Empire, and from fragments of ancient copies ('papyri') excavated in modern times from the dry sands of Egypt (see plate 9.1).

It is a noteworthy fact that although the surviving works composed during the first five centuries (*c.*740–240 BC) of ancient Greek literature (the 'archaic' and 'classical' periods and the earlier part of the 'Hellenistic' period) amount to much less than what has survived to our day from the following eight ('post-classical'), it was those earlier centuries which saw the creation of virtually all the works which we find in the syllabus of a modern university

**Plate 9.1** Fragment of a papyrus copy of Pindar's *Paeans*, second century AD. The passages in smaller writing between, above and below the main columns are critical notes derived from the commentaries

course under the rubric 'Greek', works to which modern standard surveys devote between 70 and 80 per cent of their space. This great disparity is more the product of ancient judgement than of modern prejudice. Homer's *Iliad* and *Odyssey*, archaic epics, were regarded as supreme and given a central place in education throughout the history of the ancient world. In tragic drama the distinction of three poets – Aeschylus, Sophokles and Euripides – was recognized in their lifetimes, and within a century they were treated as constituting a 'classical canon'. In the mass of writings on rhetoric and style which appeared in post-classical times virtually all the illustrative quotations are taken from authors who had died before 300 BC. There were, of course, some striking and fruitful innovations in post-classical literature – notably the novel, which was romantic, sensational, essentially 'escapist' – but taken as a whole they do not compare in scale, pace and vigour with what had gone before. It is certainly arguable that the loss of the Greek city-states' independence to the Macedonian kings (Philip II and his son Alexander the Great) in the period after 338 BC instilled in many Greeks a nostalgia, powerfully reinforced by their eventual relegation to provincial status under Roman rule, for what they saw as their past days of glory, and that imposed restraint on any inclination to depart from traditional literary forms. It must be remembered, though, that there were some genres of literature (notably tragedy) which ran out of steam well before the end of the classical period. Much the same can be said of sculpture and painting, in which the early and rapid attainment of great technical skill in representational art did not promote any exploration of new ideas about the nature and function of the visual arts. Attempts to explain why rates of change vary so greatly between different periods in the history of a culture seldom carry conviction.

## THE EARLIEST POETRY: HOMER AND HESIOD

The two earliest poets known to us (and to the Greeks themselves) are Homer and Hesiod; that they are customarily named in that order is a consequence of their relative poetic stature and does not rest on firm evidence for their dates, for we cannot do more than locate both of them in the region of 750–700 BC. Homer tells us nothing about himself, and the Greeks did not agree on where he came from. On Hesiod we are better informed, thanks to some items of autobiography in the two greatest poems attributed to him: the *Theogony*, on the genealogy of the gods, and the *Works and Days*, a didactic work which combines advice on farming with much moral preaching. The world portrayed by Homer is a distant heroic world, in which humans and gods and half-gods mingle, and in its details it blends features of Homer's own time with other features which on historical and archaeological grounds we can locate half a millennium earlier. Hesiod too assigns the 'heroic age' to the distant past, between what he calls the 'bronze' age of mankind and the 'iron' age to which he himself belongs. The early epic poets' concentration on the heroic age (and there were many epics, lost to us, in addition to Homer's) established its pre-eminent events – the Trojan War, the fate of the Greek rulers who returned from Troy, the trials and triumphs of Herakles, the misfortunes of the royal houses of Thebes and Argos – as the appropriate subject-matter for most serious poetry throughout the classical period.

Homer on more than one occasion depicts a man 'singing' narratives at the court of a ruler, and plainly the composer and the

**Plate 9.2**  A reciter of epic poetry, Athenian red-figure vase-painting, early fifth century BC. The words 'Thus once in Tiryns' (not visible here) are written as coming from his mouth

performer are one and the same person. Hesiod too speaks of himself as a composer-singer, and declares that he won a prize at the 'funeral games' of an eminent man in Euboia. That claim introduces us to several very important aspects of Greek poetry and the part it played in the life of Greek society.

Most important of all is the fact that poetry was designed for public performance to a mass audience, not for solitary reading under a tree. That is obviously true of drama, but it is equally true of narrative recitation (see plate 9.2) and of choral singing accompanied by dancing. Moreover, poetry was an ingredient of festivals, often in conjunction with athletic contests, processions and sacrifices to deities. Festivals in general were occasions on which the community attempted to honour its gods and its ancestral heroes by impressive and enjoyable activities, it being assumed that they enjoyed the same things as humans. It was considered that people gave of their best if they were required to compete in the hope of achieving the high social status of a prize-winner and escaping the humiliation which was the fate of the loser. Hence Hesiod's pride in his victory at the funeral games, which in his time were a species of *ad hoc* festival; hence too the fact that throughout the classical period the Athenian dramatists were required to compete for prizes at the dramatic festivals.

It is noteworthy that Hesiod won his prize not at a festival in his native city-state (Askra in Boiotia) but at Chalkis in Euboia. Good poets were welcome competitors away from home, and the language of epic and didactic poetry was inter-regional. From about 600 BC onwards we have an increasing number of documentary inscriptions, and they enable us to discern the dialectal features of different regions of the Greek-speaking world. On the basis of that knowledge we can say that the commonest inflections of the language of Homer and Hesiod belong to the Ionic dialect-group, spoken in many of the Aegean islands and most of the cities on the western seaboard of Asia Minor, but that is just one stratum in what is in fact a highly artificial amalgam. Alternative inflections from other dialect-groups appear constantly, together with prehistoric forms (sometimes such a form and its later equivalent may be found in the same phrase) and a fair number of forms which never belonged to the spoken language but were created by the poets for metrical convenience. A radical difference between spoken language and poetic language, a difference not acceptable to modern poetic taste, is widespread in non-literate cultures, and it persisted to the end in Greek poetry, though in very varying degrees. It meant that in some genres a poet might make predominant use of the dialect of his own region, while in others he might suppress it entirely in favour of the inter-regional language associated with the genre in question. The audience, for its part, needed either to know poetic language in addition to its own, or else to reconcile itself to a limited understanding of what it heard, rejoicing more in the sound and splendour of the occasion than in the detail of what was being communicated.

One peculiarity of Homeric language is the recurrence of large numbers of 'formulae', such as 'Agamemnon, shepherd of hosts', even whole verses, e.g. 'the sun set and all the streets were darkened'. Analogous formulae are observable in the narrative epic of some other cultures which have such a genre, and it has been argued that their purpose was to assist improvisation in the course of performance. The evidence from cultural comparisons, however, shows that the correlation between orality, improvisation and formulaic diction is extremely variable; performance which does not at any stage entail writing may nevertheless entail prolonged and careful premeditation. The use of formulae was no doubt a great help to the fluent composition of long poems in what is, by the standards of English poetry, an exacting and restrictive metrical form.

That the Homeric epics were the product of a long tradition of composition without the aid of writing is indisputable; among many other considerations, it is notable that the relative importance of Greek cities as portrayed in epic is not as it was when the Greek alphabet was invented but as it had been four or five centuries earlier than that. It is reasonable to believe that Homer was among the last of the composer-performers, and that it was the introduction of writing which engendered in him the ambition to compose epics grander in scale and more subtle in structure than anything that had gone before. After him, the public was decreasingly willing to hear what performers presented as their own; it demanded poetry attributable (even if not always rightly) to Homer.

## Choral and 'personal' poetry

In the next two centuries lived a succession of poets whose fame endured to the end of the ancient world: among them, Archilochos, Sappho, Stesichoros, Anakreon, Simonides. But despite their fame, their readership faltered in the Christian centuries, and none of their work survived intact into the Middle Ages; our acquaintance with it depends on quotations and fragments. The range of this poetry is very wide. Some of it was designed for public performance by dancing choruses at festivals, but much of it consisted of songs which can be called 'personal': boasting, vilifying, preaching, satirizing, philosophizing, and describing adventures, quarrels and sexual encounters which are all presented as if they were the poet's own, though the voice may in many cases be that of an imaginary character assumed by the poet for the purpose of the song. This kind of poetry was not meant for great public festivals, but in the first instance for private celebrations, drinking parties of people who knew each other, and then for any of the many kinds of occasion on which people sing. The language used is a blend of regional dialect and inter-regional poetic, the ratio of the two varying very greatly according to the subject-matter. The difference in character between this poetry and Homeric epic is so marked that it has tempted some scholars to believe that it reflects radical changes in Greek attitudes and sentiments, but that belief is unjustified. Song is a universal feature of human cultures and must be presumed to be of immemorial antiquity. The kinds of poetry which come into view after Homer must always have existed before him, but their function was quite different from the function of epic, and it was only with the introduction of writing that it became possible to collect, preserve and transmit, under the names of individual authors, poems of kinds which were originally ephemeral and regarded as such.

About 500 BC the Athenians made an innovation which was momentous in the history of literature: they incorporated in their annual festivals of the god Dionysos serious drama ('tragedy') and not long afterwards comedy. As we know from vase-paintings that dances by men disguised as animals or birds (a frequent feature of early comedies) already existed, and we observe also that humorous impersonations and ridicule of well-known people are a widespread feature of festive occasions in pre-literate societies, it is quite likely that comedy is by far the older of the two genres and provided a model for the creation of tragedy. Tragedy combined traditional choral song and dance with dialogue in which narration of the deeds and speech of heroes and deities was replaced by enactment, as if the actors were the persons concerned. The subject-matter of tragedy was almost invariably taken from the legends of the heroic age which had provided the matter for epic narrative and choral lyric, but in its early days there were one or two striking exceptions to the general practice; the very first Greek tragedy whose complete text we possess is the *Persians* of Aeschylus (472 BC), which portrays the homecoming of the Persian king Xerxes after a disastrous failure to conquer Greece eight years before.

In our own time tragedy is the genre of Greek poetry best known and most admired, thanks to frequent translation and performance, and it is interesting to recall that in the *Poetics* of Aristotle (who died in 322 BC) it is treated as poetry *par excellence*. It did not, however, achieve that dominance from the outset, for in fact non-dramatic choral lyric, designed for festive and ritual occasions, reached its peak during the period 500–450 BC, the period which saw the production of all the plays of the tragic dramatist Aeschylus, many of Sophokles', and the first few of Euripides'. The supreme exponent of non-dramatic choral lyric was Pindar, who composed in many different categories; the only category to have survived almost intact is his odes for victors in the major athletic festivals. A limited field for poetry, one might have thought; but though praise of the festival, the victor and the victor's native city are indispensable in such a poem, the kernel of a major ode is the telling of a myth that arises – by association, analogy or exemplification – from one or other of the indispensable ingredients. The myth in turn prompts moral and religious reflections, maxims and admonitions, and the whole ode is a cascade of metaphor, infused with Pindar's love of strength and wealth, art and skill, and visual, aural and tactile beauty and splendour.

Even the earliest specimens of Greek personal poetry available to us (about 650 BC) are very far from 'primitive', because they display striking technical sophistication in their use of rhythm. The various forms of Greek verse are not founded (as English verse is) on stress-accent or rhyme; they use one or other of a range of patterns composed of long and short syllables, and a lyric poem is made up of stanzas identical in pattern. For instance, the *Fourth Pythian Ode* of Pindar comprises thirteen metrically identical 'triads', each of 125 syllables, and the triad itself contains three sections, of which the first and second respond exactly to each other. In addition, each kind of verse can be seen to follow rules governing the points at which a word may or may not end and the treatment of a final vowel followed by an initial vowel. No audience was expected to tolerate a poet who broke formal rules and slung words together in whatever way seemed to him to express his own emotions.

## DRAMA

The principle of metrical response was inherited by drama and employed, though normally just in one pair of stanzas at a time, for the lyrics sung by the chorus which was an obligatory participant in every play (at Athens the technical term for 'offer a play for performance' was literally 'ask for a chorus'). The ancestry of dramatic lyrics is apparent also from the fact that they preserve salient linguistic features of archaic pre-dramatic lyric, whereas the language of dramatic dialogue is phonologically and grammatically nearer to ordinary speech, though nothing like so near as is expected by a modern theatrical audience. How far the classical Athenian democracy accepted a schism between a 'popular' culture of which we are ignorant and an 'elitist' culture represented by the literature which has been preserved, we cannot judge. We can well believe in the existence of folk-songs and dance-songs which were technically rather rough and not to be heard at a social level above that of village festivities; but we do know that the production of tragedies was a great occasion for the whole population, and if 'plain folk' sometimes had difficulty in understanding tragic language – archaic, elaborate, often enigmatic – public reaction did not demand that the poets express themselves in simpler style.

The use of poetic language meant that tragedy could not be what we would nowadays regard as 'realistic'. Moreover, the actors wore masks, so that an audience's understanding of a character was necessarily founded solely on voice, gesture and movement, and the author knew that no effect could be achieved through changes in facial expression. The complete silence of one character while others were speaking was sometimes used to great dramatic effect, but there was no room in tragedy for clumsily inarticulate characters. At moments when we might have expected a character to be rendered incoherent by anger or fear, hatred or love, we are apt to hear instead a speech rhetorically organized and embodying moral and (in the broad sense) philosophical reflections, no doubt under the influence of the Greeks' high valuation of fluency in litigation and political debate. It is clear from Aristophanes' *Frogs* (405 BC), a comedy in which the ghosts of Aeschylus and Euripides compete for the Throne of Poetry in the underworld, that many people felt by then that Euripides had 'philosophized' too much, and the older generation hankered after tragedy which made them feel that they were witnessing the grandeur, simultaneously elemental and superhuman, of the distant heroic past.

Drawing as they did on the great stock of inherited myth, the tragic poets had many opportunities for re-interpretation. It is our good fortune to possess three plays, one each by Aeschylus, Sophokles and Euripides, which portray how Orestes, with the help of his sister Elektra, kill their mother Klytaimestra to revenge her killing of their father, and we can see how profoundly different their characterizations of those three persons are. In the literary criticism of recent times (especially in the study of Shakespeare) the 'consistency' and 'development' of a character are often a focus of interest, and since Greek tragedy, by contrast, contains some striking inconsistencies and unrealistically abrupt developments, it has been argued that the Greek tragedian was primarily concerned with the rhetorical and theatrical effect of individual scenes and speeches. The rhetoric is undeniable, but the intractable inconsistencies are actually very few and a modern audience, despite the alien formalities of Greek tragedy, readily responds to its timeless aspects, the interaction of the characters and the critical decisions they have to make.

The freedom of the Greek tragedian in the handling of inherited myth was by no means confined to re-interpretation. Greek myth was never incorporated in a divinely inspired text which it would be impious to mistrust. The Greek world had no central religious authority empowered to prescribe what people should believe, and it was tacitly recognized that sure knowledge of the distant past was not attainable. Irreconcilable versions of the same myth co-existed in different regions, and performances of narrative and lyric poetry at inter-state festivals spread the knowledge of alternatives. For instance, well before 500 BC a remarkable modification of the story of Helen ('of Troy') was propagated, to the effect that although she ran away from her husband with the Trojan prince Paris, she spent the ten years of the Trojan War chastely in Egypt, while her place in Troy was taken by a phantom 'Helen' created by the gods in order to provoke and prolong the war. A play of Euripides, the *Trojan Women*, adopts the traditional (Homeric) version of the myth, while three years later, in his *Helen*, the playwright follows the story that the real Helen stayed in Egypt.

There was a tendency among the Greeks to evaluate a play in terms of what was presumed to be its moral effect on the audience and therefore on society as a whole. This tendency was sustained in part by the archaic tradition of didactic poetry, charged with exhortation and admonition, but Plato criticized tragedy for the bad examples it presented, and popular sentiment was easily shocked by the utterance of unconventional ideas, regardless of their context and their appropriateness to the dramatic situation. In later times, and to this day, with equal disregard for context, situation and character, the words of a play have often been treated as expressing the opinions of its author. There is some excuse for that when the words are uttered by the chorus, because in many myths there is no room for a collective body, and the poet, precluded from investing his chorus in such cases with a distinctive role, limits it to comment on the action. Note, however, that in the three major classical treatments of tragedy – Aristophanes' *Frogs*, Plato's *Republic* and Aristotle's *Poetics* – no consideration is given to the possibility that what is sung by the chorus might affect the attitudes and beliefs of the audience. Naturally we would like to know what Sophokles thought on a variety of topics, but it is always safer to say 'Sophokles represents a chorus as saying . . .' rather than 'Sophokles says . . .'.

After 400 BC the composition and production of new tragedies declined, and old tragedies of Euripides and Sophokles were increasingly revived for the dramatic festivals. In comedy, on the other hand, the opposite happened; Old Comedy underwent considerable changes within the lifetime of its most notable exponent, Aristophanes (who died about 386 BC), and continued to evolve into New Comedy, with which it had remarkably little in common.

The essence of Old Comedy is fantasy, of rather the same kind as we find in fairy-tales and fables. The laws of material cause and effect are broken whenever it furthers the plot to break them, inconsistencies and incoherences are tolerated with the same justification, and if a critical audience asked 'But how could . . . ?', there would be no answer but a smile and a shrug. For instance, in *Peace* the protagonist, Trygaios, fattens up a dung-beetle until it is the size of a horse and on it flies up to the gods to beg Zeus to restore peace to the Greek world. He finds that the gods have moved house and that War has cast Peace into a deep cave. Summoned by Trygaios, a chorus of farmers arrives (how?) and pulls Peace out of the cave. All return to earth (how? The beetle has already flown away; the breaking of dramatic illusion by a theatrical joke helps).

The comic poets, like the tragic poets, competed for prizes, and it is reasonable to suppose that the judges were strongly influenced by how often and how loudly the audience laughed. The poet has to steer a course between wit which might be above the head of the average member of the audience and gross humour which might bore the judges if there were too much of it. The humour furnished by sex and excretion was exploited uninhibitedly (with two exceptions, lesbianism and menstruation) in costume (outsize artificial genitals – see plate 9.3), action (simulated defecation), and language whose vulgarity is guaranteed for us by its presence in graffiti and complete absence from serious literature. At the other end of the scale, there is much parody of tragedies and some also of quasi-scientific and quasi-philosophical ideas which struck

**Plate 9.3**  Two members of a bird chorus dancing to the music of a piper, Athenian red-figure vase-painting, late fifth century BC

most people as laughable. Even if only a minority of the audience (and that 'if', rather than 'though', is designedly prudent) knew exactly what was being parodied, the majority could certainly recognize the *kind* of thing.

The most deep-rooted of all the differences between Old Comedy and tragedy is that tragedy portrays the heroic past, while comedy is tied to the time of the first production by topical allusions and ridicule of well-known contemporaries. Some comedies, indeed, take as their subject issues of the highest political importance, e.g. the desirability of ending the Peloponnesian War by a negotiated peace, or the style of political leadership and the operation of the democratic jury-system. This phenomenon naturally raises the question: how far was comedy intended by its authors, and received by the audience, as moral, social and political persuasion? There are plays, and portions of plays, which patently have that character, most of all in the *parabasis*, a point in the play at which the actors are offstage and the chorus addresses the audience directly, and in the triumph of a principal character who secures, by comic, fantastic means, a reversal of public policy. We can be sure that whatever the political tendency of a play, there were people within the citizen-body who agreed with it – there was never complete unanimity in the Athenian democracy on any issue – but to think of political 'parties' in the modern sense and assign Aristophanes to one of them would be mistaken. Comparison with existing citations from the other poets of Old Comedy suggests rather that the performance of comedies was a privileged occasion on which politicians, officials and commanders could be criticized, often in coarse and violent terms. The standpoint of this grumbling criticism was populist, and intellectuals were among its victims. So indeed were the gods, sometimes depicted in absurd and humiliating situations, a procedure which in other contexts could incur savage punishment.

For us, comedy goes, so to speak, half underground in the seventy years which separate our last play of Aristophanes from the emergence of New Comedy in the first we have of Menander. We have plenty of citations from comedies of those seventy years, but they give us very little idea of the nature and structure of the plays from which they were taken. In Menander we encounter the kind of comedy that has a plot, a coherent story-line which admits remarkable coincidences but does not rest on fantasy or magic. The plot is commonly romantic, concerned more with falling in love than with the sexual opportunities of Old Comedy, and happy reunions with the long-lost are an inheritance from the 'recognition scenes' of tragedy (particularly Euripides). Lovers of Aristophanes may regret the comparative sobriety and respectability of Menander, and a change in language went with the change in matter; the language of Old Comedy is highly inventive and extravagant, embracing both the poetic and the grossly colloquial, while that of New Comedy is more limited in scope but invested with a quality which it is tempting to call 'naturalness', in so far as it resembles the portrayal of conversation in prose literature. The action requires no chorus except for the purpose of dividing the play into 'acts', and what such a chorus sang, since it is absent from the transmitted text, was presumably not composed by the playwright himself. New Comedy, however, compensates in elegance and subtlety of characterization for what it lacks in audacity, and it was to this that it owed its cosmopolitan appeal. Athenian tragedy had been welcomed quite early in many parts of the Greek world, but close association with the personalities, institutions and ephemeral political issues of classical Athens was an impediment to the spread of Old Comedy. The universal character of New Comedy shed that disadvantage, and it provided the models for the Roman comic playwrights, Terence above all.

## THE ALEXANDRIANS

Non-dramatic poetry enjoyed an efflorescence of creative talent in the period from 300 to 240 BC. Its most remarkable aspect is that this was simultaneously a time of 'forward-looking' innovation and of 'backward-looking' scholarship, when the texts of the poetry of earlier periods were edited, studied and explained. Kallimachos, the greatest poet of the age, compiled an immense catalogue, classified by genres and authors, of all the Greek works which were collected (and it was intended that the collection should be exhaustive) in the library which Ptolemy I, the Macedonian ruler of Egypt, had founded at Alexandria. Apollonios Rhodios, author of a short epic on the voyage of the Argonauts, was a director of the library. The third member of a talented triad, Theokritos, was not remembered for scholarly work, but he certainly sought, and probably secured, the patronage of Ptolemy II.

Apollonios' epic uses a language that is basically Homeric, but not Homer's (or any other) 'formulae'; there is much in it which recalls Homeric passages by allusion and analogy, and the better his readers know Homer, the more they appreciate Apollonios. His portrayal of the heroic world is deeply indebted to tragedy, exploring the emotions of his characters with greater subtlety than is found in Homer's comparatively brusque depiction of emotion. There is nearly always more of significance in a passage of Apollonios than can be gathered without pause for reflection; more, that is to say, for the reader than for the hearer.

Both Kallimachos and Theokritos shared with Apollonios a wide knowledge and deep understanding of the poetic tradition which they inherited, but their versatility and inventiveness were displayed more obviously. It was bold on their part to use Doric dialect (Kallimachos was from Cyrene in North Africa, Theokritos from Syracuse in Sicily) in combination with epic and elegiac metrical form, and Theokritos launched a new genre, 'bucolic', in which poetry of great elegance was seasoned with a rusticity not always prettified. The Alexandrian poets in general were erudite in mythology and local cults, and this has encouraged a belief that they wrote, so to speak, for one another and read with an encyclopedia of mythology handy. However, there is abundant evidence for an increase in the competitive performance of song and recitation at local festivals, and if we think of the classical audience's tolerance of enigmatic language and recondite allusion in tragedy and choral lyric, it is not hard to imagine Hellenistic audiences applauding poetry in which they did not understand everything aright.

From the 700 years after what I have treated as 'the Alexandrian triad' we possess epics of late date, ranging from giant to dwarf, and we hear of many more; we possess also some didactic poetry and, again, hear of much more; yet, in all that time, there was no one who could reasonably be called a *great* Greek poet. Undoubtedly the ability to compose verses was an intrinsic element in Greek culture, and it was exercised in ever longer epitaphs on tombs, but even there the dead hand of poetic tradition lay heavily. The spirit of innovation found a home only in the miniaturists, the composers of neat and witty epigrams.

## READING AND RHETORIC

It is self-evident that however few people in the archaic and classical periods actually read poetry (see plate 9.4) and possessed copies of written texts, there were enough of them to ensure its survival; but the extent of the ability to read, let alone the scale of the 'reading public', even by 400 BC (when we first hear of a book-trade), is a different matter. Some Athenian political and administrative procedures appear, from about 500 BC, to have presupposed universal ability to read and write. That presupposition may have been remote from reality, but to conclude from comparative anthropological considerations that it *must* have been does not take

**Plate 9.4**  A boy reads from a papyrus roll held by a teacher. The text, with shaky spelling, is shown in gigantic letters running (unrealistically) from top to bottom of the roll, Athenian red-figure cup-painting, early fifth century BC

sufficient account of some important variables: simplicity (e.g. Greek) or complexity (e.g. Sumerian) of script, straightforwardness (e.g. Italian) or absurdity (e.g. English) of spelling, and above all the attitude of the uneducated – 'it's not for the likes of us' or 'you a xxxxxxx philosopher, or sump'n?' or 'well, why shouldn't I?' It should be observed that in Aristophanes' *Knights* (424 BC) a character who is portrayed as social scum declares that his culture is limited to 'letters' (i.e. reading – and writing?) 'and even they are very bad'; he does *not* say that he cannot read at all.

From about 650 BC onwards we have some fragmentary inscriptions in prose, from many parts of the Greek world, bearing laws and regulations, but prose literature was a late arrival on the scene. We know of none before about 500 BC, when the first philosophical, mythographical, geographical and quasi-scientific works were composed, and we have no complete prose texts until 430–420. Those texts are: what Herodotos calls the 'exposition' of his 'inquiry' into the conflict between Europe and Asia which reached its climax in the unsuccessful Persian invasion (480–479 BC) of the Greek mainland; a tract on the Athenian democracy, written from an anti-democratic standpoint ('The Old Oligarch'); almost certainly (but which ones is not agreed) a few of the medical texts attributed *en masse* to Hippokrates; the first examples, initiated by the Athenian Antiphon, of speeches delivered in assemblies or lawcourts and subsequently circulated in written form; and some speeches composed as rhetorical exercises for imaginary occasions.

Surviving citations from the earliest prose writers point to the use of two very different models: one, bald oral reporting, in which no elaboration or variation of style was sought; and the other, the aphoristic ingredient of poetry, sometimes expressed in elliptical, even enigmatic, form. Yet more important than either was a third model whose character has to be inferred, for it cannot be directly observed: unwritten oratory. It is clear from Homer that in the society which he portrays the good public speaker is admired both for the wisdom of his matter and the aesthetic pleasure afforded by his manner; the complimentary adjective *ligús*, applied to a fluent speaker, is used also of singers and musical instruments. In a classical democracy, such as Athens or (part of the time) Syracuse, persuasive speaking was absolutely crucial to the attainment of high political standing and success in litigation. Much political conflict was pursued in the lawcourts – where decisions, not subject to appeal, were taken by mass juries without guidance from a judge – and the persuasiveness of a speech rested not only on argument from evidence but also on the effectiveness with which the speaker conveyed an impression of integrity, and on the reaction of the audience to his speech as a work of art. Once Antiphon in the 420s had allowed a copy of a speech of his to go out of his hands as a written text – for that was 'publication' in the ancient world – oratory expanded as a major branch of literature, and it embraced not only speeches delivered in assemblies and lawcourts or on ceremonial occasions but also *jeux d'esprit* designed as entertainment and political essays originally read to a very limited circle. The purpose of 'publishing' speeches was manifold: to gain in esteem as an artist, to injure adversaries by prolonging the life of unpleasant allegations against them, and to attract the notice of people whose goodwill might be profitable as forensic clients or (in some cases) pupils.

We cannot know the relationship between the text we have and what its author actually said in court, and it is reasonable to suppose that the former was normally an improvement on the latter. What we can observe is a degree of attention to formal detail which is extraordinary on any reckoning and intelligible only if the speech is *sound*, not ink on paper. Within a few years of the death of Antiphon in 411 BC we see clear signs of a tendency to avoid 'hiatus', the placing of a word which begins with a vowel immediately after a word ending with a long vowel or diphthong (a *short* vowel at the end of a word can usually be elided altogether). Avoidance of hiatus became an obsession with Isokrates, whose long life ended in 338 BC, and his much younger contemporary Demosthenes (for ever after regarded as the supreme orator) normally permitted hiatus only where the sense required some degree of pause. Demosthenes also had a strong tendency to avoid a succession of more than two short syllables. Post-classical literary critics attached great importance to rhythm, above all at the beginning and end of a sentence. We see here the burgeoning of an art-form to which the culture of our own time would be regarded by the ancients as barbarously insensitive.

In the post-classical centuries rhetoric, the art of persuasive speech, was a mainstay of middle- and upper-class education, and the public performance of orations took the place of drama; indeed, it *was* a form of drama, in so far as gesture, movement, and modulations of the voice contributed to its success or failure. And although the orator's art could be exercised in litigation or in petitions to men of power, he was not in a position, as Demosthenes was, to persuade an assembly to take major political decisions, and the topics he chose for performance were either of a familiar general type (e.g. town life versus country life) or hypothetical dilemmas, some drawn from Greek history. The great rhetorician-performers of the Empire, such as Dion of Prusa in the first century AD, Aelius Aristides in the second, Libanius in the fourth, account for a significant fraction of the Greek literature which has survived. Fate does not allow us to trade some of their work in for a lost play of Aeschylus.

## HISTORIANS

To turn back now to the earliest historians: Herodotos, whose work, put into circulation about 430 BC, is the first to survive intact, claims to have travelled widely, even to Egypt and the Black Sea coasts. The second half of the work deals with the direct conflict between Persia and the Greeks, the first half with the growth of the Persian Empire, and that first half is enlarged by a mass of geographical, ethnological and zoological material. Herodotos' principle, to which he refers twice, is to 'tell what is told' without committing himself to believing it (though he sometimes permits himself scepticism). It was hard for him to do otherwise, because in the Greek city-states as he knew them documentation was very sparse indeed, in great contrast to the archival system of the Near Eastern monarchies, and what a Greek believed about the past was derived from narrative poetry and oral tradition. 'Oral tradition' is a broad term; it includes what an individual heard from his father and grandfather, and what he hears from friends; genealogies, of which there may well be rival versions; and the incorporation of historical personages into pre-existing stories. Once a society has adopted writing, the orality of a tradition cannot be guaranteed. A may acquire a datum from a poem and communicate it to B, who passes it on to C; for C it is oral tradition, but its origin lies in poetic invention. Herodotos is very fond of citing collective tradition, e.g. 'the Samians say . . . but the Milesians say . . .', and we have no way of knowing whether or not they did. Sometimes a collective attribution of this kind is grossly implausible, e.g. the 'learned Persians' who expound the origins of the conflict between Asia and Europe in terms of Greek mythology, and there is a serious possibility that Herodotos does not tell the truth about his oral sources, even when we interpret 'the Samians say' as 'someone told me that a Samian had told a friend of his'.

Moreover, there are often serious difficulties in believing that Herodotos saw what he says he saw, especially when we can see for ourselves how wrong he is. Yet whatever doubts may be expressed about his integrity, there is not much room for doubt about his genius as a narrator: clear, cool, rarely allowing his own moral evaluation to obtrude, dramatic without melodrama. His work is full of dialogue, with some longer speeches, and that feature is one of many which make us think of Homeric epic. It also looks forward to the historical novel; no minutes were circulated after meetings of Persian nobles, and the 'creative' historian had free reign.

The second great historian of the classical era, Thucydides, belonged to the generation after Herodotos. It is inevitable that they should be contrasted, but important to remember that much of the difference between them is owed to the difference between their subjects. Thucydides wrote the history of a war – the Peloponnesian War (431–404 BC) – through which he lived as a mature adult, and did not live to finish the work, for although he did not die until some time in the 390s BC his history stops at 411, with seven years of the war still to go. His sources, necessarily, were participants in the war, and since he was exiled from Athens for a large part of it he found informants on both sides; but he never identifies them – here there is a real contrast of technique with Herodotos – very rarely mentions any obstacles encountered in his investigations, and in general casts his narrative in terms of magisterial finality, even when people's motives, hopes and fears are in question. His stated reason for going into the causes of the war 'so that no one in future need enquire into them' is characteristic.

In his introductory chapters he divided his matter into 'what was said' and 'what was done', recognizing that what was done resulted from the impact of persuasive speech upon those bodies, whether democratic assemblies or meetings of delegates, which had the power to decide. In consequence he sometimes chose to portray crucial debates by putting speeches into the mouths of proponent and opponent, while at other times there is only one speaker, and in the famous 'funeral speech' of Perikles the device is used to display simultaneously the power of Perikles' oratory and the sentiments on which the Athenians prided themselves. Thucydides claims to have kept as close as he could to the argument of 'what was actually said' on such occasions, but the style in which he composed the speeches, together with some of the generalizing passages in his narrative, is distinctively concentrated and abstruse, alien to the surviving forensic and political speeches of the orators and sometimes baffling to later critics. A reader of his own time confronted with a written text of Thucydides (which would have no accents or punctuation) must sometimes have lost his way in the course of a complex sentence – but would not have lost it had he heard it recited by the author himself, with all the intended phrasing, pauses, emphasis and intonation, and had he at the same time seen the author's accompanying gestures and facial expression. Paradoxically, Thucydides asserts that his work is not designed as 'a competitive performance for an audience to hear on one occasion' but 'a permanent possession' (*Histories* 1.22); yet he showed little mercy to the readers who would possess it, for he expected them to understand things which, however obvious to him, could not be obvious to them.

We hear of several hundred Greek historians after Thucydides, and it is clear that his influence was enduring; Greek interest in rhetoric ensured that the historian's composition of speeches, however grossly fictitious, was acceptable to readers. In the classical period, Xenophon is the only post-Thucydidean historian whose works have survived complete. He was a man of great versatility, and in addition to an eccentrically selective history of the Greek mainland and Aegean from 411 to 362 BC and what may reasonably be called a historical novel, *The Education of Cyrus*, he compiled *Recollections of Sokrates*, whose trial and execution occurred when Xenophon was about thirty. The *Recollections* steer clear of difficult philosophical questions, and focus on the good moral teaching which Sokrates imparted to his friends. Some of it reminds us of the genre 'sayings of wise men', found in many cultures (and not without influence on parts of the Gospels): 'and when So-and-so asked him . . . , he said . . .', or 'when he met So-and-so . . .'.

## PHILOSOPHICAL WRITINGS

Sokrates left nothing in writing, and it is only through others' portrayal of him that we know him. Xenophon's portrayal, despite its many interesting features, is thin stuff compared with what is presented by his coeval, Plato. Before Plato philosophical texts had been *ex cathedra* pronouncements, some of which started life as lectures, intellectual performances for which fees were paid. He, on the other hand, composed dialogues between a Sokrates who professes ignorance and earnest puzzlement and a variety of interlocutors of whom some are impatient and intolerant, others patient and fired with Sokrates' own passion for discovery of the truth. Whether this kind of dialogue was invented by Plato or by an otherwise wholly unknown Alexamenos, to whom Aristotle makes one reference, is disputable; in any case, its roots lie in the theatre, in prose 'mimes', in writers of memoirs such as Ion of Chios (who died when Plato was six), and in the problems which rhetoricians set their pupils for discussion.

Its purpose, like that of other philosophical writing, is to persuade the reader that the author is right, and Plato's Sokrates does not allow his axiomatic belief that the government of the universe is divine, wise and good, to be undermined. But undeniably, Plato still casts a spell on his readers, and that is owed to the vitality of his writing, particularly in what it is customary to regard as his 'early' and 'middle' periods. There are always subtle nuances, often humour, in his portrayal of his characters and their interaction. The logic of philosophical argument demands consistency of terms, without which there is always a risk of ambiguity and obscurity; but Plato is willing to take that risk, and in consequence the philosophical discussions which he sets before us (except occasionally, when he moves into a didactic mode and the minor participant is reduced to 'Yes, indeed') read not like a textbook but like the conversation of people whose eloquence is effortlessly vivid. Yet, when moved by earnest passion, he can rise to a climax of colourful poetic language.

Given Plato's skill as a writer, it is singular that in his *Phaedrus* he represents Sokrates as arguing that writing is not *serious*; having said what it has to say, a book cannot respond to questioning. Progress towards philosophical truth is best achieved by the dialogue of two people capable of its pursuit and tirelessly committed to co-operation and mutual criticism. Yet it would be precipitate to charge Plato with implicit self-contradiction. To relegate written texts to second-best status is not incompatible with recognizing that they alone could reach a significant proportion of his interested public (some references in contemporary comedy indicate a degree of awareness of Platonic philosophy) and serve to prompt in the minds of good men a recollection of the knowledge which according to the *Phaedrus* the soul possessed before its union with a body.

Aristotle, who as a young man had been closely associated with Plato, was an author of prodigious versatility. He himself drew a distinction between works written for the general public and 'philosophical' works. The former having perished, it is from the latter that we know him; above all, his contributions to logic, metaphysics, moral philosophy and (though with a somewhat philosophical slant) biology, together with his penetrating analyses of poetic and oratorical effect. He sometimes refers to the addressees of such works as 'hearers', not 'readers', and we often have the impression that we are reading not exactly 'lecture-notes' but written versions, arid and concentrated in style, of matter which had been dealt with in a more relaxed and expansive way in the lecture-room. Aristotle, like Plato before him, assembled a 'school' of collaborators and bright pupils, and we find in his transmitted texts repetitions, digressions and apparently irrelevant sections which are best explained on the hypothesis that reconstructions of his lectures at different times by different pupils played some part in the formation of the Aristotelian corpus.

## LATER PROSE

In the generation after his death (in 322 BC) some of Aristotle's pupils turned to the history of literature and the lives of authors, a line of inquiry which he himself had instigated when he made available in book-form the list of competitors at the dramatic festivals which was preserved in the archives at Athens. The era of study and learning, inaugurated by Aristotelians, was consolidated by Alexandrian scholars. Acquaintance with literature and facility with language, central to Greek culture thereafter, ensured a progressive divergence between spoken language (which, as always, went its own way) and the language of literature. That is apparent when we contrast pagan Greek literature of the first century AD with the Gospels, whose colloquial character is attested by the private documents of the period from Roman Egypt. There were even, at one stage, purists who regarded the language of classical Athens as the only 'correct' Greek for literary prose. Those apart, literary Greek evolved at a very leisurely pace, while colloquial speech proceeded at a gallop in the direction of Modern Greek.

If this chapter had been intended as a summary history of Greek literature in all its aspects, a substantial fraction of it would have been devoted to Plutarch (born c.AD 45) and Lucian (born c.AD 120). Both were heirs to an immensely rich historical and literary tradition, and reading them makes us aware of the essential continuity of Greek culture. What religious and philosophical doctrines either of them 'believed' in those later centuries of paganism – the quotation-marks are justified by the supremacy of sentiment and practice over creed among the Greeks – eludes precise definition. The flippancy, parody and satire prominent in Lucian remind us, more than anything, of the strand of irreverence in classical comedy towards myth and philosophy. Lucian could be said to observe his own civilization as an amused and amusing bystander. Plutarch's work, by contrast, belongs to the Sokratic-Platonic tradition, morally serious and committed to pious observance, but infused with greater humanity. To what extent Plutarch and Lucian performed as public lecturers or at least read a composition to an audience of friends before allowing it to go into circulation is uncertain, but the analogies which can be drawn from the culture of the age, both Greek and Roman, leave us in little doubt that they conceived what they wrote in the first instance as spoken words.

### FURTHER READING

Easterling, P. E. and Knox, B. M. W. (eds), 1985: *The Cambridge History of Classical Literature, vol. 1 Greek Literature.* Cambridge: Cambridge University Press.

Gould, J., 1989: *Herodotus.* London: Weidenfeld and Nicolson.

Green, J. R., 1994: *Theatre in Ancient Greek Society.* London: Routledge.

Kennedy, G., 1963: *The Art of Persuasion in Greece.* Princeton: Princeton University Press.

Kirk, G. S., 1962: *The Songs of Homer.* Cambridge: Cambridge University Press.

Russell, D. A., 1983: *Greek Declamation.* Cambridge: Cambridge University Press.

Rutherford, R. B., 1995: *The Art of Plato: Ten Essays in Platonic Interpretation.* London: Duckworth.

Taplin, O., 1978: *Greek Tragedy in Action,* London: Methuen.

Thomas, R., 1992: *Literacy and Orality in Ancient Greece.* Cambridge: Cambridge University Press.

# 10 / EXAMINING LIFE

*Edward Hussey*

Scientific and philosophical thinking, in something like their modern form, were invented by Greeks of the Ionian coastline (western Asia Minor) in the sixth century BC. Why and how this great step forward took place just then and just there can only be guessed. From the older civilizations of the Ancient Near East, the Greeks had already learnt many things: religious and cosmological speculations, as well as practical mathematical and astronomical methods. Many Greek cities were relatively free at this time, and above all not subject to the domination of kings or of organized priestly castes. Finally, the introduction of alphabetical writing made it easy to preserve, criticize and improve upon complex lines of thought.

The first person known to us by name as a proto-scientific thinker is Thales of Miletos (active *c.*575 BC). Thales speculated that everything is a form of water. The observational supports of his theory can be guessed: water is known as a liquid, but freezes to a solid, and boils away to a gas, so that it can exist in all three forms. Water is necessary to life, so it is a good guess that it is the origin of life.

What was new in the style of Thales' thinking was its concern with explanatory generality and economy, and the concept of an absolutely uniform 'nature' of things, which was supposed to be present (and observable) in everything. It is these features that link Thales and his successors to modern science. They were not fully scientists in the modern sense, above all because, though they appealed to facts of observation to support their theories, they had no systematic experimental method.

From these beginnings in the sixth century BC, there flowed different lines of development, which were often interwoven. First, a number of specialized sciences developed, which combined the systematic collection of observations with attempts at general theories of ever-increasing sophistication (and mathematical power) to explain them (see the section on Mathematics and science below). Second, there grew up a tradition of cosmological theorizing, which made repeated, though premature, attempts at a general science of the whole realm of 'nature' and of the universe as a whole. Third, it quickly became clear that the whole proto-scientific enterprise of the Ionians was bedevilled by problems of method and foundation. It claimed to give knowledge; but how could that claim be justified? It favoured simple, economical, unifying theories; but how far could such demands be pushed in the face of the observed complexities of the world? Reflection on these foundational problems of science led to the birth of philosophy.

## PYTHAGORAS AND THE PYTHAGOREANS

At the point where these three lines of development were about to separate, stands the elusive figure of Pythagoras (active *c.*520–490 BC).

What is clearest about Pythagoras is that he offered a new version of religion, and a new way of life, in response to the growing dissatisfaction, felt around this time, with traditional religious beliefs and practices and their traditional justifications. Pythagoras is represented, in the earliest testimony about him, as a person claiming magical powers and occult knowledge. It is certain that he founded a sect based on acceptance of his teachings and his rules for life. The most characteristic doctrine was 'metempsychosis': that people are immortal souls, which always exist and which as punishment go through successive re-incarnations in different animal and human bodies.

But Pythagoras can also be connected, though less certainly, with the proto-scientific and proto-philosophical movement of his time, and the three lines of development from it. He seems to have been a polymath, interested in the detail of all branches of knowledge. The 'metempsychosis' doctrine brought an entirely new conception of what human beings really are, which was a stimulus to philosophical reflection. There are indications, too, that he also emphasized the importance of mathematical structure in the universe, as evidenced by, for instance, the mathematical ratios involved in musical intervals. One way and another, Pythagoras (a legendary figure already in his lifetime) was later looked back to as the originator of ideas which were to have a long and influential career in Greek thinking (see plate 10.1).

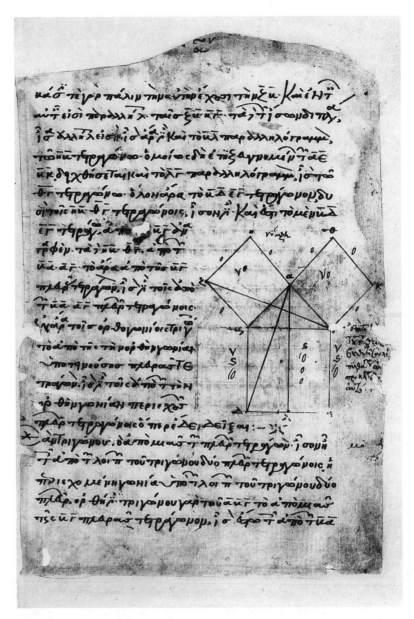

**Plate 10.1** A twelfth-century manuscript of Euclid's *Elements* showing Pythagoras' theorem (Book 1, 47)

## Early metaphysics: Herakleitos, Parmenides, Zeno of Elea

The puzzles and paradoxes with which all reasoning is infected began to be noticed at this early stage. Herakleitos (active at the end of the sixth century BC) pondered on the river that stays the same river only in virtue of changing constantly, and the road that is both an uphill road and a downhill road at once. Herakleitos' remarks show him groping for a general logic of 'unity in opposites' and of 'sameness through difference'. Parmenides of Elea (c.520–c.450 BC) claimed to demonstrate, by logical arguments derived from the very notion of truth or reality, that there could be no real diversity or change, and that the universe must be essentially an unchanging unity. His follower Zeno of Elea (active c.460 BC) discovered the astonishing paradoxes of the infinite, as they arise naturally in the attempt to analyse time and change. How, for example, does anyone (a runner, say, on a race-track) ever manage to pass through any given distance? Before going the whole distance, one must first go half the distance; after that, one must go half of what remains; then, half of what remains after that, and so on *ad infinitum*. This Zeno dramatized further in terms of a race between a fast runner ('Achilles') and a slow one ('the tortoise') who is given a start. Achilles must first run to the starting point of the tortoise; then to where the tortoise is then; then to where the tortoise is *then*; and so on. Again an infinite series of runs appears: how can Achilles ever get through them all?

## The early atomistic theory: Demokritos

One of the high points of the cosmological-physical tradition was the atomistic theory, created in the late fifth century BC by Demokritos and Leukippos of Abdera. According to this, everything consisted of 'atoms and void': atoms were indivisible material particles, and void was the empty space they moved through. On this purely materialistic basis, Demokritos claimed to be able to account for all phenomena whatever, and wrote at length in support of his claims. Though none of his writings has survived, we know that he furnished explanations on atomistic lines of, for example, magnetism, mental phenomena, pre-cognitive dreams, 'gods' – which he explained as long-lived superhuman beings in outer space – and ethical values. 'I would rather discover a single scientific explanation,' he wrote, 'than be king of Persia'.

The atomistic hypothesis was the right way for a developing physics to go, in the then state of knowledge. Though modern physics is not fundamentally atomistic in the exclusive and simplistic way of Demokritos, Greek atomism in the Demokritean spirit can be seen, with hindsight, as its precursor, and it served as an example and an inspiration to the seventeenth-century creators of modern physical thinking.

## 'EXAMINATION OF LIFE' IN THE LATE FIFTH CENTURY: SCEPTICISM, SOPHISTS AND SOKRATES

Reflection on the problem of knowledge quickly produced the first known examples of some persistent types of philosophical thinking. There were those who questioned whether any claims to knowledge could be justified, at least beyond the reach of immediate experience. There were those who tried to show, on the contrary, that knowledge of the general nature of things could be discovered by reason alone. By the end of the fifth century BC, traditional Greek religion and values had been subjected to searching sceptical criticism, not all of it purely destructive (there were also attempts to build up an empirically defensible account of 'good' and 'bad' in human life).

This sceptical and empirical tendency was combined with, and fed by, a growing awareness of other civilizations, neighbours to the Greek world but with sharply different customs and laws and often (at least in appearance) different values. It came to be a commonplace of Greek thought at this time that there was a fundamental contrast between the uniformity of nature (*phusis*), and the vast variety of human societies with their disparate customs and values (*nomos*). The *nomos/phusis* contrast was a double-edged weapon. Many theorists took it to show that all human values were merely relative, with no validity outside the particular society which supported them. Others, though, took it as a cue to look beneath the surface appearances, in order to find the real foundations of law, morality and human society in nature itself.

The prime agents and catalysts of these ways of thinking, in the later fifth century BC, were a group of people who came to be known as 'sophists' (the word originally meant simply 'expert', and had at this time positive as well as negative connotations). These were itinerant suppliers of all kinds of up-to-date higher education, for which a big demand was beginning to be felt, and no other provision existed. The city of Athens, at the height of its power and prosperity, presented itself self-consciously as a model of an open, tolerant and cultured society. It became the natural intellectual centre of the times.

The three outstanding figures of this period, Protagoras, Thucydides and Sokrates, had much in common. All were concerned, in different ways, to examine dispassionately traditional and conventional ideas on human nature and society, to reject everything that could not stand up to rational criticism, to reinterpret suitably whatever survived, and to build a radically new edifice of theory on intelligible foundations.

Protagoras of Abdera (active *c*.450–420 BC), the most prominent and influential of the sophists, expounded an empirical and pragmatic approach. His famous slogan, 'man is the measure of all things', was not meant as pure relativism. It stood rather for the thought that any claims to truth and knowledge must be tested by appeal to actual human experience. In particular, any claims about what is good and bad must be tested by appeal to what people actually experience as good or bad. This by itself gives only a method, not a theory. Protagoras' substantive theory of human nature and society, so far as it can be reconstructed from Plato's criticisms, seems to have been optimistic in tone and democratic in tendency: when people are released from non-rational constraints, they will naturally evolve towards a state of democratic consensus.

Thucydides (*c*.460–*c*.390 BC), an Athenian from a rich and politically powerful family, wrote contemporary history in a sceptical and empirical spirit. In his account of the Peloponnesian War, of the decline and defeat of Athens, he drew for his substratum of general ideas on various aspects of the sophistic period, including the contemporary medical theorizing of the Hippokratic school (see the section Mathematics and science below). Human nature was, in spite of appearances, a universal constant. Human society was naturally a battleground of opposed forces; its multiple forms and changes, like those of the human body, were to be understood in terms of the relative strengths of those forces. Thucydides applies these ideas in the intentionally dispassionate, clinical and realistic analysis of political and military situations which is characteristic of his work.

The concerns of this period, particularly the attempt to give traditional values an intelligible foundation, were followed yet further and deeper by Sokrates (*c.*470–399 BC), another citizen of Athens. Sokrates perfected a new and powerful method of philosophical inquiry, which consisted in the examination of one's own or others' beliefs by a systematic process of question and answer. Sokrates' questioning proceeded step by step, to establish just what could be said and what not, and demanded clear, precise and relevant answers. The aim was, in the first instance, to reach agreed definitions of key terms, and to isolate the essential properties of things from what was merely incidental, as indispensable steps on the way to a firmly based knowledge. But the usual effect of grinding up people's beliefs in this logical mincing-machine was to reveal them as badly based and badly thought out, and unfit to serve as the basis for rational discussion.

Though his questioning made some resentful, and others sceptical, Sokrates persisted because it seemed to him to be the only possible method in philosophy. Though perhaps nothing of substance could be proved, it would at least become clear which were the possible theories, and which of them accorded most closely with the truths of experience. Sokrates focused his inquiries on ethical questions, because those were the only ones which seemed to him of any importance. He assumed (like Pythagoras and his followers) that each person consisted essentially of a reasoning 'soul', and that the fate of the soul might depend on the quality of its actions. For Sokrates therefore the fundamental question was 'how should one live?' From this time onwards, Greek philosophy was seen, above all, as a source of systematic ethical theorizing and advice. For many people, some brand of philosophy took the place of religion (and traditional religious belief and practices were given philosophical reinterpretations).

Sokrates gave his own particular twist to this inquiry by his assumption that the state of the soul depended entirely on its possession, or lack, of knowledge, which led him to the paradoxical position that 'no-one knowingly does wrong'. Sokrates was not afraid to proclaim paradoxical and unpopular opinions: in democratic Athens, he insistently raised doubts about the moral and practical value of democracy, which led to his judicial murder (through the administering of hemlock, see figure 10.1) in the restored democracy at the end of the Peloponnesian War.

**Figure 10.1** Illustration of Hemlock (*conium maculatum*) from a sixth-century AD manuscript of the herbal of Dioscurides (first century AD), a medical reference work summing up ancient botanical knowledge

## PLATO: THE VISION OF A
### MATHEMATICAL UNIVERSE

The first of the two great philosophers of the fourth century BC was Plato (428–347 BC), a disciple of Sokrates. Plato (drawing heavily on Pythagorean ideas) began with dramatic representations of Sokrates at work, and his evolution into an original philosopher began with the attempt to systematize the insights and methods of Sokrates, and establish them on a firmer basis.

Plato half-formalized Sokratic inquiry as a process of methodical investigation ('dialectic') with its own inner logic. Dialectic was intended to reveal a timeless realm of abstract objects, about which precise and certain knowledge was possible. The price of this certainty was that the truths accessible to the philosopher would never exactly fit the actual world.

The practical message of Plato's mature philosophy would seem to be that as far as possible one should withdraw oneself from the world of experience, and live in the timeless one of knowledge and reality. But Plato himself did not rest in this very un-Sokratic conclusion. In his later works, he goes back to looking for ways to understand, know and deal with the delusive world of ordinary experience.

Plato's psychological and philosophical critique of human nature and values was closely connected with his political thinking. He developed Sokrates' doubts about democracy into a full-scale, root-and-branch attack on democratic politics and ways of thinking. In its place, he advocated, as the only ethically acceptable model for organizing human society, an inflexible totalitarian state, to be ruled by disinterested philosophers for the common good.

## ARISTOTLE: THE SYSTEMATIZATION OF KNOWLEDGE

Aristotle (384–322 BC), the other great philosopher of his century, set a pattern in a different way from Plato; in the long run it was even more influential. Aristotle created a framework of logical and metaphysical concepts, within which he tried (with the aid of his students) to subsume all the sciences, and the entire corpus of existing knowledge. It was an extraordinary effort of system-building imperialism, unparalleled before or since.

Outstanding among Aristotle's diverse achievements were: his scientific work, involving original and important contributions to physics, chemistry and above all biology (see the section Mathematics and science below); his creation of formal logic; his ethics; his explorations in the area of metaphysics and philosophy of science.

Aristotle reshaped the earlier cosmological tradition, in the light of Sokrates' and Plato's criticisms and his own deeper explorations. His concept of *nature* and of the natural world, and his analysis of the factors required to give explanations within this world, gave a workable philosophical basis not only for his science of the inanimate and animal realms, but for his discussions of human nature and values as well. His ethics carries over as much as possible of traditional Greek upper-class values, but recasts and presents them as the necessary result of the attempt to achieve a worthwhile life, within human society and the fixed limits of human nature.

Aristotle, like Plato, founded his own school of philosophy with an organized programme of 'undergraduate' and 'graduate-level' studies, and an all-inclusive programme of research for his followers. These schools, and the others that were to succeed them, were the closest approaches in the ancient world to anything like a university.

## IN SEARCH OF TRANQUILLITY OF MIND: CYNICS, SCEPTICS AND EPICUREANS

While Plato and Aristotle, starting from the inspiration of Sokrates, moved in the direction of ever more sophisticated theorizing, at the same time there also sprang up more popularly accessible philosophies of life, preached in a more down-to-earth way. Most of these traced the evils of the human condition to the artificially created complications of civilization, and claimed to teach the attainment of true happiness through the conquest of unnecessary fears and desires. It was these philosophies that dominated the Greek world in the new world of the Hellenistic period.

Beginning with their founder-saint Diogenes 'the Dog' (*c*.400–*c*.325 BC), the Cynics (the word means 'doglike') advocated the utmost simplicity and 'naturalness' of life, rejecting social institutions and conventions as 'not natural'.

The Sceptics professed a systematic scepticism, such as that of Pyrrho (*c*.365–*c*.275 BC). This was another attempt to cut through convention and dogmatism, and lay out simply and clearly the requirements for a truly happy life. The prescription was to aim at 'being free from disturbance'. They held much of human disturbance to come from attachment to false beliefs and values, and recommended a critical abstention from beliefs and values going beyond immediate experience and practical purposes.

The most widely popular of these sects were the Epicureans. Epicurus (341–270 BC), a voluminous theorist, preached what was meant to be a simple message. According to Epicurus, atomism was the correct physical theory, and it could be proved from atomistic physics that the soul was mortal and death not to be feared, which was the only good reason for studying physics. Hence for a good life it was necessary and sufficient to study physics and

**Plate 10.2** Part of the great inscription set up by Diogenes of Oenoanda, found at Oenoanda (central Turkey), in which Diogenes explains Epicurean philosophy as the source of happiness

philosophy to a certain extent; beyond these limits they were of no use. The Epicurean, concerned to live well on this earth, could do so, when freed of irrational fears, by living quietly and cultivating the natural pleasures, of which, Epicurus held, the greatest was friendship (see plate 10.2).

## THE STOICS

Both Cynics and Epicureans show a clear tendency to reject civic life, which had traditionally been the focus of the free Greek male's activities, and the centre of his sense of identity. Perhaps in response to the decay of democracy and city-state autonomy in the Hellenistic Greek world, Cynics, Sceptics and Epicureans were all anti-civic or even anarchistic in the implications of their ways of life.

In sharp contrast, the other leading philosophy of the Hellenistic period, Stoicism, advocated a very different rule of life. Stoicism had many varieties, but what was common to them was the understanding of human nature and destiny in terms of 'citizenship of the universe' (from which concept our word 'cosmopolitan' is

derived). Human beings were seen by the Stoics as beings endowed by God with rationality and a conscience, so that they
could play their appointed part in the universe, like good citizens
in the city. This role imposed duties, to perform which might
involve hardship and suffering of various kinds. In theory at any
rate the good person would always be able to rise above such evils.
The Stoic sage was supposed to be able to enjoy life even when
being tortured, provided that he was conscious of having done
what was right (hence the English word 'stoical').

Again unlike the Epicureans, the Stoics took logic and physics,
as well as ethics, seriously, and made original contributions to
them.

## The Neo-Platonists

In its final period, under the Roman Empire, Greek philosophy
became more academic and specialized, but generally less original.
Plato's theories enjoyed new influence, and the most impressive
work in this period was due to the later followers of Plato (the
'neo-Platonists'). Plotinos (AD 205–70), a great philosopher in his
own right, struggled to clarify what he took to be the essence of
Plato's insights. Proclus (AD 410–85) reduced them to a highly
organized metaphysical system involving a hierarchy of levels of
existence. Neo-Platonic philosophy, increasingly baroque in construction, and tinged with mysticism, supplied those who did
not accept Christianity with the only coherent alternative which
was both intellectually and religiously appealing. Conversely, many
Christian philosophers in the same period acknowledged their debt
to Platonism, and emphasized its closeness to Judaism and Christianity on many points ('what is Plato but Moses speaking Attic
Greek?' asked one enthusiastic Christian writer).

## Mathematics and science

Ancient Greece made impressive advances in pure mathematics,
and in some branches of pure and applied science, particularly
astronomy (observational and theoretical), mechanics, optics, biology and medicine. The pattern is roughly the same for all of these.
There was a first period of initial discovery and grand theorizing,
in the sixth and fifth centuries BC. That gave way to more thorough,

professional and specialized work, much of it in the fourth and third centuries BC, and rather more sporadically thereafter.

A good example is pure mathematics (geometry (see plate 10.1) and theory of numbers). The Babylonians had developed arithmetic and geometry, but only as a collection of methods for practical calculations. By the fifth century BC, the Greeks had created pure mathematics as an abstract science. There was rapid development in the fourth and third centuries BC, culminating in the work of Apollonios of Perge (later third century BC) and Archimedes (*c*.287–212 BC), who in developing geometrical methods came close to the ideas of the integral calculus. There was then a long 'afterlife', with sporadic new discoveries being made down to the third and fourth centuries AD.

The companion sciences of mathematical astronomy and geometrical optics followed a parallel course. In the fifth century BC, unknown Greeks transformed astronomy by discovering the explanation of the phases and eclipses of the moon, and the sphericity of the earth. Eudoxos (*c*.390–*c*.340 BC) made an early attempt to apply mathematics to the detail of physical phenomena, giving a mathematical model to explain planetary motions. The work of Hipparchos (*c*.190–*c*.120 BC) was a great advance in accuracy of observation, sophistication of method and theoretical achievement. The tradition culminated and was summed up in the great systematic work (the 'Almagest') of Ptolemy (Claudius Ptolemaeus, active *c*.AD 140).

All of these astronomers accepted the geocentric assumption (that the sun, moon, planets and stars circle round a fixed earth). The only known serious attempt to break free of it was made by Aristarchos of Samos (active early third century BC), but it was not successful.

Other mathematical sciences (mechanics, statics) made at least beginnings, but were hampered by the lack of calculus. They had some influence on mechanical technology; some striking achievements were complex geared devices, such as the Antikythera 'computer' (see plate 10.3), and ballistic engines.

The life sciences, apart from medicine, had a shorter span. Aristotle's biological field-work and theorizing were amazing but

**Plates 10.3a–b** (*opposite*) The geared mechanism (early first century BC) from the Antikythera shipwreck; the earliest surviving example of a working model of the movements of the sun, moon and planets

a

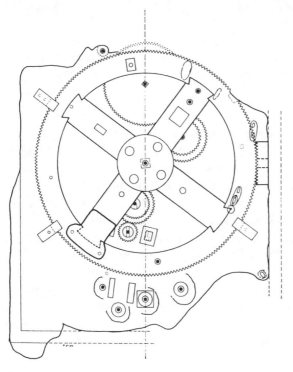

b

**Plate 10.4** Illustration of the reduction of vertebrae by traction, windlass and human pressure; tenth century AD copy of an ancient drawing, from the commentary of Apollonios of Kition on Hippocrates

isolated achievements, which were not followed up; the same is true of the botanical work of his pupil Theophrastos (cf. figure 10.1).

In medicine, there was an enormous burst of theorizing in the fifth century BC and at the same time an accumulation of a mass of precisely observed case histories, of distilled clinical experience, and of dissections. These achievements, associated with the name of Hippokrates of Kos (active later fifth century BC), were connected with the existence of continuing schools of medicine (see plate 10.4). The researches of Erasistratos and Herophilos at Alexandria (third century BC) are the scientific high-point, but the voluminous medical writings of later antiquity, especially those of Galen (second century AD), show that the theoretical arguments continued, even if new experimental insights did not.

FURTHER READING

Akrill, J. L., 1981: *Aristotle the Philosopher*. Oxford: Oxford University Press.

Hussey, E., 1972: *The Presocratics*. London: Duckworth (reissued in 1995).

Irwin, T., 1989: *Classical Thought*. Oxford: Oxford University Press.

Lloyd, G. E. R., 1970: *Early Greek Science: Thales to Aristotle*. London: Chatto and Windus.

Lloyd, G. E. R., 1973: *Greek Science: After Aristotle*. London: Chatto and Windus.

Long, A. A., 1986: *Hellenistic Philosophy* (2nd edn). London: Duckworth.

Melling, D. J., 1987: *Understanding Plato*. Oxford: Oxford University Press.

de Romilly, J., 1988: *Les Grands Sophistes dans l'Athènes de Périclès*. Paris: Editions de Fallois (*The Great Sophists in Periclean Athens*, trans. Janet Lloyd. Oxford: Clarendon Press, 1992).

Sambursky, S., 1987: *The Physical World of the Greeks*, trans. M. Dagut. London: Routledge and Kegan Paul.

Sharples, R. W., 1996: *Stoics, Epicureans and Sceptics: An Introduction to Hellenistic Philosophy*. London: Routledge.

Vlastos, G., 1991: *Socrates: Ironist and Moral Philosopher*. Cambridge: Cambridge University Press.

Wallis, R. T., 1972: *Neoplatonism*. London: Duckworth.

# 11 / TRADES AND CRAFTS

## *Alison Burford*

### INTRODUCTION

Within the limits of resources and techniques available, the trades and crafts practised by the Greeks of the classical period satisfied a wide variety of demands, and at their best met the highest standards of design and efficiency. Their products included everything from intricately wrought wares in precious metals, monumental architecture and sculpture, whose proportions were reflected in the lesser art of fine pottery, to shoes, farm tools, armour, domestic buildings, roof tiles, ships and last but not least, given its place in constructions of many kinds, sun-dried mud brick. The work that every kind of craftsman did was determined by two things: the potential, or conversely the limitation, of his craft, and the customer's expectations. It is very hard to gauge the balance between these two factors in the skilled worker's relations with the public.

We tend to assume that the makers of works of art were distinct from the producers of purely utilitarian objects, that the two groups hardly communicated, and that, whereas the general public could not hope to emulate the artists, it had some sympathy with the village blacksmith, cobbler or house builder. The evidence suggests on the contrary that the manufacturers as a whole comprised a cohesive body distinguished by its professional expertise. At the same time the Greeks differentiated sharply between the maker and the object made: if a life-size bronze statue was aesthetically and culturally more valuable than a woven basket, the bronze statuary was not necessarily considered more worthy than the basket-weaver. The modern distinction between artist and craftsman did not exist; both were seen as merely artisans or technicians.

### WORKSHOPS AND APPRENTICESHIP

The centre of a craftsman's life was his working environment, the workshop, consisting in the first place not of an industrial structure but of his fellow workers: the master-craftsman (who might either own the business himself, or manage it as the slave or freedman of a non-participating owner), the craftsman's assistants and a pupil or two. The collective knowledge of the craft handed down within the workshop taught the new worker techniques which in essence remained unchanged throughout the Greek period; most developments consisted of small-scale adaptations made within the established canon. Nevertheless these strongly traditional practices did not, in the hands of a really able craftsman, stifle important stylistic advances.

Admission to a workshop was best gained through being born the son of a craftsman. Plato remarks that 'the sons of skilled handworkers learn their craft from the fathers' (Plato *Protagoras* 328a), and the genealogy of the magician carpenter Daidalos ('Well-wrought') suggests this relationship, for he was the son of Metion ('Forethoughtfulness') and the grandson of Eupalamos ('Skilful-handed'); in the same way the Homeric shipwright Phereklos' father was Tekton ('Carpenter') and his grandfather Harmonides ('Joiner'). Numerous references show family tradition in the crafts; the sculptor Skopas of Paros was himself the son of a sculptor and the forebear of others, while the sculptural connections of the Athenian family of Praxiteles can be traced for several generations. It seems therefore that when the sculptor Kallonides put his name to a statue as 'Kallonides the son of Deinios', he meant to indicate that he was a properly accredited sculptor; and so 'the sons of Brentes' acknowledged their debt to parental training too, in this self-effacing signature to their work. Family connections can also be detected in the more mundane crafts, as the grave relief of the shoemaker Dionysios shows (see plate 11.1).

Training presumably started early; some occupations, like mining, would in any case have benefited from the aid of small nimble bodies, as would the jeweller's or gem-engraver's from sharp young eyes. When a young relative was lacking, the craftsman might apprentice another man's son or slave, or buy his own child slaves to train, if he could not afford really qualified adult slaves or hired workers; for the rule of the workshop made no distinction between free Greek and slave barbarian – all were craftsmen first and foremost, and the work they did was indistinguishable, such were the traditional strengths of craftsmanship. The building accounts of the Erechtheion (see plate 11.2) shows that within the six teams of masons who channelled the Ionic columns on the east front, citizens worked alongside metics and slaves. Three teams were led

**Plate 11.1** Attic marble votive relief showing shoemakers at work, dedicated by the shoemaker Dionysios and his children to the hero Kallistephanos and his children, fourth century BC

by citizens; Theugenes had perhaps two family members working with him, while Laossos and Phalakros owned the slave in their teams. In the two metic-led teams, Simias owned four of the five slaves and two metics. All were paid at exactly the same rate for exactly the same kind of work.

Discipline within a good workshop was no doubt equally harsh for all, whatever their status, especially when expensive materials and fragile products were concerned, or where carelessness might endanger fellow workers.

We might suppose that the high quality of the best artefacts was only achieved by means of narrow specialization, and that the masons of the Erechtheion, for example, had never worked in other materials or on less monumental projects. This is unlikely, not only for economic reasons but because it was versatility and

**Plate 11.2** The Erechtheion on the Athenian Acropolis (from the east), built in the later fifth century BC

breadth of expertise that characterized all first-rate craftsmen – among the greatest, the sculptor, bronze statuary, gold-and-ivory image-maker and architectural co-ordinator Pheidias and his brother Panainos, silversmith and painter, are cases in point. Narrow specialization could have been necessary for a pupil in training, in that he would doubtless start with one or another simple process, graduating as he learned each step to more complex tasks; and it would be now that a particular aptitude (or limitation) became apparent, so that he might ever after concentrate on carving hands or feet, painting decorative borders on pots, or drilling holes in beads. Yet the aim generally was to form a master-craftsman who could carry out every technique of his craft.

Specialization certainly occurred, as a means of making high-quality goods, but not, primarily, from the wish to make more of them. Xenophon (*The Education of Cyrus* 8.2.5) emphasizes quality, not quantity, in his analogy between the Great King's kitchen and the specialist shoe-shops of the Greek city, whose work he contrasts with the merely utilitarian products of the village cobbler.

The workshop scenes on Athenian painted pottery indicate a division of labour of the kind suggested above; the bearded and

**Plate 11.3**  A foundry, Athenian red-figure cup-painting, early fifth century BC

therefore older members of the workshop make the pot or rivet together and finish the various sections of a bronze figure, while the younger workers fetch and carry or help to hold things in place, meanwhile observing the process as a whole (see plate 11.3). These scenes also suggest that the workshop generally numbered a mere half-dozen or so workers; we hear of other workshops of about this size, so that when the literary sources mention men who owned 'factories' of twenty knife- or sword-makers, thirty-two inlaid-ivory bed-makers, or 120 shield-makers, it may be that each one consisted of several small work groups in the usual sense. Other craftsmen such as weavers, jewellers or village cobblers might have worked in still smaller establishments or even on their own.

## TECHNIQUES AND WORKING CONDITIONS

Often enough the craftsman's place of employment was set in rural isolation. Potters for instance found it convenient to locate their workshops near their source of clay, regardless of its relation to the centre of settlement; at Corinth and Athens, however, two of the best known potters' quarters were situated on their cities' outskirts, and potters and makers of terracotta figurines were also established well within the city of Athens itself, close to the *agora*. The techniques of pottery manufacture had evolved well before the Greek period, but marked stylistic developments occurred in shape and in decoration, for example in the interplay of black and other glazes with the red fabric of the fired pot. Athenian black-figure and red-figure decoration depended not on a ceramic revolution but simply on the skilful adjustments of the kiln's temperature during firing. Whether it was the potter or the vase-painter who initiated such changes is unclear; the functions of making and decorating were usually divided between them, but neither craftsman can have been so specialized that he did not share in the concerns of the other.

The broad utility of terracotta was such that workers in clay could generally afford to confine themselves to either decorated ware, or cooking pots, or storage jars, ceramic beehives and other special lines, or roof tiles, drainpipes and so on. Some sixth- and fifth-century Athenian potteries are known to have concentrated on a limited range of fine ware, but a rural pottery on the island of Thasos produced many types of pottery and roof tiles too, presumably to meet local demand. Moulds were used for some products such as relief-decorated vessels and figurines, where the aim was not to mass-produce but to create a particular effect; whereas the only sensible way to make roof tiles which, to serve their purpose, were needed in some quantity, was to turn them out from simple moulds. Otherwise, mass-production of poor-quality figurines and painted pots was achieved by cutting corners – as numerous featureless statuettes and unattractive vases testify.

The use of fire entailed risks for potter and product alike, risks such as the so-called 'Potters' Hymn' vividly evokes, with its references to destructive demigods at work in the kiln, and to the faces of those peering into the kiln being blackened by a blowback. Both potters and smiths who were even more at risk from burns are shown in various illustrations of their crafts to have hung up apotropaic masks over kiln, forge or furnace; someone, perhaps Pheidias himself, devised an apotropaic graffito in his chryselephantine workshop at Olympia.

The smiths' workshops were rarely near the source of their material, which generally reached them from distant mines through trade as ingots of copper, tin, alloyed bronze, iron, silver or gold. Even when the source was local, as in Attica, the miners and smelters of silver comprised, certainly by the classical period, a separate labour force, predominantly slave, which was kept in 'villages' nearby; the lessees of the mines were mainly businessmen, not silversmiths. The smiths' workshops on the other hand tended to be much more accessible to the general public in city or village – so Hesiod (*Works and Days* 493–5) refers to the pleasures of loitering by the blacksmith's fire in winter; some smiths worked close to the sanctuaries, conveniently placed for those requiring metallic objects as temple offerings. The range of the smith's expertise included refining and sometimes alloying, pouring, and hammering his material, whatever metal he worked in; there was doubtless specialization to the extent that blacksmiths would hardly change over to working gold jewellery, while bronze statuaries would only under exceptional circumstances have worked as armourers. But at the same time the statue-maker must work in other materials too – clay, wax or wood, for the model and matrix of his cast bronze figure – while other crafts continually challenged the blacksmith's inventiveness by requiring boot-nails, door fittings, clamps and dowels for stone masonry, and so on.

Stone working of a simple kind was age-old, but monumental stone architecture and large-scale sculpture came new to the Greek world during the seventh century BC. These techniques were not Greek inventions but were learned from the Egyptians; however, the Greek craftsmen immediately made their own adaptations, but always within the confines of what each worker had acquired from his teacher. Finding suitable sources of material was, especially at first, an experimental undertaking in itself, and connection with a good quarry always remained important. Not surprisingly Paros almost from the beginning produced both the finest marble and many of the most famous sculptors. Masons too benefited from personal knowledge of local stones; an Argive mason and his two sons provided and worked for the tholos at Epidauros a dark Argive stone in which they perhaps had a family interest of long standing. Work in the quarry required skill almost equal to that of constructing and finishing; each block was cut close to its final dimensions, and only a protective layer was left on it until the mason set it in place and dressed it down to the finished surface. Quarryman and mason may often have been one and the same.

Many sculptors and masons spent some of their working life on building sites, but when privately employed in the production of dedicatory pieces or funeral monuments, they would maintain workshops in the city. Evidence has been unearthed to show that a sculptor Mikion had an establishment very close to the Athenian *agora*. Versatility was necessary, for statues would be modelled first in other materials, while features of the finished statue were picked out with gems, metal work, fabrics, and sometimes pigments. The community of interests among monumental stone workers was probably close, the best mason's work being very near to that of the sculptor – but perhaps the builder of well-cut ashlar walls had little to say to the man who laid pebble-mosaic floors in private houses.

The eminently useful crafts of leather-working and weaving drew largely on pastoral resources, as far as possible local. In large communities the tanning of leather had probably long been a separate occupation, involving if not the actual slaughter and skinning of the beasts, then the treatment of the hide with various foul liquids; tanners were unpopular (as the association of the brash politician Kleon with this unlovely trade makes clear), and were doubtless expected to locate their workshops outside the city. But the shoe-maker's shop, like the blacksmith's, could become a social focus; one such has almost certainly been identified, again close to the Athenian *agora*, as belonging to the Simon who is said to have entertained Perikles and Sokrates. Shoes were both custom-made and ready to wear; if in big-city shops pupils worked exclusively on one or another part of the shoe, as Xenophon suggests (*The Education of Cyrus* 8.2.5), they must eventually have mastered all aspects of the craft. As Xenophon also suggests, the village shoe-maker made rough-and-ready versions of many other leather goods, perhaps even harness and farm labourers' tunics, which in the city would have come from specialist workshops.

Domestic production always accounted for much woollen cloth, but there were also professional weavers, men and women (some of whom had doubtless been domestic slaves and employed as textile workers). How far the process came to be divided among shearers, cleaners, spinners, dyers, weavers and finishers is unclear, although dyeing may often have been a separate undertaking – classical and later dyeworks have been found, some in the country convenient for wind, water and natural dye ingredients. Embroidered and woven designs enhanced clothing and hangings, with motifs similar to those found in other media; we cannot judge, however, what initiative, if any, the textile workers had in the introduction of new ideas. Other branches of the craft dealt with linen, silk-like material and sail-cloth, information about which is curiously lacking in the light of its importance to a sea-going society.

The most ancient traditions of craftsmanship resided in the wood-worker's craft, which is why the co-ordinator of public works was not a master mason but a master carpenter or *architekton*. The competence of the carpenter always remained broad, and encom-passed everything from domestic houseframes, fittings and roofs, to ships, furniture, carts, tools and the prototypes of monumental stone statuary and architecture. At the lower end of the profession, the woodcutter and forester provided not only timber suitable for the carpenter's use but raw material for the charcoal burners who produced the fuel commonly used in furnaces and domestic stoves, and who are glimpsed in Aristophanes' comedy *Acharnians*.

Little can be said of the shipbuilders, apart from the names of individual shipwrights recorded in Athenian naval lists, but pre-sumably the same characteristics prevailed here as in other crafts. There was the same need to incorporate a range of materials – bone glue, pitch, metal fittings, rope, canvas – just as the house builder combined wooden elements with stone and mud-brick walls, plaster and pitch-sealed roof-tiles. Family interest in shipbuilding is suggested by the Athenian records, and is vouched for in the builder's craft by the Delian sanctuary's records of a carpenter's family, a father and three sons (two of them architects).

## CRAFTSMEN AND THEIR PATRONS

The craftsman's working life was prescribed not only by the nature of his craft but also by the need to earn a living. This meant heeding the customer's wishes. At the same time the patron's demands were subject to the inevitable limitations of the crafts. Was it then primarily at the public's prompting that craftsmen produced fine work of the quality demonstrated in the Erechtheion's decorative elements (see plate 11.2) or in well-shaped painted pottery (see plate 11.4)? Or did the public's awareness that there existed the capacity for achieving such effects encourage the de-mand for them? Or was the patron simply a passive recipient of the craftsman's excellences?

Some sense of the relation between craftsman and patron emerges from the evidence of public works. Responsibility for structures like fortifications, fountainhouses, theatres, council chambers,

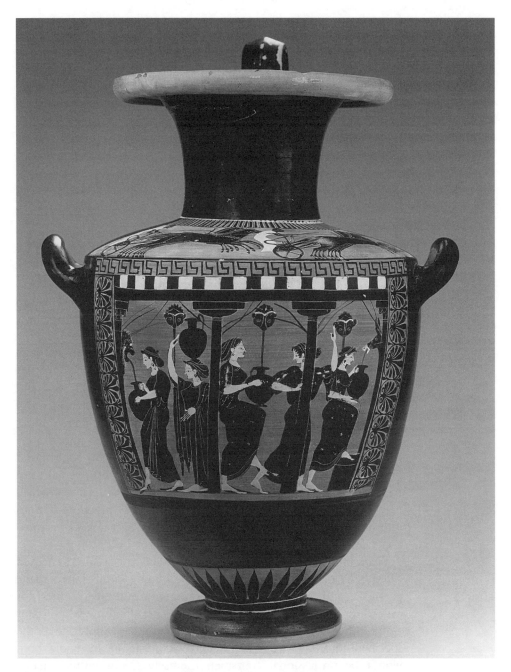

**Plate 11.4**  Women at a public fountain, Athenian black-figure vase-painting, late sixth century BC

temples and market halls lay between the (expert) architect and the (layman) body of city or sanctuary officials which financed and administered the project. The precise contribution made by either party to the solution of technical and aesthetic problems is unclear, but when plans were published they surely generated critical discussion among the general public too. Designers rarely had a free hand as to the layout or scale of the plans, for bounds were set by traditional, cultural and functional requirements such that the maker, in recognizing the user's dictates, must limit his own initiative.

The success of public works depended on communication between the craftsman and the general public at a purely practical level: nowhere at the commencement of a public works programme did a fully fledged force of professional monumental builders exist. When local talent was wanting, skilled workers must be drawn in from elsewhere; and although some recruitment surely occurred through interstate contacts within the craft community itself, commercial and diplomatic channels would also have been of use. When in the fourth century BC the comparatively small state of Epidauros needed to match its hitherto modest sanctuary of Asklepios to the god's recently acquired international status, local labour was only able to provide and fit stone for the temple foundations, cart imported material up from the harbour, build the sculptors' and decorators' workshop, make simple metal fittings for masonry and doors. So the building commissioners turned to craft communities abroad, in Corinth, Argos, Athens and Paros, for the finer materials and the skilled workers (architects included) who could build properly ordered temples. Here, as at Delphi and other small centres, foreign craftsmen worked under contract, the forms of which may have owed something to private business practices and to international law, such as existed to regulate agreements between a city and foreigners so that contracts might be binding.

Work under contract was strictly controlled; the architect checked the quality of work done, while the building commissioners made payments and imposed penalties, sometimes quite heavy ones, for exceeding the time limit, failing to correct badly done work, damaging other parts of the structure, or employing fewer than the specified number of workers. Hence the contractors, many of whom would be professional craftsmen themselves, not entrepreneurs, would have imposed firm discipline on their fellow workers.

Where a large labour force was already concentrated, as at Athens in the mid-fifth century, the building commissioners made very limited use of contracts (perhaps only for decorative elements), and chose to hire workers direct for the bulk of construction. Quarrymen, carters, carpenters, operators of the stone lift (from the base to the upper surface of the Acropolis) received a set day-wage, more specialized work was paid for by the piece, relief-sculptors for example receiving a flat rate of sixty drachmas per figure, or 240 drachmas for a composition containing two human figures and a chariot, while carpenters and masons were paid per block or timber. Under this system individual craftsmen could not make their own deals as they surely did when offering bids for work offered on contract.

Indeed what monetary value did the community put on the work done by those who provided its public monuments? Day-wage workers earned about the same as the citizen-soldier serving on campaign – one drachma; this was also what architects received in both fifth-century Athens and fourth-century Epidauros, but the architects, though professionals in a sense, constituted state officials in receipt of an honorarium rather than full-time wage-earning craftsmen. As for piece-workers, we do not know how long they needed to complete their assignment (modern work-comparisons can only be very approximate), or what other employment they had privately during the same period. The six teams of masons who fluted the columns on the east front of the Erechtheion received varying amounts of pay per *prytany* (a thirty-six to thirty-seven day period), depending presumably on the number of 'flute-inches' they had completed to date; none of these payments equalled a day-wage of one drachma, and not all six teams worked during every *prytany*, further suggesting that they were earning their living from private commissions meantime. Surviving records of contract payments do not show rates of pay per worker, or provide a sure basis for deciding whether a standard rate for certain building processes came to be applied at temple sites generally. Possibly craftsmen who came in from elsewhere to small or remote places could get better terms than hired or piece-rate workers in busy centres like Athens. But even at Athens temple-building was an occasional, not a continuous, undertaking; it is equally likely then that the comparative rarity of employment available to monumental builders balanced their own scarcity value, so that there were limits to even the most famous craftsman's hopes of rich rewards.

The delicacy of the balance between employment on offer and skilled labour available, not financial or political imperatives, may often have decided a project's progress. When defence was concerned, the city might order its craftsmen to work, and so the Athenians decreed that shipwrights should go to the timber yards of Macedonia, and requisitioned masons, carpenters and bakers for the great expedition to Sicily. But some skilled workers might prefer to accept offers of work elsewhere, professional mobility being their chief insurance against unemployment and destitution.

Evidence for craftsmen's personal wealth is sparse; votive reliefs like that of the shoemaker Dionysios (see plate 11.1) are rare, and anecdotal evidence suggests that comparatively few – sculptors and painters patronized by such as Alexander the Great – became more than comfortably off. Apart from some architects, hardly any craftsmen are known to have held public office. However, craftsmen could assess the value that the public, their patrons, put on their work by the kind of recognition they were allowed through being able to put their name to the work they did (see plate 11.5). It is also clear from many of these 'signatures' that the patron too felt his own reputation to be enhanced by association with the craftsman he had employed. The statue of a winged victory at Olympia was therefore inscribed:

> The Messenians and Naupaktians dedicated [this] to Zeus
> the Olympian as a tithe from the enemy.

> Paionios of Mende made it [the statue],
> and was victorious in making the roof
> decorations (*akroteria*) for the temple.

## CRAFTSMEN AGAINST SOCIETY

Despite the sympathy of interest that could arise between craftsmen and their patrons, various factors militated against their general acceptance as full members of society. Popular suspicion of the craftsmen's arcane knowledge, combined with their essential professional preoccupations, set them apart and encouraged the rise of prejudice against them. Just as the very real physical dangers inherent in mining, smelting, forging, firing pots or crouching over a work bench prompted the idea that they were all deformed, so they could be considered dim-witted too, as the philosophers chose to suggest. The conventional aristocratic scorn for manual workers

**Plate 11.5**  A sixth-century Attic funerary stele of Aristion, signed by the maker Aristokles, late sixth century BC

is forcefully expressed by Xenophon's Sokrates (*Household Management* 4.2–3):

> In fact, the so-called 'banausic' occupations are both denounced and quite rightly held in very low esteem by states. For they utterly ruin the bodies of those who work at them and those of their supervisors, by forcing them to lead a sedentary life and to stay indoors, and some of them even to spend the whole day by the fire.

Thus the smith god Hephaistos, divinely skilled though he was, could be laughed at for his limping, bulky form. But whatever the public's attitude, it appears that the solidarity which Greek craftsmen enjoyed with their fellow workers armoured them against all scorn. The existence of industrial districts, for example the one close to the Athenian *agora*, would have enhanced that solidarity while at the same time encouraging the very exchange of designs and techniques together with the competitive spirit which contributed so much to good craftsmanship. Sculptors and painters competed among themselves and for public commissions (see above); at Athens potters entered contests staged by the city; vase-painters emulated one another and the sculptors and painters of their day; temple architects strove each to go a little beyond what his predecessors had achieved. Because the desire to excel pervaded all the crafts, the epitaphs of a foreign-born mine worker and an Athenian lumberman could state, of the one that 'no-one rivalled me in the knowledge of my craft', and the other, 'By Zeus, I never saw a better woodman.'

## FURTHER READING

Burford, A., 1969: *The Greek Temple Builders at Epidauros*. Liverpool: Liverpool University Press.

Burford, A., 1972: *Craftsmen in Greek and Roman Society*. London: Thames and Hudson.

Camp, J., 1986: *The Athenian Agora: Excavations in the Heart of Classical Athens*. London: Thames and Hudson.

Coulton, J. J., 1977: *Greek Architects at Work: Problems of Structure and Design*. London: Paul Elek.

Lauffer, S., 1979: *Die Bergwerkssklaven von Laureion* (2nd edn). Wiesbaden: Franz Steiner.

Mossé, Cl., 1966: *Le Travail en Grèce et à Rome*. Paris: Presses Universitaires de France (*The Ancient World at Work*, trans. Janet Lloyd. London: Chatto and Windus, 1969).

Noble, J. V., 1988: *The Techniques of Painted Attic Pottery* (2nd edn). London: Thames and Hudson.

Philipp, H., 1968: *Tektonon Daidala: der bildende Künstler und sein Werk im vorplatonischen Schrifttum*. Berlin: B. Hessling.

Randall, R. H., 1953: 'The Erechtheum workmen', *American Journal of Archaeology* 57: 199–210.

Rasmussen, T. and Spivey, N. (eds), 1991: *Looking at Greek Vases*. Cambridge: Cambridge University Press.

Sparkes, B. A., 1991: *Greek Pottery: An Introduction*. Manchester: Manchester University Press.

Stewart, A., 1990: *Greek Sculpture: An Exploration*. New Haven: Yale University Press.

White, K. D., 1984: *Greek and Roman Technology*. London: Thames and Hudson.

# 12 / ARCHITECTURE AND SCULPTURE

## Olga Palagia

### MONUMENTALITY AND THE BIRTH OF THE CLASSICAL

Although the minor arts never ceased to flourish in Greek lands, monumental architecture and sculpture in stone only began to develop after the middle of the seventh century BC. The stimulus was provided by renewed contact with Egypt, when *c.*660 BC the Egyptian King Psamtik I invited Greek mercenaries to assist him in his struggle against the Assyrians. This was soon followed by commercial contacts, mainly through the trading post of Naukratis on the Nile, established towards the last quarter of the seventh century. Egyptian temples in ashlar masonry and colossal statuary in hard stone seem to have served as models to the Greeks who attempted to imitate not only their techniques but also their scale. Influence no doubt travelled via indirect routes. We can trace the origins of Greek monumental architecture in the north-eastern Peloponnese, home of the Doric order, while stone sculpture on a grand scale appeared almost simultaneously in Crete and the Cyclades. The Cretan workshops, however, proved something of a dead end since their local limestone could not compete with the luminous Cycladic marble which proved a very marketable commodity until the end of the high classical period, while Athenian domination ensured the widest possible distribution of Pentelic marble in the fourth century.

Egyptian stoneworking tools and materials were adapted to Greek needs; in contrast to Egypt, the Greeks dispensed with the magic properties of art, gradually abandoned the practice of inscribing the bodies of their sculptures, adopted nudity for the male figures and allowed their art and architecture to develop at what by Egyptian standards was a breathless pace. Unlike their Oriental counterparts, Greek sculptors did not remain anonymous but advertised their individuality by signing their works (see plate 11.5). Formally, both sculpture and architecture were subject to development through the gradual perfection of certain strict types (for example, the Doric order of architecture, the standing male nude known as the *kouros*, the standing dressed female known as the *kore*), repeated *ad nauseam* for over a century and a half. Sculptures and temples were, however, soon pared down from the awesomely colossal to a more human scale, and limestone was superseded by marble.

The archaic phase of Greek art in the seventh and sixth centuries was essentially related to Egypt and the Near East in form and design though adapted to the functions of archaic Greek society, dominated as it was by great aristocratic families forming a Panhellenic network across the boundaries of city-states. The inception of democracy in Athens with the reforms of Kleisthenes in 508 BC had little impact on the visual arts. It is often said that the great revolution of classical art was due to the political freedom of the new democratic regime; our material evidence, however, suggests that classical art was born as a result of the repulse of the Persian invasions of 490 and 480/479 BC. It was freedom from foreign domination that liberated the Greek imagination and enabled it to create the first naturalistic style in human history. While struggling to create images that looked visually convincing and did not merely rely on conceptualization to be understood, the Greeks also invented art history. We have it on their own testimony that sculptors of the classical period were self-conscious to the extent that they built life-like images by combining direct observation of nature with the Geometric principles of balanced postures (*rhythmos*) and ideal proportions (*symmetria*), as well as the composition of harmonious movements (*eurhythmia*) and the expression of suitable feelings (*ethe semna*).

Many classical artists were articulate. From the fifth century onward, sculptors and architects were known to analyse their techniques through treatises, usually involving the creation of a particular building (Iktinos on the Parthenon and Pytheos on the temple of Athena at Priene) or statue (Polykleitos on the Doryphoros). The representation of gods and heroes could be used as a pretext for the expression of the artist's aspirations and experimentations. Such tendencies brought about a streak of secularization in the arts which culminated in historical painting, the erection of citizens' portraits and finally a few architectural friezes with a contemporary subject. Oddly enough, artistic freedom was still subject to strict rules, and classical sculpture continued to advance through the ever more naturalistic development of statuary types.

## MAN AS THE MEASURE OF ALL THINGS

The principal subject of classical sculpture was the human body. Men were preferably shown nude, always with the physique of athletes, a reflection of the leisured classes' preoccupation with physical exercise. Women were dressed until the mid-fourth century, when Praxiteles boldly revealed female nudity in his Knidian Aphrodite. His real-life model was predictably a financially independent courtesan: unlike modern perceptions of female nudity in the visual arts, the predominance of clothed women in ancient art was not a sign of women's liberation. Even so, the classical sculptors' obsession with athletic nudes which were freely displayed in public places has its parallel in advertisement photography of our own times. Like their modern counterparts, Greek nudes, male as well as female, exude an erotic quality which is perhaps not immediately apparent to jaded twentieth-century sensibilities.

The onset of the early classical style in sculpture c.490–480 BC was highlighted by a more naturalistic rendering of hair, veins and muscles, combined with a new, stationary pose where the figure bends a leg, thus dividing the body vertically into taut and relaxed sides. The new formal language advanced by fits and starts and the early classical phase is often criticized for stylistic inconsistency on account of the incongruous combination of conservative and innovative traits. The best preserved group of original sculptures of the early classical style are the pediments and metopes of the Doric temple of Zeus at Olympia, dated to the second quarter of the fifth century. The middle of the east pediment, showing the preparation for the chariot race between Pelops and Oinomaos, is a regular repertory of early classical types and poses. Zeus on the axis is revolutionary, shown for the first time in a himation leaving the chest bare (this will become the standard Zeus iconography). He is flanked by two helmeted warriors, Pelops and Oinomaos, who are in turn accompanied by two peplos figures, Oinomaos' wife Sterope and his daughter Hippodameia. The robust musculature of the men and the spare, vertical folds of the women's clothing are characteristic of the style, so is Oinomaos' hand on his hip and his half-open lips in a lively attempt to speak. Despite its severity, this phase is full of life, noise and bustle as is evident in the battle of Lapiths and centaurs in the west pediment of the same temple (see plate 12.1). Apollo in the centre monitors the triumph of the Lapiths, a figure of calm in the midst of fierce fighting and shocking

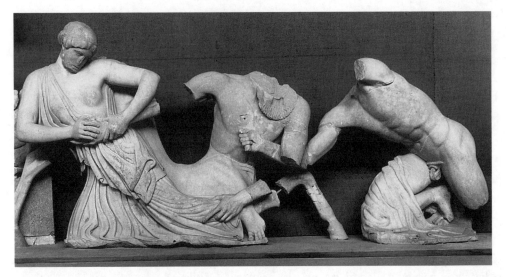

**Plate 12.1**  The battle of the Lapiths and Centaurs on the west pediment of the Zeus temple at Olympia, *c*.460 BC

violence against women and children. The balanced compositions and harmonious proportions of the east pediment figures are here replaced by a confusion of lines and shapes, faces disfigured by pain, bodies and limbs distorted, truncated or elongated by inept attempts at foreshortening. Not surprisingly, these pediments enjoy a special popularity with the modern public.

## CLASSICAL MARBLES

The realistic tendencies of early classical sculpture, evident in Olympia, had no following. Art took a new direction in the mid-fifth century when the Athenian democracy began to rebuild the sanctuaries on the Acropolis devastated by the Persians in 480. An ambitious building programme was initiated by Perikles, and according to the ancient sources the sculptor Pheidias was appointed overseer of the works. Thus in the second half of the fifth century a number of sacred buildings were set up on the Acropolis, forming the most successful example of classical architecture in the ancient world. Some carried architectural sculptures of the finest quality carved by teams of marble workers from all over Greece. The Parthenon (see plate 12.2) was built in 447–432 BC by Iktinos and Kallikrates, the Propylaia in 437–432 BC by Mnesikles, the

**Plate 12.2**   The Parthenon, Athens (447–432 BC)

temple of Athena Nike in the mid 420s by Kallikrates, and the
Erechtheion (see plate 11.2), also attributed to Mnesikles, was
begun in the 430s and completed in 405 BC. Pentelic marble was
employed throughout. The Parthenon and the Propylaia combine
the Doric and Ionic orders, while the Erechtheion and the Nike
temple are purely Ionic. Marble polychromy was discretely employed by the addition of grey Hymettian marble in the Propylaia
and black Eleusinian limestone in the Erechtheion.

Technical innovations abound, for example the use of structural
iron in the ceilings of the Propylaia and the pedimental floors
of the Parthenon. New architectural orders were invented (the
capitals of the maidens' porch of the Erechtheion; some believe
that the Corinthian capital was invented for the interior of the
Parthenon). Optical refinements are abundant in the Parthenon,
where irregularities in the individual dimensions of blocks and
departures from the straight line impart a sense of life into the
building. The architects were not averse to changes of plan as witness
the east porch of the Parthenon, and the Propylaia remained
unfinished at the inception of the Peloponnesian War. In contrast
to the classical grandeur of the sacred buildings on the Acropolis,
the Periklean building programme included the exotic Odeion on
the south slope, its roof imitating the Persian king's tent. Perikles

commissioned this building borrowing the architectural forms of Athens' defeated enemy, a practice which continues to this day.

The Parthenon was lavishly decorated with architectural sculptures, two pediments (each carrying about 25 statues), 92 metopes and $c.160$ m of frieze running around the exterior wall of the cella. The design of the sculptures of the Parthenon is attributed to Pheidias, assisted by his pupils Alkamenes and Agorakritos. Pheidias was also responsible for the colossal cult statue of Athena Parthenos covered in ivory and gold in the cella of the Parthenon (446–438 BC). In the process of creating the Parthenon sculptures and the Athena Parthenos, Pheidias and his associates invented the high classical style (445–390 BC), a blend of early classical tendencies tempered with elements of harmony, imperturbability and grandeur inherited from an earlier age. Pheidias' personal style can be glimpsed through Roman copies of details of his cult statues of Athena Parthenos in the Parthenon and of Zeus at Olympia. The Amazonomachy on Athena's shield is perfectly adapted to the circular frame since the Amazons are shown climbing the walls of the Acropolis; the action spreads up and down the field, in single combat, except for a majestic hero, perhaps identified with Athens' mythical king Erechtheus, struck with an arrow by an invisible opponent (see plate 12.3). The 'Erechtheus' motif is developed further in the frieze of the slaughter of the Niobids from the armrests of Zeus' throne at Olympia. Poses and draperies are here exploited to the full to depict the flight and the agony of Niobe's doomed children.

But the finest examples of the high classical style that have come down to us are the pedimental statues of the Parthenon (see plate 12.4). The virtuosity of the marble carvers breathes life into draperies and muscles which are made to express the agitation and awe of the Olympian gods and the heroes of Attica during the violent moments of the birth of Athena in the east pediment and the contest of Athena and Poseidon in the west. The pedimental figures of the Parthenon are the finest extant marble statues of the classical world, their vitality and originality even transcending the classical style. The Parthenon frieze depicts the Panathenaic procession on the occasion of Athena's birthday: it is a celebration of Athenian youth and the Olympian gods' informal grandeur. Gods and men mix easily in a world of unruffled calm which reflects Athenian self-confidence. This is the first non-mythological frieze ever to adorn a Greek temple.

Among Pheidias' most prominent followers, Agorakritos was

**Plate 12.3**  A Hadrianic copy of one of the figures from the shield of Athena Parthenos (446–438 BC) (the so-called 'Capaneus')

responsible for the cult statue of Nemesis at Rhamnous in Attica, a goddess associated with the repulse of the Persians by the Athenians at Marathon in 490 BC. The statuary type is related to Aphrodite in the east pediment of the Parthenon, while the statue base tells a story about the origins of the Trojan War, a mythological episode symbolizing the actual Persian Wars in Athenian popular imagination. Since the frieze was designed during the Peloponnesian War, an additional twist to the story is the attempt to claim Sparta's

**Plate 12.4** Leto, Artemis and Aphrodite from the east pediment of the Parthenon (430s BC)

main deity, Helen, as Athens' own. The battle of Marathon was represented on one of the friezes of the Nike temple, a first in sculpture, though a painting of the battle had been set up in the Painted Stoa nearly half a century earlier.

While the Attic school of sculpture, headed by Pheidias, catered for the needs of sanctuaries, preferring to work in marble and precious materials like ivory and gold, the Argive School, represented by Polykleitos, specialized in the male nude in bronze, capturing the market for statues of victorious athletes, particularly of Olympic victors. Polykleitos devised a canon for the perfectly balanced body, poised in a precarious moment of walking, with one foot drawn back, its visual effect dependent on the intricate network of taut and relaxed muscles. He aspired to create perfect proportions, and once he had created the desired model, he barely departed from it. His work was clearly admired not only in the Peloponnese but also in Athens, where he had an impact on the balanced composition of statues. His followers flourished into the fourth century and beyond.

The high classical style was carried over into the first decades of the fourth century. Iktinos' second surviving temple, that of Apollo Epikourios at Bassai, is again an imaginative combination of the

Doric and Ionic orders, with strong emphasis on the articulation of the interior by the addition of engaged Ionic columns and an internal frieze. The engaged columns were forward-looking, since they came to be liberally employed in the fourth century. The fact that this temple strikes the spectator as profoundly different from the Parthenon may be attributed to the effects of local materials (limestone instead of marble) and builders, trained in another tradition. Its sculptured frieze, dated to the beginning of the fourth century, retains echoes of the sculptures of Pheidias and the Parthenon, which are, however, less refined with clumsy proportions but with a tremendous sense of action and movement.

## LATE CLASSICAL AND THE EXOTIC

Athens' defeat in the Peloponnesian War in 404 produced a diaspora of artists who gradually ventured across the Aegean to find employment in the Hellenized barbarian courts of Lycia and Caria and the revitalized cities of Ionia. A second classicism emerged after the 380s, nostalgic for the glories of the past, partly retrospective, introducing the new element of pictorialism and a love of nature, youth, childhood and the idyllic. New canons of proportions in sculpture and architecture show awareness of the subjective factors of spectator and location.

The grandest monument of the age was the tomb of Mausolus, dynast of Caria, known as the Mausoleum, in Halikarnassos. It served the un-Greek purpose of deification of its owner but was entirely designed and executed by prominent Greek artists and architects, mainly from Athens, in the finest late classical style. Quantities of Pentelic marble were used. The Mausoleum was an Ionic temple set on a high podium and crowned by a stepped pyramid. It was lavishly decorated with sculpture in the round and in relief glorifying the deeds of the owner and his family, with an additional sprinkling of Greek mythology. The magnificent portrait of a Hellenized Oriental nobleman, possibly Mausolus himself (see plate 12.5), is a powerful composition of exotic traits garbed in a Greek idiom. The architect of the Mausoleum was Pytheos, chief exponent of the pure Ionic style in fourth-century architecture.

The salient trends of fourth-century sculpture can be traced through the styles of its most prominent artists. Praxiteles of Athens specialized in the representation of women and children,

**Plate 12.5**   'Mausolus' from the Mausoleum at Halikarnassos, *c.*350 BC

exploiting the luminosity of marble for the rendering of softness and inventing off-balance poses that required additional supports, often in the form of tree-trunks, in order to suggest out-of-doors settings. His Apollo Sauroktonos, a harmless little boy leaning against a tree, is a playful allusion to the god's capacity as pest exterminator. Praxiteles revolutionized sculptural practice by the introduction of the female nude and the employment of live models like the notorious Phryne.

Praxiteles' preoccupation with monumental images of children leaning on supports was shared by another member of the Athenian School, Skopas of Paros. His Pothos was part of a three-figure group of the children and companions of Aphrodite (Eros, Himeros and Pothos) in Megara. He was also an architect, responsible for one of the finest fourth-century temples, that of Athena Alea at Tegea. He took particular care with the articulation of the cella by means of a two-tiered colonnade of engaged columns running along three sides of the interior. The bottom row was Corinthian, the top possibly Ionic, introducing the first ever combination of two superimposed orders. The use of interior half-columns eliminated their structural purpose, thus reducing them to a decorative feature. Skopas was inspired by Athenian architecture, not only in his combination of Doric exterior with Ionic interior but also in his reproduction of many of the dimensions of Mnesikles' Propylaia and his imaginative adaptation of Iktinos' interior articulation of the temple at Bassai.

But the greatest achievement of fourth-century sculpture was the new set of elongated proportions along with the three-dimensional stance developed by Lysippos of Sikyon in the last decades of the century. He was a bronze sculptor in the tradition of Polykleitos; his statues acquired longer limbs and smaller heads, sometimes ventured into the spectator's space, and were posed according to the 'pendulum' stance, giving the impression of being in the process of shifting their weight from one foot to another. The posthumous portrait of the Olympic victor Agias (see plate 12.6) at Delphi is probably a contemporary marble version of a bronze by Lysippos. Lysippos' achievement heralded the Hellenistic style (*c.*323–30 BC) which in many respects broke with the classical tradition, leading to new discoveries in art.

## MONUMENTAL BRONZES

Monumental statuary in bronze was developed in Greece around the middle of the sixth century. From the fifth century onward, thanks to the indirect method of lost-wax casting, large figures were cast piecemeal and reassembled in separate sheets of thin metal held together with iron pins. The production required full-scale models in clay out of which piece moulds were taken in clay or plaster. It was these moulds, filled with wax and applied over a clay core, that were used in the actual process of bronze casting. The models survived for the reproduction of more than one original. The statues were mostly hollow, retaining fractions of their clay core. The thickness of the metal sheets and the bronze alloys vary.

Greek sculptors seem to have developed the use of bronze primarily for its texture and colour (additional colouring was achieved by copper or silver inlays and the occasional gilding); they were slow to realize the potential for bolder poses and greater freedom

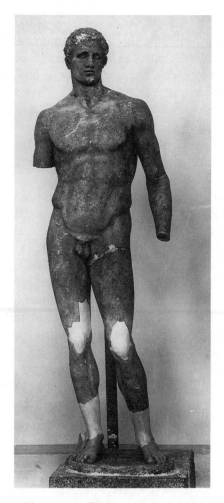

**Plate 12.6**  A marble statue of Agias set up in the sanctuary of Apollo at Delphi, *c*.338–332 BC

in space. Bronze was more precious than marble and became the predominant material of free-standing sculpture from the fifth century onward. The ancient sources distinguished local bronze workshops according to the alloy used, for example Aigina, Delos and Corinth. Out of the vast numbers of bronze statues produced in antiquity, only a handful remain, usually preserved at the bottom of the sea or buried after they were damaged in antiquity. Many famous bronzes were copied in marble in the Roman period. No stone copies, however, can reproduce the exceptional quality of the original bronzes.

**Plate 12.7** A bronze statue ('A') found in the sea off Riace Marina, *c*.460–450 BC

A few rather second-rate bronzes survive from the first half of the fifth century, like the Delphi Charioteer and the Artemision god. By far the finest bronzes that have come down to us are the two heroes ('A' and 'B') from the sea off Riace, dated to the mid-fifth century. They are fully armed yet nude, which suggests heroes rather than gods; their similarity to Pelops and Oinomaos from the east pediment of the temple of Zeus at Olympia is quite striking. They are clearly part of the same group, of identical poses, height and alloy, yet stylistically 'A' (see plate 12.7) looks earlier than 'B'. This is explained by the fact that several sculptors used to collaborate

**Plate 12.8**   A bronze statue of Athena found in the Piraeus, *c*.350 BC

on many-figured monuments. It has also been suggested that they issued from the same rough model to which adjustments were made before casting.

Several large bronzes are preserved from the fourth century, many of them of exceptional quality. An unusual Athena (see plate 12.8) was found in the debris of a storehouse in Piraeus which was burnt down during Sulla's sack of 86 BC. The same cache included two rather similar statues of Artemis, of which the little one, albeit in poor condition, is of remarkable beauty. The enigmatic Apollo, long thought to be the earliest large-scale bronze in existence, is now deemed an archaistic work of the second century. The Boy fished off the Bay of Marathon is miraculously poised in mid-air, demonstrating the tensile quality of bronze. Its identity and pose, however, remain unexplained. Although after the fourth century techniques developed further, the statues could be less imaginative, like the Eros from the Mahdia shipwreck, which is an eclectic combination of Polykleitan and Lysippan traits. Hellenistic sculptors were quick to exploit the possibilities of serial production afforded by the lost-wax casting method: popular types like the sleeping Eros were reproduced and sold at will.

### FURTHER READING

Boardman, J., 1991: *Greek Sculpture: The Classical Period*. London: Thames and Hudson.

Boardman, J., 1995: *Greek Sculpture: The Late Classical Period*. London: Thames and Hudson.

Clayton, P. A. and Price, M. J. (eds), 1988: *The Seven Wonders of the Ancient World*. London: Routledge.

Dinsmoor, W. B., 1950: *The Architecture of Ancient Greece* (2nd edn). London and Sydney: B. T. Batsford.

Jenkins, I., 1994: *The Parthenon Frieze*. London: British Museum.

Mattusch, C. C., 1988: *Greek Bronze Statuary: From the Beginnings through the Fifth Century BC*. Ithaca and London: Cornell University Press.

Mattusch, C. C., 1996: *Classical Bronzes*. Ithaca: Cornell University Press.

Mattusch, C. C. (ed.), 1996: *The Fire of Hephaistos*. Cambridge, Mass.: Harvard University Press.

Moon, W. G. (ed.), 1995: *Polykleitos, the Doryphoros, and Tradition*. Madison; The University of Wisconsin Press.

Palagia, O., 1980: *Euphranor*. Leiden: E. J. Brill.

Palagia, O., 1993: *The Pediments of the Parthenon*. Leiden: E. J. Brill.

Palagia, O. and Pollitt, J. J. (eds), 1996: *Personal Styles in Greek Sculpture* (Yale Classical Studies 30). Cambridge: Cambridge University Press.

Ridgway, B. S., 1993: *The Archaic Style in Greek Sculpture* (2nd edn). Chicago: Chicago University Press.

Robertson, M., 1975: *A History of Greek Art*. Cambridge: Cambridge University Press.

Stewart, A., 1990: *Greek Sculpture: An Exploration*. New Haven: Yale University Press.

Tournikiotis, P. (ed.), 1994: *The Parthenon and its Impact in Modern Times*. Athens: Melissa.

# 13 / CRAFTS IN THE PRIVATE SPHERE

## *Brian Sparkes*

### INTRODUCTION

Whether in a sanctuary, a public square or a cemetery, architectural and free-standing sculpture, in the round or in relief, was set up for all to see. The reasons for its installation were many: religious gratitude, political chauvinism, personal pride, a demonstration of public or private wealth, an expression of family or civic grief. The making of the figures and compositions was costly and time-consuming, whether the material was bronze, stone, or in a few cases, gold and ivory, and for the friezes, metopes and pediments that graced the temples the fashioning needed a team of craftsmen under an overseer who might move from one commission to another.

When we consider the objects made for private use, we move to small workshops that mainly served the needs of individual customers, whether for personal use in the home or outside it, for dedication in a local or national sanctuary, or to be buried alongside a member of the family. The craftsmen usually fashioned small portable objects which could be either used locally or more rarely transferred to the far ends of the Mediterranean. We must imagine that in most settlements in different parts of Greece there were workshops that served the everyday needs of the local community. Each craftsman would be a specialist in his own craft, having learnt the traditional skills and designs as an apprentice in the family workshop, introducing his own individuality to the task and in time passing on his knowledge to the next generation; but in some crafts, specialization did not prohibit versatility altogether, as a number of craftsmen are known to have practised a variety of skills (see chapter 11).

### EVIDENCE

Our understanding of the diverse crafts stems from a number of different sources. First, the survival of the objects themselves, from which information on techniques of manufacture etc. can be derived, depends on various factors – e.g. the initial scale of their production, the nature of the material of which they were made, their intrinsic value (hidden in times of trouble or taken as booty), their use and deposition (funerary goods are always likely to be better preserved than those that were in daily use). Nature, man and chance have all had their effects. The locations of workshops (with the tools of the trade) have occasionally been excavated; some needed only a small space, perhaps situated in the centre of a settlement, others demanded extensive premises, in some cases set near the source of supply of their materials (see chapter 11).

There are some illustrations, mainly on painted pottery, of objects being made (e.g. furniture, shoes (see plate 13.1), helmets, pots). The workers are mainly men, but the making of cloth at home shows women at the task. Sometimes the craftsmen are elevated to divine status when the workman is shown as a god, e.g. Hephaistos in his forge making the arms of Achilles, often in the presence of Athena. The painted scenes on pottery also reveal the various objects in everyday use.

Written evidence in literary works, technical manuals (e.g. Pliny's *Natural History*) and encyclopedias, and on inscriptions such as the inventories of articles in temple repositories, all add to the general picture of craftsmen and craftsmanship.

To be a worker involved a degree of servitude. Whether slaves in reality or not, all artisans (*banausoi*) were dependent for their living on the work they had to do. It was this lack of independence that placed the craftsmen low down on the social scale, no matter how well or badly paid, whether making luxury goods or necessities. Such men had no moral worth, no political standing, no masculine stature (see chapter 11). However, they are not all mere ciphers; we know the names of some craftsmen from the fact that they signed their work, on carvings (see plate 11.5), on pottery, on coins, on gems, but these are rare lights in the gloom of anonymity.

## CONTEXTS

The demand for items from the craftsmen, whether by the state or by private clients, can be set in four major categories: home life, public life, sanctuaries and cemeteries (the export of goods is not treated here).

**Plate 13.1** A scene at a shoemaker's shop, with shoes being made to measure, Athenian black-figure vase-painting, late sixth century BC

Within the home, members of the family themselves furnished some of the basic products. The women – mothers and daughters – worked at the loom to weave the clothes and the bedding. In some families, depending on their status and wealth, the coarse and plain household pottery would be made at various times of the year, and some furniture might also be home-made. However, calls on the skill of various artisans were still many. For personal adornment the women needed the services of a jeweller, to provide necklaces, earrings, etc. (see plate 13.2); the men called on the gem-engraver to cut a design in a gem for use as a seal with which to mark property and endorse documents (see plate 13.3). Bronze mirrors were also popular items. Painted pottery was most likely bought from a potter's shop, and this could serve the needs of the women (scent bottles, trinket boxes) or of the men (mainly drinking vessels). As for metal containers, the poorer people might have a bronze mixing bowl or bucket; some households would be rich enough to purchase objects of silver or gold (see plate 13.4). For the children there would be a call for dolls and toys (carved from wood or shaped in clay), some again doubtless made 'in house', others bought in from outside. Most rooms in Greek houses were sparse, with earth floors and roughly coated walls; but in some instances mosaic floors were laid in the room where the master of the house entertained his male guests. We also read of the rich Athenian Alkibiades having his house walls painted by Agatharchos, a famous artist of the day (Plutarch, *Alkibiades* 16).

Men's lives were lived in the public domain: the political and judicial arena (assembly, council, lawcourt), the gymnasium and palaestra, the markets, the battlefield. Each had their paraphernalia supplied by the artisans. For the political meeting places and the lawcourts in Athens where citizen involvement was most intense, there was a call for official bronze identity tickets (see plate 7.2), bronze voting discs for jurors, pottery and wicker urns in which to collect the discs, etc. Some of the pottery cups and bowls that were used for public dining on various official occasions carried a ligature scratched on the surface (DE, i.e. *demosion* ('public property')), to indicate that the dinner service was provided by the state. For the gymnasium and palaestra, the athletes needed equipment (discus, javelin, etc.) for their practice, and bronze strigils and terracotta and bronze flasks for the oil with which to clean themselves. In the markets all sorts of different containers were naturally in evidence, both for buyers and sellers, and once again

**Figure 13.1** Back piece of a bronze cuirass with elaborate incised decoration (human figures, animals and monsters), found at Olympia, seventh century BC

as with the public dining articles, the markets of Athens had official measures for dry and liquid goods marked with the same ligature. Away from the city centre, on the battlefield, man faced his fiercest competition and his greatest test of personal valour. He was furnished by the armourers with offensive weapons (spear and sword) and defensive armour (breastplate (see figure 13.1), helmet, greaves and shield).

Greek sanctuaries, which today are free of all but their buildings and their visitors, in antiquity were cluttered with public and private offerings, and as time went by, they were often cleared of the bric-a-brac of past years which was buried on site. The smaller objects that individuals offered were precious personal souvenirs that had been in the family for years or ex-votos made close by the shrine and bought at the entrance gate. The range of offerings is extensive: small, cheap terracotta figurines and hastily made votive cups that had no use beyond the act of giving; painted pottery, some poor, some of the best quality; small solid bronze figurines of men (see plates 7.4 and 8.1), women and animals; massive bronze bowls and tripods; gold and silver dishes; ivories, gems and jewellery. The temple inventories of the Parthenon and Erechtheion on the Athenian Acropolis inscribed on stone, which provide annual lists of material stored in the temples, give an indication of the wealth of some material, whether of the vessels used in ritual such as offering dishes (*phialai*) or of dedications (gold and silver cups, weapons, coins, furniture, clothes, jewellery, etc.).

At the boundaries of each settlement lay the cemeteries, traversed by local inhabitants and visitors as they entered or left the town, and visited at times of funerals or of anniversaries of remembrance by members of the families whose ancestors rested there. The Greek tradition of placing in the ground different offerings with the dead at the time of burial gave the craftsmen other outlets for their skills. Some of the offerings were old family possessions, perhaps the personal property of the dead (armour, jewellery, etc.), but many were made especially for the occasion. Pottery was a popular item, doubtless to give the dead the illusion of a continuation of their lives. Some of the painted shapes specially made for the grave (e.g. Athenian white ground lekythoi (see plate 14.4), the red-figure vases made in Greek South Italy) carry everyday and mythological scenes that make direct reference to death and the life beyond; others allude to death through the medium of divine and mythological figures. The richer graves are the earlier (archaic and before) when expense was conspicuous; by the classical period the goods in average Greek graves were usually meaner and cheaper. It is the graves of neighbouring peoples (Thracians, Skythians, etc.) that in the classical centuries were still lavishly furnished with expensive accoutrements (gold and silver plate, bronze bowls, jewellery) and for which Greek craftsmen still supplied the products of their skill.

## MATERIALS, TOOLS AND TECHNIQUES

The various materials, tools and techniques that the craftsmen used give us some idea of the skills they brought to bear on the items they produced.

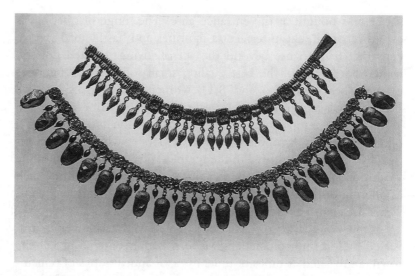

**Plate 13.2** Electrum and gold necklaces found in graves at Nymphaeum (Crimea), fifth and fourth centuries BC

The makers of jewellery handled costly materials, gold and silver, together with semi-precious stones, and worked at close range at an anvil with hammers, punches, stamps, bronze and stone blocks, etc. with a charcoal fire and a clay crucible. The techniques included modelling, repoussé, granulation and filigree. Gold, because it survives best, was considered the preferred material (see plate 13.2), but silver (and indeed bronze) were popular; it was only in the Hellenistic period that necklaces, bracelets, diadems, etc. depended for their effect on the use of coloured stones. The intricate designs centred on flowers and fruit, leaves and seeds, insects (bees, cicadas, etc.) and figures of gods, goddesses and personifications such as Victory. There are one or two rare pieces that carry the signature of a jeweller.

Some of the jewellers' finger rings were set with small incised gemstones, and in general makers of gemstones doubtless worked closely alongside the jewellers. As well as acting as a personal seal, some stones were used as ornaments and amulets. The holes through some of the stones show that they could be suspended on strings of wire or be set to swivel on metal hoops. There was a variety of stones worked; the most popular were cornelian, chalcedony (see plate 13.3) and rock crystal, others were steatite, green jasper, coloured quartzes, agate, ivory, and red and green serpentine; in the Hellenistic period, when the spread of Greek contacts was

a

b

**Plates 13.3a–b**   Blue chalcedony scaraboid and impression of a figure
of Victory setting up a trophy, fourth century BC

wider, especially in the East, some rarer stones (such as garnets and amethysts) came into use. The gemstones were carved into a variety of shapes: lentoid, glandular, round, some shaped into scarabs with the beetle back carved on top, others scaraboid with smooth back. The underside of the stones was carved intaglio (cameos were not carved until the Hellenistic period). The gem-engraver's tools included a bow drill, a wheel, a file, emery powder and abrasives. The designs were varied: monsters, animals, fish, figures of religion, myth and everyday life. Occasionally the gems have a name carved on them: some are of the owners, others of the craftsmen responsible for the work, e.g. Sosias, Onatas, Dexamenos; more than one name is found on both gems and silver coins and may indicate a connection. Herodotos' well-known story of Polykrates, the sixth-century tyrant of Samos, and the ring that he tried to throw away (3.41–2) mentions the maker: 'a signet-ring set in gold, an emerald, the work of Theodoros son of Telekles of Samos'.

Whereas gems were personal property and could act as private seals, coins were the official seals of city-states. Again we are looking at a craft in which all the work was done by hand, no Greek coins were mechanically minted. The tools needed were an anvil into the top of which was fitted a thick metal disc carrying an intaglio design, a punch with another intaglio design carved on the face, and blank discs of metal (silver was the most usual) of the correct weight which were heated in a fire until malleable. Less usual metals for coining were gold, electrum and bronze. The use of silver for coins indicates that coinage was mainly used for payments to and by the state; for the first generations of manufacture (*c*.600 BC onwards) coins were not the small change of individual transactions. The designs on the obverse and reverse of the coins can often be seen to carry a punning reference to, or local symbol of, the state which issued them (a rose for the island of Rhodes, Poseidon for the Greek city-state of Poseidonia (Latin: Paestum) in south Italy). Most coins are unsigned, but some (particularly those of Greek Sicily) carry signatures, e.g. Eukleidas, Euainetos, Kimon (all of Syracuse), Herakleidas (of Katane). The best-known site of a mint is that at the south-east corner of the Athenian *agora*.

Other workers in precious metals were the goldsmiths and silversmiths making plate: mixing bowls and cups of assorted shapes, jugs, dishes, mugs (see plate 13.4), and animal-shaped horns for drinking or ritual. The numbers that survive are few, as the gold

**Plate 13.4**   A silver and black mug, from Dalboki (Bulgaria), *c.*400 BC

and silver was melted down and reshaped; it is mainly those that were buried in the graves of peoples that bordered the Greeks (Thracians, Skythians, etc.) that give us any idea of the elaboration of the finished articles. The references to gold and silver plate in literary sources show us the extent of our loss. Thucydides, writing in the fifth century BC, recounts (*Histories* 6.32.1) that when the Athenian fleet was ready to set sail for Sicily in 415 BC, 'the soldiers on board and the commanders poured libations from gold and silver cups' and Diodoros, the Greek historian of the first century BC, even adds (*Library of History* 13.3.2) that on the same occasion silver mixing bowls lined the whole of the circumference of the Piraeus. The work was carried out in workshops equipped with crucibles and fires, and the metal was hammered into shape. If decoration was to be added, incised designs were cut on the interior of cups or on the outer walls of closed vessels, or relief compositions were applied. The silver shapes often had gold leaf added to the surface. The subjects of the compositions varied from floral designs to complex mythological subjects.

Bronze was less valuable than gold or silver but has survived in greater quantities, even though the survival rate is still low. The bronzeworkers produced mixing bowls and cups, etc. that paralleled those that issued from the gold and silver workshops; they also produced utensils, tools, water jars, basins, and the massive tripod-cauldrons that are some of the most impressive offerings of the archaic period in sanctuaries such as Olympia and Delphi. The techniques were much the same as for silver and gold and, just as silver was enhanced with gold, so bronze was sometimes plated with silver. The bronzesmiths also made brooches and hand mirrors (with handle or cover) for the women, and for the men breastplates (see figure 13.1), shields, greaves and helmets which they decorated with incised and repoussé compositions. Crete is now known to have been one of the most energetic centres of production in the seventh century. In the archaic period these compositions were very elaborate, and the straps that crossed the inside of shields from top to bottom sometimes carried a series of small scenes from myths. Some scenes, made in the same moulds, are found on both shield bands and on the handle plates of bronze mirrors, thus showing that the same shops were producing both mirrors and armour. The mirror-discs and the armour were hammered into shape; the bodies of the containers were usually hammered, but their handles and feet were cast solid, as were the mirror handles, with figures as handles and animal paws as feet. Also cast solid were the small figurines that were offered in their hundreds in sanctuaries: gods, humans (see plates 7.4 and 8.1), animals.

Both the containers and the figurines of gold, silver and bronze might have inscriptions cut on them, to indicate the name of the deity to whom they were being offered, and/or of the dedicator: a gold bowl, c.600 BC, found at Olympia, carries the inscription '[dedicated] by the sons of Kypselos [tyrant of Corinth] from the spoils of Herakleia' and a Corinthian-style helmet, of the early fifth century BC, also found at Olympia, reads '[dedicated] to Zeus by Miltiades [presumed to be the victor of Marathon]'. Very occasionally the name of the maker is incised, e.g. Telestas on the handle of a bronze water jar of the sixth century (in Mainz) and Aristodamos of Argos on a shield strap of the early sixth century (in Malibu). Craftsmen's signatures appear infrequently and are of no discernible pattern of incidence.

The accidents of survival have made it difficult to assess the precise place that wood held in the Greek world – certainly it was of far more importance than the exceedingly meagre remains indicate. To survive wood needs a constant climate and unchanging conditions, wet or dry. Some pieces of furniture and fragments of musical instruments have survived, and an exiguous number of wooden statuettes, though we read of large statues of wood, and there are some vase-paintings that show how they might have

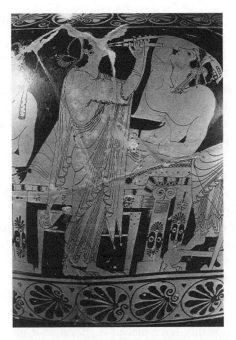

**Plate 13.5** Inlaid couch and patterned bedding, Athenian red-figure vase-painting, late sixth century BC

looked. A carpenter's equipment included bow-drills and adzes, axes and saws, lathe and glue, and his woods were maple, beech, willow, citrus, cedar and such. The vase-paintings show us wood-workers at their tasks and the objects they made are to be found in scenes of mythology and everyday life (chairs and tables, beds and chests, chariots and ploughs). Some pictures show wooden furniture inlaid with other materials (ivory, gold and precious stones; see plate 13.5); some flat shapes for ivory inlays have survived, and the tumulus that contains the tomb of Philip of Macedon at Vergina has preserved small ivory figurines, carved in the round and in relief, that decorate wooden biers.

Other crafts that have left little or no material evidence are naturally those where the medium is even less able to resist the exigencies of time, nature and the destructive hand of man. On the more elevated plane wall- and panel-painting were highly praised in ancient literature with detailed descriptions of some composi-tions (the Painted Colonnade in Athens, the club-house (*lesche*) of the Knidians at Delphi) that help towards an understanding of their effect. The small assortment of mosaic pavements that survive give some idea of the materials, techniques and subjects of the designs executed by workers in that craft. At a lower level tanning was a basic task, for leather was used for clothing of various sorts, for shoes (see plate 13.1), as containers for liquid, etc. Although wicker-working may have been carried out at home for the making of chests and baskets, it is likely that this was an itinerant craft as well. Many textiles also are likely to have been home-based creations: cushions, bed-covers, cloaks and dresses. Every house would have had a loom (see plate 14.3), with the accompanying equipment such as loom-weights, spindles and knee-guards. Pictures and literature that deal with clothing and bed coverings indicate that some could be very fancy, with intricate patterns and figured scenes. There were also centres that specialized in making dresses, e.g. the island of Amorgos which produced diaphanous cloth.

A material that survives in abundance is terracotta. When baked, clay is almost impossible to destroy and hence features more fully in our image of Greeks' public and private lives than its relative status would in reality have placed it. Because it is so malleable in its unbaked state, clay can be fashioned in many shapes for all sorts of purposes. A major product was bricks, either simply sun-dried in frames or baked in kilns, a major element in building; also useful were baked roof-tiles, decorative antefixes for roofs shaped into palmettes or figures, and the humbler water-pipes.

On a smaller scale, there was an abundant production of terracotta figurines, modelled by hand or made in moulds or in a mixture of the two (the front moulded and the back hand-modelled) or partly wheel-made. Some of the figurines were solid and were fashioned as toys for children, offerings for the dead or votives for the gods (e.g. horses, riders, birds, humans, deities). Some hollow figurines were fancy receptacles for perfumed oil, sometimes in the shape of clothed females, animals and birds, or naked males (see plate 13.6). The figurines were baked like pottery but were often covered in a white slip before firing and had colours added after firing: red, blue, yellow; others were treated in the same way as pottery. Some workshops (e.g. on Melos and at Locris) manufactured relief plaques that could be attached to the wall or act as a decorative covering for caskets.

The most basic use of terracotta was of course as a container, and it is as pottery that it mostly survives today. The making of pottery could be carried out in the home as a small-scale operation

**Plate 13.6**  Terracotta figurine in the shape of a youth as victor, made to contain perfumed oil, *c*.540–530 BC

to fill the gaps in the store of family crockery, in small businesses and in larger factories. The pots were either made freehand or shaped by the use of a beater and anvil or fashioned on a wheel, and then fired in an open bonfire or in a kiln. In texture they could be thin and gritty for use in cooking on an open fire, or plain and coated with black slip (see plate 13.4) to act as storage jars or mixing bowls for the preparation of food and other household tasks. Other varieties of container that were essential items were storage jars (*pithoi*), large transport jars, beehives and lamps for indoor illumination.

Today the best-known products are the fine and carefully shaped pots that carry either incised, impressed, or painted designs, or a combination of techniques, with compositions that include geometric, floral and figured details. The paint (a clay-based solution) was applied before the firing, and it was the stages in the firing that generated the contrast of black paint and red clay that was the basis for the black-figure technique and its later reversal into red-figure. These pots may have been used in the home (perhaps most likely for the husband entertaining his friends), as dedications in sanctuaries, and as offerings in tombs, where they would have accompanied the dead on their journey. In form some clay pots resemble the more expensive metal shapes (see plate 13.4), and in cities where both potters and metalworkers operated, there was likely to have been a healthy, and doubtless keen, exchange of ideas. In some cases it can be seen that moulds were taken from silver dishes and reproduced in clay. Despite the low position in society that potters held, some (mainly Athenian) pots carry personal names of makers and painters, e.g. Sophilos, Exekias, Douris, Meidias. Some names (e.g. Brygos ('the Phrygian'), Skythes ('the Skythian'), Onesimos ('the Useful')) argue for slave status.

Not surprisingly the figured scenes on the Greek vases, particularly those of Athenian black- and red-figure, have attracted a good deal of attention, for not only do they provide us with information on painting styles and the world of Greek images, but they also furnish scenes that help to enlarge our understanding of those other crafts that time has almost obliterated.

## FURTHER READING

Boardman, J., 1970: *Greek Gems and Finger Rings*. London: Thames and Hudson.

Burford, A., 1972: *Craftsmen in Greek and Roman Society*. London: Thames and Hudson.

Charbonneaux, J. 1958: *Les Bronzes grecs*. Paris: Presses. Universitaires de France (*Greek Bronzes*, trans. Katherine Watson. London: Elek Books, 1962).

Higgins, R. A., 1967: *Greek Terracottas*. London: Methuen.

Higgins, R. A., 1980: *Greek and Roman Jewellery* (2nd edn). London: Methuen.

Kraay, C. M., 1976: *Archaic and Classical Greek Coins*. London: Methuen.

Rasmussen, T. and Spivey, N., 1991: *Looking at Greek Vases*. Cambridge: Cambridge University Press.

Richter, G. M. A., 1966: *The Furniture of the Greeks, Etruscans and Romans*. London: Phaidon.

Richter, G. M. A., 1968: *The Engraved Gems of the Greeks, Etruscans and Romans. Part One: Engraved Gems of the Greeks and Etruscans: A History of Greek Art in Miniature*. London: Phaidon.

Rolley, C., 1986: *Greek Bronzes*, trans. P. Howell. London: Sotheby's and Chesterman.

Snodgrass, A. M., 1967: *Arms and Armour of the Greeks*. London: Thames and Hudson.

Sparkes, B. A., 1991: *Greek Pottery: An Introduction*. Manchester: Manchester University Press.

Sparkes, B. A., 1996: *The Red and the Black: Studies in Greek Pottery.*
London: Routledge.

Strong, D. E., 1966: *Greek and Roman Gold and Silver Plate.* London:
Methuen.

Vickers, M. and Gill, D., 1994: *Artful Crafts: Ancient Greek Silverware
and Pottery.* Oxford: Clarendon Press.

Williams, D. and Ogden, J., 1994: *Greek Gold: Jewellery of the Classical
World.* London: British Museum Publications.

# 14 / WOMEN IN
# CLASSICAL ATHENS

## *Sue Blundell*

## INTRODUCTION

In the *poleis* of ancient Greece, as in other human societies, roughly
half the children born were female. Until fairly recently historical
studies of these states focused almost exclusively on political and
military activities, and the female section of the population received little attention. But in the last thirty years several factors
have combined to bring the women of the period, real or represented, increasingly into the picture. These factors include the rise
of women's studies, the adoption by historians of a more sociological approach to their subject, and a growing interest in ancient
societies' symbolic systems. The change, though it has certainly
not transformed ancient history, has been fairly pervasive, so that
nowadays Greek women are often to be encountered in writings
which are not specifically labelled 'Women in . . . '. In this book,
for example, they put in an appearance in a number of chapters,
such as the ones on religion and on sexual mores. The purpose of
this particular chapter, where they do feature in the title, is to
examine what it meant to be a woman, and what women meant to
men, in the *polis* of Athens during the fifth and fourth centuries BC.
Unfortunately, all the evidence for this topic is derived from works
produced by male writers and artists, so that we need to be aware
that the male view of women is far more accessible to us as an
object of study than the reality of women's day-to-day lives. No
Athenian woman of the classical age is able to speak for herself.
Nevertheless, enough information is available for us to be able to
construct at least an outline of the place accorded to women in
Athenian society.

'Let no-one think of me as lowly, or weak, or submissive. I am
of a different type, dangerous to my enemies, and kind to my
friends. A life conducted in this fashion wins the most glory'
(Euripides *Medea* 807–10). This heroic declaration is pronounced
by the tragic heroine Medea, an abandoned wife, as she embarks

on her mission to win revenge against her erstwhile husband, Jason, by murdering his new bride, the bride's father, and her own dearly loved sons. One comment that is frequently provoked by images of women such as this one is that there appears to be a remarkable discrepancy between the outgoing, energetic and sometimes violent females of fifth-century Athenian tragedy, and the real-life women resident in Athens during the same period. The behaviour of the latter, it is thought, is more accurately encapsulated in a maxim found in Xenophon's treatise on household management, written in the early fourth century: 'So it is seemly for a woman to remain at home and not be out of doors; but for a man to stay inside, instead of devoting himself to outdoor pursuits, is disgraceful' (Xenophon *Household Management* 7.30). If the women of Athens were kept in virtual seclusion, people ask, how could Euripides ever have dreamt up a character such as Medea? What hidden fears about women were being expressed in these tragic viragos?

Both Medea and the seemly woman who remains indoors, are extreme cases, and even in themselves require qualification. Xenophon is presenting an ideal, and is not necessarily describing the way in which a real woman would have operated. And Medea, who is definitely an imaginary woman, is also a foreigner, not an Athenian or even a Greek; and as such she would have been expected to behave to some extent in an abnormal fashion. The truth about the women of Athens may have lain somewhere between these two extremes. But we should not expect this 'truth' to be a uniform one. In classical Athens there were females of many kinds and conditions – rich and poor Athenian-born women, resident aliens and slaves, submissive women and outspoken ones, women who joined exotic religious cults, and women who earned a small fortune having sex with wealthy clients. Moreover, times changed, and new political and economic circumstances brought new attitudes and new roles for women. In attempting to achieve an understanding of 'the women of classical Athens', we have to take account of all these variations. At the same time, however, we should not lose sight of the discrepancy between Medea and the seemly woman. Though they may be unrepresentative, they were both products of Athenian culture, and they point to an anomaly in the Athenian conception of women, and possibly in the lives of women themselves, which will need to be investigated.

## GIRLHOOD AND MARRIAGE

Although it is debatable whether their condition amounted to one of seclusion, there can be little doubt that the wives and daughters of Athenian citizens spent most of their time indoors. The sexual division of space outlined in Xenophon's maxim would have been recognizable to everyone. Whereas many Athenian boys between the ages of 6 and 14 attended small private schools, girls seem to have been educated entirely at home, though some at least (probably a minority) learned to read and write. At the stage when a young man was beginning to be initiated into the civic and military duties of a future citizen, a young woman would have been undergoing the most fundamental transition of her life: her marriage generally took place not long after puberty, somewhere between the ages of 14 and 18. Her new husband, who was usually about 30, would have been chosen for her by her father, who as her guardian or *kyrios* was her representative in all matters with a legal significance. In some cases she may scarcely have known the man she was marrying; in others there would have been at least some social contact, since marriages between first cousins were relatively common.

The event was marked by a number of ceremonies. One of the most important, the betrothal or *engue*, took place shortly before the wedding. At this the bride-to-be's guardian pronounced the words, 'I hand over this woman to you for the ploughing of legitimate children' (Menander, fragment 720K; see chapter 8, p. 138). This formula employs a common metaphorical allusion to a female as a piece of land, calling to mind both the woman's fertility and her husband's territorial control over it. But the ceremony most frequently depicted by Athenian vase-painters was the wedding procession, in which the bride and groom were transported at nightfall, in a cart or chariot, from the house of the bride's father to their new home. There they were greeted by the groom's mother, who was carrying torches. The scene in plate 14.1 is a 'stretched out' version of a painting which decorates a circular cosmetics jar or *pyxis*, so that the door on the left is in fact both the starting-point and the destination of the procession. This device serves to emphasize, like the public display of the real-life procession, the way in which two households were being brought together by the marriage. We can also see that the transfer of the bride involved a transfer of property, with the wedding-gifts

**Plate 14.1** A wedding procession, Athenian red-figure vase-painting, *c.*430 BC

carried by the women on the left symbolizing the much more substantial item, the dowry, which a woman took with her when she was married. Once inside her new home, the bride was formally escorted around the hearth, its focal point; and it was probably after this that in a ritual gesture she removed her veil which was used in art to denote not just a bride but any married woman (see plate 14.2). It signified both the modest covering which shielded a wife from the gaze of other men, and the uncovering of her body in the presence of her husband, a symbolic prelude to sexual intercourse and reproduction.

When she married, a woman passed into the guardianship of her husband. Legally she was a minor for the whole of her life, and although she may technically have owned her dowry – which was generally a sum of money – she was effectively prevented from spending it by a law which placed a low limit on the value of contracts which could be legally entered into by a woman. Her husband did have the right to dispose of the dowry, although, if he had any sense, he was cautious in the extent to which he exercised this right. On divorce, which was easy and relatively common, the dowry had to be returned in full to the wife's father or next-of-kin.

## WOMEN'S ROLES

### THE DOMESTIC DOMAIN

'It's difficult for a woman to get out of the house. What with dancing attendance on her husband, keeping the serving-girl on

**Plate 14.2** Mistress and slave girl on an Attic funerary stele, late fifth century BC

her toes, putting the baby to bed, bathing it, feeding it'
(Aristophanes *Lysistrata* 16–19). No female reader will be sur-
prised to learn from this comment in a fifth-century Athenian
comedy that, irrespective of any ideal of seclusion, a married woman
had plenty of work to keep her inside the home or *oikos*. In addition to childcare and the supervision of slaves she was responsible
for the storage and distribution of household goods, a job which
in some cases involved the management of the family finances; and
in poorer households with no servants she also had to take care of
the cooking, cleaning and washing. Most Athenian husbands may
not have valued this kind of work very highly, but there were at
least two domestic functions – wool-working and childbearing – to
which they attributed considerable social and symbolic importance.

Spinning and weaving were viewed by Greek men as the quin-
tessential feminine accomplishments. Women of every class participated in these activities, supplying not only all the clothing
requirements of their households but also most of its soft furnish-
ings: the wall-hangings, cushions and couch-covers displayed in
particular in the men's dining-room, the most public part of the
house (see plate 13.5), would have testified to the skill and devotion to duty of the female members of the family. In poetry the
symbolic value which had attached itself to wool-working was
underlined. In Homer's *Odyssey*, for example, when Penelope re-
sists her suitors' entreaties by pretending to weave a shroud for her
father-in-law, she demonstrates not only her loyalty to her absent
husband, but also her cunning intelligence or *metis*. As the products of female ingenuity textiles were also seen as the basis of a
system of knowledge and power which was exclusive to women, an
idea illustrated by several females, in the *Odyssey* and in Athenian
tragedies, who learn the secret of a man's identity through a piece
of material which they themselves wove in the distant past. The
power which women acquire through their wool-working is often
seen as dangerous to men. Prominent among the disastrous textiles
featured in Greek literature are the poisoned garments with which
Euripides' Medea and Sophokles' Deianeira (in *Women of Trachis*)
inflict terrible deaths on the recipients of their gifts.

In vase-painting (see plate 14.3) there are allusions both to a
woman's ability to work wool and to her childbearing capacity. In
one respect the scene on plate 14.3 is an unusual one, since it is
relatively rare for men and women to be shown together in an
indoor environment. However, the stick held by the husband

**Plate 14.3**  Family scene, Athenian red-figure vase-painting, *c.*430 BC

indicates to the viewer that his true place is in the outdoor world of public activity. His sojourn in the home is a temporary one, but while he is there, he gazes at his wife and surveys the signs of her creativity; there is a loom in the background, and the woman is handing over a male baby to a nurse. For Greek men, sons were by far the most important product which their wives supplied. The overriding significance of this female function is demonstrated, for example, by the prescriptions presented in a number of medical treatises. One of them informs its readers that, 'if (women) have intercourse with men their health is better than if they do not' (*On the seed* 4). In the absence of this therapeutic treatment, the womb is liable to become dry and contracted, and in the most serious cases it will begin to wander about the body, causing drowsiness, suffocation, or foaming at the mouth. Sex and pregnancy were thought to be the ultimate cures, and had the effect of creating in a woman an unimpeded interior space which matched the domestic interior with which she herself was so often associated.

Sexual activity in a woman was all too frequently, in the view of Athenian men, accompanied by sexual desire. Indeed, an inability to control one's lusts was often seen as one of the psychological characteristics which distinguished females from males (see chapter 15). Women were thus subjected to the double bind of being limited to a largely biological role, and being condemned if they showed too much appreciation of it. Laws which safeguarded the chastity of married women were introduced in a number of Greek states; in Athens the adulterous wives of Athenian citizens were punished by compulsory divorce and exclusion from all religious festivals, while their male lovers could be fined or even put to death. Measures such as these are indicative of the state's recognition of the vital contribution made by women to the stability of its political and social structures. Through their provision of legitimate sons women helped to secure the smooth transmission of wealth and power to the next generation. In a typical Greek *polis*, where the majority of people earned their living from the land, and where land-owning was limited to citizens who participated actively in the government and defence of their state, both processes were seen as crucial. The greater the political privileges which a community accorded to its adult male members, the more important it became to ensure that these privileges were confined to a narrowly defined citizen body. Hence in democratic Athens legislation aimed at guaranteeing the Athenian paternity of its future citizens by prohibiting adultery was supplemented, in 451 BC, by a law stipulating that in order to qualify for citizenship a man had to be of Athenian parentage on both sides, and not just, as previously, on that of his father. One of the effects of this law would have been to deter men from marrying non-Athenian women; the increased social significance which Athenian-born females acquired in this way would have intensified the pressure to control their sexuality.

In ancient Greece, it seems, democracy was not particularly good for women. It was in democratic Athens that male writers and artists produced a plethora of piquant but cautionary fantasies about women's capacity for sexual excess; and it was here that the ideological polarization of public (male) and private (female) spheres of operation received the most emphasis. No Greek state ever enfranchised women; but in Athens, where male citizens were increasingly defined by their active participation in political life as well as by their involvement in collective pursuits such as warfare and athletics, the gulf between the masculine domain and the feminine world of the *oikos* seemed especially wide.

In Athens in particular, then, a wide range of political, social and cultural controls were in place to counteract the potential for female power implicit in the mature woman's ability to make wool and babies. But the restriction of women to a largely domestic role seems to have fuelled rather than allayed anxieties about female behaviour. An abundance of negative imagery testifies to the latent unease with which married women were viewed – witness the poisoned garments and murderous mothers so vividly highlighted in Athenian tragedy. Such unease may be attributed, at least in part, to the anomalies of a system which accorded women a crucial role in reproducing the existing social order, while at the same time relegating them to a position of political and economic subordination within the community.

Whether or not the domestic domain did in reality provide women with an alternative arena for the exercise of power is a matter for speculation. In some of Aristophanes' comic plays, such as *Lysistrata*, women are able to get their own way by nagging, or by doing things behind their husbands' backs, or by refusing to have sex with them. Plato informs us that the dowry system made women arrogant and robbed men of their freedom (Plato *Laws* 774c); and in some of the speeches made in the Athenian law courts we learn about females who played an active part in managing the family property. But such women are few and far between. Legally and ideologically the *oikos* was ruled by the male head of the household; and though it is pleasing to conjure up an image of the home as a hidden preserve of female assertiveness, too much should not be made of the issue of women's domestic power.

## RELIGION

But there was one area of activity where women unquestionably wielded authority, and where they were accorded moreover a high degree of public prominence. In ancient Greece participation in

a                                    b

**Plates 14.4a–b**  Mourning the dead, Athenian white-ground vase-painting, mid-fifth century BC

religious rituals was one of the principal means by which the solidarity of the social group was created and reaffirmed; and it was through this medium in particular that women were integrated into the communities whose reproduction depended upon them. Within the *oikos*, women took part in the daily worship of the household's deities, and they were also intimately involved in rites marking transitional stages in the human life-cycle, especially those related to marriage and death. The laying out of a corpse and its ritual lamentation through the singing of dirges and the tearing of hair were duties which fell largely on the female members of a family (see plate 14.4). Women were also members of religious associations devoted to the worship of particular divine beings, and in some of them, most famously those which practised the mysteries of the god Dionysos, they were remarkably conspicuous. But it was in the public cults, celebrated in particular in elaborate civic festivals, that women's presence would have been most striking. Here they might participate on three different levels – as ordinary worshippers, as the performers of ritual tasks such as producing

**Plate 14.5**   Girls in the Panathenaic procession on the east frieze of the Parthenon, *c*.440 BC

garments to be presented to a deity's cult statue, and finally as priestesses, the officials who were specially chosen to supervise the cult of a goddess and administer her sanctuary. Some indication of the tremendous importance attached to these roles is given by the prominent positioning of female attendants at the head of the religious procession represented in the Parthenon frieze (see plate 14.5): in this way the part played by women in the Great Panathenaia, a festival held in honour of the city's patron deity Athena, was commemorated on the outstanding monument of the classical age (see chapter 8). There were also some major religious events which were exclusive to the female members of the population, most notably the Thesmophoria, a festival of the goddess Demeter celebrated in Athens and many other parts of the Greek world (see chapters 6 and 8).

## WOMEN OUTSIDE THE HOME

Clearly, then, religion was one aspect of experience where the seclusion of women within the home ceased to be a valid consideration. Young women whose sheltered lives had made them 'ashamed to be seen even by relatives' (Lysias 3.6–7) would have been expected to shed their modesty and emerge into the public world in order to participate in the civic cults which guaranteed a community's well-being. In other contexts women's appearances outside the home may have been viewed less positively, but would have been tolerated as an economic necessity. 'We do not live in the way we would like' (Demosthenes 57.31) is the heartfelt assertion of one speaker in the law courts whose mother, in the difficult years following Athens' defeat in the Peloponnesian War, had been forced to earn her living as a nurse and a ribbon-seller. Other women of the citizen class found work as midwives, washerwomen, and casual agricultural labourers; and in households where there was no well and no slave to fetch water, they would have made regular trips to the public fountain. Female friendships, less talked about than the more prestigious male variety, certainly existed, and women visited each other in their homes to borrow salt, assist at a confinement, or celebrate the birth of a baby. An easing of the pressure to remain indoors may have begun to occur during the Peloponnesian War (431–404 BC), the major conflict with Sparta which forced the Athenians to evacuate the countryside and bring its rural population inside the city walls. The absence of many men at the war, the more free-and-easy ways of countrywomen, and a growing need for some women to go out to work would all have been factors contributing to a manipulation and gradual erosion of the ideal of seclusion which continued into the next century.

## RESIDENT ALIENS, SLAVES AND PROSTITUTES

The comparative freedom of movement enjoyed by Athenian women of the poorer classes would also have been an element in the lives of metic, or resident alien, women. The majority of these were the wives and daughters of non-Athenian men – most of them Greeks from other states – who had been given permission to reside in Athens and who mostly worked in manufacturing or retail industries or as tenant farmers. Since metics were excluded from citizenship, and their womenfolk could not give birth to future Athenian citizens, codes of behaviour featuring female chastity may well have been less rigorously applied in their case. But there was only one significant group of women in Athens who enjoyed economic as well as physical freedom. Most *hetairai*, or high-class prostitutes (see chapter 15), belonged to the metic class, and some at least were valued for their intellectual as well as their sexual companionship. Aspasia, the long-term mistress of the statesman Perikles, had come to Athens as a *hetaira*, and was renowned – or rather notorious – for her clever and persuasive talk and her political astuteness. While ignorance, inexperience, and speechlessness were qualities which were generally prized in Athenian women, foreign females who had taken on an active sexual role were also permitted to subvert other norms, and were tentatively admitted into the masculine world of discourse and dialogue. But, like the clever and outgoing females of tragedy, such women would always have been seen as dangerous. Aspasia was widely regarded as having influenced Perikles' domestic and foreign policies, and was the object of some vicious caricatures and political attacks.

But women like Aspasia were exceptional. The majority of prostitutes were slaves (see chapter 15) and like their sisters who worked as domestic servants they would have been allowed very little freedom. The females who staffed the low-grade brothels were sometimes brutally treated by their clients, while household slaves might be whipped or locked in their quarters if they misbehaved. However, the latter did sometimes enjoy the compensation of becoming their mistresses' confidantes or the much-loved companions of the children they had nursed; and in wealthier households they could at least aspire to more responsible managerial positions as housekeepers.

## WOMEN AS 'THE OTHER'

So far in our investigations we have encountered a number of women who departed, to one degree or another, from the ideal of the passive, chaste and submissive female who was bound to the confines of the domestic interior. The woman who popped outside to visit a neighbour or draw water from a fountain existed at the lower end of a scale of female transgressions which culminated in extraordinary figures such as Aspasia, or some of the women worshippers of the god Dionysos. The extent to which the latter actually engaged in the kind of ecstatic dancing on the mountainside which is described in Euripides' tragedy *Bacchae* is open to question; but vase-paintings depicting these women (see plate 8.2) demonstrate, as does Euripides' play, that the tendency to pass

**Plate 14.6** A maenad in a bacchic frenzy, Athenian white-ground cup-painting, *c*.490 BC

over into a wild and uncontrolled state of being was a trait which the male imagination readily attributed to the female of the species. The Bacchic woman's abandoned pose, her loosened hair and animal-skin cloak, and her physical contact with the snake and the panther (see plate 14.6) are all signs of her affinity with a natural sphere whose values are opposed to those of the ordered political community. In this way the female could be used to underpin the Athenian male's definition of himself as civilized and self-controlled by providing him with an image of the 'other' – of everything which he believed he was not.

But at the same time the female could present the male with challenges. Women who slipped across the boundary separating human culture from the untamed world of nature could also exceed other limits, exhibiting on occasions an alarming propensity for adopting masculine modes of behaviour. In real life Aspasia may well have fulfilled such a role in the eyes of her male antagonists. In the realm of fantasy there were the Amazons, a mythical race of warrior women who lived in a self-governing all-female state, and were repeatedly represented in temple sculpture, in wall-paintings and on pottery. The fact that these highly successful fighters were in the end always defeated by Greeks suggests that this particular narrative would have been safely interpreted by most spectators as a purely cautionary tale – 'women who adopt a masculine lifestyle and try to survive without husbands are naturally doomed to failure.' But the similarly outgoing female characters of Athenian tragedy were far too subtly presented to be summed up so straight-forwardly. When Euripides' Medea utters sentiments borrowed from the masculine code of honour as she steels herself to murder her sons, when Klytaimestra in Aeschylus' *Agamemnon* slaughters her faithless consort and takes control of the state, when Sophokles' Antigone defies the head of her household and ruler of her country in order to perform the masculine task of interring her dead brother – when, in short, tragic women begin to behave more like men – then the male members of the audience were surely being invited to look at themselves and their standards of conduct from a new and disturbing perspective.

Most Athenian men would have wanted to draw a firm line between their own wives and daughters, and the Aspasias, Amazons and Medeas who populated their imaginative world. The rules and regulations which they had invented for their womenfolk indicate that on one level they were able to do this. But the uniformity of the symbolism with which females were associated in Athenian culture – for example, the indiscriminate application of the wool-working motif to wives, prostitutes and goddesses alike – suggests that on a deeper level Athenian men were responding to the conviction that all women, irrespective of their social status, shared the same fundamental feminine characteristics. The fear may always have been present that 'the seemly woman who remained at home' might one day erupt into a tragic heroine unless masculine controls over her behaviour were rigidly applied. Fortunately for the women of classical Athens, the wide-ranging political and economic changes which occurred in the latter part of this period meant that these controls were increasingly hard to maintain. In the course of the fourth century the constraints which had been imposed on women when Athens was at the height of its wealth and power were already beginning to ease.

FURTHER READING

Blundell, S., 1995: *Women in Ancient Greece*. London: British Museum Press/Harvard University Press.

Cameron, A. and Kuhrt, A. (eds), 1993: *Images of Women in Antiquity*. London: Routledge.

Cohen, D., 1991: *Law, Sexuality and Society: The Enforcement of Morals in Classical Athens*. Cambridge: Cambridge University Press.

Garland, R., 1990: *The Greek Way of Life: From Conception to Old Age*. London: Duckworth.

Halperin, D. M., Winkler, J. J. and Zeitlin, F. I. (eds), 1990: *Before Sexuality: The Construction of Erotic Experience in the Ancient Greek World*. Princeton: Princeton University Press.

Just, R., 1989: *Women in Athenian Law and Life*. London: Routledge.

Pomeroy, S. B. (ed.), 1991: *Women's History and Ancient History*. Chapel Hill: University of North Carolina Press.

Reeder, E. D. (ed.), 1995: *Pandora: Women in Classical Greece*. Baltimore: The Walters Art Gallery, Baltimore and Princeton University Press.

Zeitlin, F. I., 1996: *Playing the Other: Gender and Society in Classical Greek Literature*. Chicago: University of Chicago Press.

# 15 / SEX IN CLASSICAL ATHENS

## Brian Sparkes

### INTRODUCTION

It is a truism that one must never accept at face value anything others may say about sex, especially with regard to themselves. When statements primarily concern attitudes and practices of more than 2,000 years ago, then the need for caution is so much more acute.

Sexual behaviour and attitudes to it varied in different areas of Greece at different times, and although there were inevitably some basic similarities, it has seemed best to concentrate on one group, the Athenians of the classical period (sixth to fourth centuries BC). There are two main reasons for this. The Athenians were the most literate of all Greeks, and hence we can read what they said and thought in the various literary genres. They have also left a wide variety of visual images which stand alongside the imagery of Japan and India as being the most explicit in matters of sex. However, neither the written word nor the visual images can be taken on trust. The literary works are lacunose and partial; they were composed by men for men and reflect for the most part the dominant masculine aristocratic ideology that prevailed at the time. Also, the different genres of literature obeyed their own rules. Drama provided strong female characters who intruded into the male world where in reality they had no place, whether in myth (e.g. Klytaimestra, Medea, Antigone) or in everyday life (e.g. Lysistrata, Praxagora). Comedies also needed to raise a laugh at the sexual foibles and peccadilloes of contemporary Athenians, but jokes are not always reliably grounded in the everyday world. Philosophical writers tended to construct prescriptive standards of behaviour, whereas reality was undoubtedly much less tidy and more unruly. Orators, who provide us with much information on popular attitudes, presented cases that would be intelligible and acceptable to the expectations of their male jurors, but had to enhance their client's cause with persuasive arguments. Also, most of the literary output arose within the context of an urban environment; there is little to help us to understand the customs that applied in other areas. As for the visual images, though they are of great number, they are similarly centred on city life for the most part, and it is still necessary to keep in mind what truth they were likely to tell and for whose eyes and for what occasions they were fashioned. Whereas sculpture privileges the naked male form above all others, Athenian vase-painting, whether the earlier black-figure (mainly sixth century BC) or the later red-figure (mainly fifth and fourth centuries BC), presents scenes of sexual pairings of all varieties (male, female and animal) and is the fullest, even if still incomplete, evidence for sexual behaviour. The fact that explicit scenes of sexual congress on painted pottery grow fewer after the middle of the fifth century is a comment on taste and not on social practice.

Whether one thinks that all varieties of sexual behaviour are universal, biological imperatives, or whether they are socially constructed (and the differences in patterns of behaviour evident between classical Athens and more recent Western/Christian societies present an argument for some degree of social construction), it is impossible to consider classical Athenian practices outside the society in which they were enacted.

## A walk round Athens

The external face of sexual attitudes could be seen in the streets and public places of the city. Outside the doors of private houses, in public meeting places and in sanctuaries were placed *hermai*, statues of the god Hermes consisting of a bearded head on top of a rectangular pillar with an erect phallos on the front (see plate 15.1). Hermes was the guardian of ways and cross-roads; beware of any journey taken that omitted offerings or greetings to him. A modern visitor to ancient Athens (whether male or female) would be startled at having to greet, or be greeted by, a rampant god at the garden gate and in the centre of town, but for the Athenians it was an expression of the strength of the male force. Women were not shielded from the sight of naked male statues, though few in such an erect state as the *hermai*.

Depending on the time of year, there may be a religious procession in which a massive phallos was carried. Such a procession was in honour of Dionysos, the male god whose area of concern involved liquid – not only wine, but vital juices of all sorts. The theatre was also his sphere, and after sitting through the serious

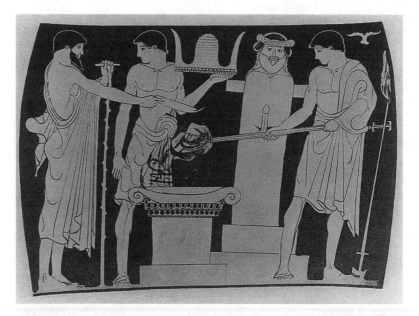

**Plate 15.1**  Sacrifice at an altar with a statue of an ithyphallic Hermes in the background, Athenian red-figure vase-painting, *c*.470 BC

tragedies, the audience would be faced in the comic and satyr plays which followed with characters dressed in costumes that included a large phallos attached to a pair of trunks, whilst scatological jokes rang round the auditorium (see plate 9.3). It is not surprising that, in view of the secluded life women led, their presence at such performances has been questioned, and the evidence is indeed ambivalent. In the *gymnasia* the sight that greeted the visitor was that of young men exercising in the nude, and in the *stadia* the athletic events were entered in the same naked state.

## SEX IN THE HOUSEHOLD

That Athens outside the house was an aggressively man's world, in sexual matters as much as in politics, is a justified claim. The adult male citizen was the dominant figure. Even within the house, the man was master (*kyrios*). The women stayed at home much of the time, looking after the children and slaves and managing the household (no light task), but all within the family were the property of the male head. It was the man who was the citizen, and in Athens to be a citizen you had to be born of an Athenian family (usually both mother and father) to give the children a chance to inherit property, for the sons to take part in public life, for the daughters to marry other Athenians, indeed to have any standing in society. Male law and order provided protection and security – but at a price. The head of the household had power over everything and everybody within his family, could have sex with anybody he liked (except his mother, daughter or full sister) and dictated the sex lives of any under his roof. Slaves were particularly vulnerable, they were owned by the master and could not refuse any demands made on them; they were in no position to reject violence or sexual assault from the master.

Marriage was for the cultivating of children, and the children must be legitimate, hence the careful watch kept on the chastity of the wife and mother. If a wife was raped or seduced (and the relative gravity of the two offences was balanced between the effect on the woman's feelings and on the husband's honour), the legal, if not moral, victim was the husband in whose house the woman lived. Adultery (*moicheia*) shamed the husband and father, his honour which he prized was tainted, he had proved incapable of keeping guard on his family and had lost face. So the husband was allowed to kill the adulterer, if caught *in flagrante*, without legal penalty; more commonly he prosecuted or physically humiliated his rival and divorced and thus dishonoured his wife.

When at home wives and daughters were kept out of sight of those male visitors who were not members of the family, and if men were invited home to a party by the master of the household, the women took no part in it. However, there were occasions when women were allowed out of the house and might meet potential lovers, if that was their inclination. The image that men projected was that women were thirsty for sex all the time (as indeed for drink) and must be kept under control; they were weak and irresponsible, ever ready to yield to temptation and lacking the self-control that men possessed. Visits to the natal home or to the home of a relative (married sister, etc.) might provide occasions for deviation from chastity, and there were also family funerals in which women had a large part to play, as well as public festivals in many of which women were essential participants. It was on the women of the upper classes that such a keen lookout was kept, for, as Aristotle asks (*Politics* 1300a6–7) 'who could prevent the wives of the poor from going outside?' The virginity of daughters was specially carefully guarded, and a marriage was often arranged for them at or before the menarche. Marriage was the socially acceptable state, nor should we imagine them all to be loveless. Only the jaundiced would consider all the epitaphs for wives insincere:

> Chairestrate lies in this tomb. When she was alive
> her husband loved her. When she died he lamented.

## Birth control

For the married couple, there was initially no choice but to 'increase and multiply'. Breeding was needed to display the husband's virility (boys for preference), to replace those who had died through such disasters as famine and war, to create a younger generation to look after the aged and tend the family tombs, and also to combat the high mortality rate (ten times higher than now). But that done, what measures were adopted to limit the family?

To treat any sexual activity not aimed at procreation as wrong is an attitude found in some pagan philosophers, but it comes late in antiquity. Of the ways of controlling the numbers in the family (contraception, abortion and abandonment or infanticide), contraception was surely the most difficult to manoeuvre. It is a product of will plus technique, allied to an understanding of the principles of procreation in the first place, knowing the most fecund time of the month and calculating the connection between intercourse and length of pregnancy. Many may have felt that avoidance of pregnancy was beyond human control. The evidence for such methods as the safe period (unfortunately it was claimed that the most fertile time was immediately after the period) and coitus interruptus is very meagre; they were also inconvenient for the master of the household. Extra-marital sex for the men was likely to have been the commonest escape route, though pessaries and potions were known, and some seem to have been efficacious. Magical charms and amulets would also have had their place, though condoms seem not to have come into use until the sixteenth century.

Abortion went against the Hippokratic oath, but the oath had no official standing amongst the common people. Aborting was always a dangerous practice, and how could you be sure that you would have any further children, should the need arise through deaths in the family? Methods in antiquity are likely to have ranged from purgatives of various sorts, pressure on the stomach, riding in a cart on the rough Greek roads, and recourse to magic recipes. The choice was stark.

Abandonment or infanticide was safer for women than abortion, even though it understandably caused acute emotional distress. Also, the sex of the child was then known, and a boy could be kept alive, if desired, and a girl exposed or killed. Exposure of infants was authorized by law in some areas, but such authority was not always needed. Sometimes the exposed babies were found and reared as slaves, and if identifying tokens had been left with the baby, then later in time when grown up, the man or woman might return to the original home, with tragic consequences as for Oedipus or, after Miss Prism-like revelations, with joy and tears. Although the later return of an exposed baby was a staple of Athenian New Comedy of the fourth century BC, the attitude to infant exposure adopted in many of the sources suggests that it was an object of concern for them, and it is difficult for us to gauge the frequency with which it actually happened.

## EXTRA-MARITAL SEX

Marriage came early for the girls, from about the age of 14, the menarche; for the man the age of marriage was usually about 30, twice the length of time to wait. This meant that young married women were surrounded by men of their own age who were unmarried for many years to come. Although it was a wife's duty to be faithful to her husband, no moral stigma attached to a husband who sought sexual gratification outside marriage. He had no duty to be faithful, perhaps just not to flaunt his extra-marital affairs in front of his wife and her family. There were girls (and boys) who plied the streets and stood outside the many brothels in Athens, to entice the customers inside. For men to use the slave girls in brothels was considered safer for casual encounters, as the consequences of being discovered in an adulterous affair with a woman married to a citizen, however thrilling the adventure, were extreme. The prostitutes (*pornai*) enjoyed certain legal safeguards but had to pay a tax, whether living privately or in a brothel. Some compositions on red-figure pottery show men offering women purses of money or presents and making gestures that declare their intentions; they have been interpreted as men buying sexual favours. Some men had mistresses (*pallakai*) whom they owned as they also were slaves; concubinage was obviously more expensive than one-night stands, and was the privilege of the wealthy. At the top end of the scale and having no part in brothel life were the high-class courtesans (often called *hetairai*), the female companions who were frequently well educated and able to make intelligent conversation in male company. The distinction between these and the concubines was that many *hetairai* were non-Athenian; they came to Athens from other areas of Greece. Perikles is the best-known public figure to have had a mistress of this type, Aspasia, who bore Perikles a son. She came from Miletos, the Greek city on the west coast of Asia Minor, and is reputed to have been a woman of high intellect. Comic poets made fun of their relationship and painted Aspasia as a madame with a string of girls.

Much less exalted were the girls who were hired out for all-male drinking parties; they were expected to play musical instruments and dance and also to complete the evening as the sexual partners of the men on their couches. The parties that we know most about are the *symposia*, the gatherings which were not without political affiliations. As indicated earlier, there were levels of society in Athens, and one has not to imagine that fishmongers and carpenters were provided with, or could pay for, such gatherings, though not all *symposia* were aristocratic. But it is these aristocratic *symposia* that the literary sources (mainly Plato and Xenophon) recall: high-minded parties at which philosophical discussions bulked large. On many occasions there were recitations, games, riddles, and extempore versifying, not to mention the singing, playing of instruments and dancing by the girls. The evidence from vase-painting would suggest that these drinking parties usually ended with sex, some of it discreetly hidden by the painters (see plate 15.2), some more blatantly exposed. Some of the more extreme pictures show the drunken conclusion to an evening's drinking when the girls were sometimes forced into simultaneous oral and genital or anal sex. In a world where men ruled and slavery was the norm, women submitted with grace or were forced against their will.

In brief, according to one prosecutor in an Athenian court (and we must keep in mind the setting):

> For this is what living with a woman as one's wife means –
> to have children by her and to introduce the sons to the
> members of the clan and of the deme, and to betroth the
> daughters to husbands as one's own. We keep courtesans

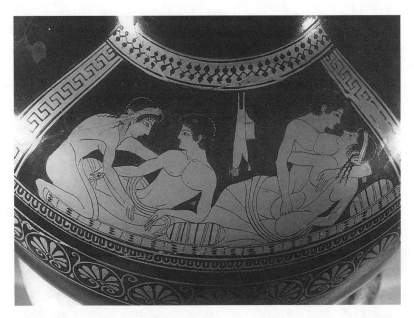

**Plate 15.2** Sex at a symposion, Athenian red-figure vase-painting, *c.*500 BC

(*hetairai*) for the sake of pleasure, mistresses (*pallakai*) for the daily care of our bodies, and wives (*gynaikes*) to bear us legitimate children and to be faithful guardians of our households. (Pseudo-Demosthenes *Against Neaira* 122)

This was likely to have been a cumulative practice rather than a mutually exclusive one.

## HOMOSEXUALITY

There was, however, another aspect to sexual behaviour. Much is made, both in antiquity and in modern studies, of 'Greek love', same-sex association between males. Given the social organization mentioned earlier with its emphasis on the separate lives lived by men and women, it is perhaps not surprising that male bonding was of great importance and publicly acknowledged, if not sanctioned.

On the basis of a combination of different types of evidence, mainly Athenian and concerning aristocratic practice, modern study of Greek homosexuality has produced a model which might be

**Plate 15.3** Man and youth in homosexual courtship, Athenian black-figure cup-painting, *c.*520 BC

characterized as 'culturally sanctioned pederasty'. The model is as follows:

> *The sexual relationship was between an* erastes, *a young adult active partner, and an* eromenos, *an adolescent passive teenager. The* erastes *was the dominant, pursuing figure, offering gifts (but not money) and helping the youngster on his way to becoming an adult member of society, giving him status as the chosen companion of a member of a distinguished family. By contrast, the* eromenos *had the subjective role, accepting the* erastes' *advances with reluctance or at least with discrimination and showing no overt joy at his approach (see plate 15.3). The physical union of the older with the younger man was not anal, but intercrural, the rubbing of the erect penis between the thighs. When the boy became a man, it was his turn to act as the pursuing* erastes *and by the age of 30, the accepted time for marriage, men abandoned their homosexuality for 'normal' married life. Public opinion castigated those men who continued to act as submissive* eromenoi *in adult life as effeminate, and if they received money for their services they could be deprived of their civic rights.*

Though much is true in this model, it is too cosy and too sanitized a version of a reality that was altogether more complex. Students of ancient Athens may be disposed to accept it as it tones down the homosexual basis of Athenian life. However, the literary evidence gives an altogether wider view and a less compartmentalized picture. For instance, homosexuality was to be found in the army, its social home, when both partners were older. Indeed, in some areas of Greece (e.g. Thebes) the pairing of male lovers as comrades-in-arms, fighting next to one another, was considered an incentive to military efficiency, for both wished to show their courage in front of each other. The images of homosexual 'courting' and congress provide varied information. There are many scenes of 'courtship', fewer of actual intercourse. In the case of courtship there are scenes of gifts being given to the adolescents, of their chins and genitals being touched in entreaty and encouragement. There are also scenes by contrast in which both figures are beardless youths, not an older and younger male, suggesting that the present model is too restricted. The older man is often shown being physically excited by the touching, the younger man is usually shown as the unaffected recipient of the advances. However, some images reveal the *eromenos* as not so demure in his reactions, and the older man receives a warmer welcome than he had expected (of historical figures, Alkibiades comes to mind here). In the matter of intercourse, the majority of images do indeed present face-to-face congress with penetration between the thighs. Anal penetration is rarely shown, but literary sources speak of sodomy as the usual form of gratification. As the more common position for male-female intercourse seems to have been *a tergo*, being sodomized was tantamount to being treated as a woman and therefore was humiliation for a male. It was considered a shameful act and contrary to nature.

Pederasty, for which the laws and customs differed between states, was a part of aristocratic upbringing in classical Athens. It cannot have been an easy transition through puberty for the Athenian youngsters still in their mid-teens who might find themselves good-looking enough to attract their older contemporaries but who had to avoid the stigma accorded to those who submitted to anal intercourse. For the emotionally undeveloped youngster, homosexual behaviour must have been like walking a tightrope; social disapproval and gossip would have been quick to make itself felt. So much in Athenian aristocratic life depended on presenting the correct public image and maintaining social connections between important families.

As for love between Athenian women, the picture is even less clear. We nowadays tend to call female pairing 'lesbianism', but that was not the Greek term for such female association. 'To play the Lesbian' seems to have referred to oral sex, *fellatio*, an obligation placed on the girls at the *symposia* and in the brothels. That females related sexually was accepted as a fact of life but was not given the same prominence as the male-to-male pairing. The verses of the Lesbian Sappho herself express the physical effects of passion for other women, and some lines would suggest more than unrequited pining for her female friends. The comic poets assumed that the sexual desires of the women would be satisfied by slaves employed in the household, or by the muleteer or the local cobbler. Vase-painters rarely, if ever, drew scenes of female congress, but one must recall that the painters were men who were likely to draw the scenes for other men.

## SELF-GRATIFICATION

Sexual self-gratification, both by men and women, seems to have been considered the last resort of those deprived of a partner. Comic playwrights treat it as a boorish practice and a suitable subject for farcical comment. There are a few images of men at work, so to speak, not all painters treating the practice as a joke, some indeed quite sympathetic or at least free from comment. Sometimes the male is alone, but quite often in what one might call competition; in pictures where group sex is represented (e.g. at a *symposion*), when there is no partner (either male or female) to share the experience, they are shown dealing with their desperation themselves.

Evidence for lone women and sex is slight, but given that women were considered by men to be highly sexed, in the absence of any partner the woman might resort to a dildo (*olisbos*) (see plate 15.4). These leather articles, which are jokingly said to have been borrowed by neighbours and pronounced firmer than the real article, were said to come from, or be made by craftsmen from, the Greek settlements on and off the west coast of Asia Minor (e.g. Miletos and the island of Chios). In the vase-paintings the dildos are shown as huge (with an eye), the male painters perhaps fantasizing about

**Plate 15.4** Woman using dildos, Athenian red-figure cup-painting, *c*.500 BC

their own prowess. In scenes of group sex the women, when not involved with the men, are sometimes shown exciting and consoling themselves.

## WISHFUL THINKING

The divine myths, which were handed on from generation to generation, told of the amorous adventures of the gods and goddesses: Zeus pursuing mortal women as well as the young Ganymede (the original form of the word 'catamite'), Aphrodite and Ares enjoying one another, Apollo raping unfortunate victims of his lust, the nymphomaniac Eos, the personification of Dawn, chasing young men. Aphrodite herself gave her name to sexual conduct (*ta aphrodisia*), so women were at the root of the activity. Amongst the heroes there was Herakles for whom rape seems to have been an almost daily occurrence. Many an aristocratic family was proud to trace its ancestry to a god or hero who had fathered a child on an unwilling young woman. Such stories gave sanction to men's behaviour (as at an all-night festival), and the divine and heroic perpetrators acted as role-models for mortal men. Although there is little in Homer's *Iliad* to suggest a homosexual relationship between Achilles and Patroklos, it was read into the epic by later Greek writers, even though the whole of the *Iliad* was predicated on the theft by Agamemnon of Achilles' concubine. The fact that there is confusion (in both literary and visual evidence) of which of this pair was the *erastes* and which the *eromenos* demonstrates the difficulty even in antiquity of comprehending male–male relationships.

Greek imagination, whether verbal or visual, also invented stories that served to act out the desires and dreams of human beings. The nearness of the animal kingdom to their lives brought close to home such stories as the transformation of Zeus into a bull and a swan to effect his purpose. However, the Greeks also devised hybrid creatures such as the Pan figure for whom they carved phallic images to be set up in the countryside. The most popular figure of the imagination was the ithyphallic satyr, a mainly human figure with animal associations (most often a tail and pointed ears), that seems to express male sexual aspirations, if not accomplishments. They chase after nymphs but are usually repulsed (see plate 15.5). They are also shown performing anatomical tricks that would defeat mere mortals. If they can't catch the women, they either engage in competitive masturbation or mount a passing animal. Transfer of such bestial acts to fantasy figures should not hide the fact that many shepherds spent months in the mountains with only sheep or goats for company and would seek relief whichever way they could.

There is no corresponding female creature to the satyr, but one of the strangest fantasy figures with which women are involved is the phallos bird – a  phallos (with eye) used as the head of a bird, what has been called 'an animated dildo'. The vase-painters provide a number of variations: the bird may be large enough for a naked woman to ride (see plate 15.6), or small enough to be carried. However, the meaning is clear – this is a disembodied expression of female desires as imagined by men. We are here in the complex realms of imagination and imagery, a world away from the usually much more basic transcriptions of Greek sexual behaviour.

**Plate 15.5** A maenad repulsing a tumescent satyr, Athenian red-figure cup-painting, *c*.480 BC

**Plate 15.6** Woman riding a phallos-bird, Athenian white-ground cup-painting, *c*.520–500 BC

FURTHER READING

Boardman, J. and La Rocca, E., 1978: *Eros in Greece*. London: John Murray.

Buffière, F., 1982: *Eros adolescent: La pédérastie dans la Grèce antique*. Paris: Les Belles Lettres.

Cantarella, E., 1988: *Secondo Natura*. Rome: Editori Reuniti (*Bisexuality in the Ancient World*, trans. C. Ó. Cuilleanáin. New Haven and London: Yale University Press, 1992).

Cohen, D., 1991: *Law, Sexuality, and Society: The Enforcement of Morals in Classical Athens*. Cambridge: Cambridge University Press.

Davidson, J., 1997: *Courtesans and Fishcakes*. London: HarperCollins.

Dierichs, A., 1993: *Erotik in der Kunst Griechenlands*. Mainz: von Zabern.

Dover, K. J., 1978: *Greek Homosexuality*. London: Duckworth.

Eyben, E., 1980/1981: 'Family Planning in Graeco-Roman Antiquity', *Ancient Society* 11/12: 5–82.

Halperin, D. M., 1990: *One Hundred Years of Homosexuality*. New York and London: Routledge.

Halperin, D. M., Winkler, J. J. and Zeitlin, F. I. (eds), 1990: *Before Sexuality: The Construction of Erotic Experience in the Ancient Greek World*. New Jersey: Princeton University Press.

Johns, C., 1982: *Sex or Symbol: Erotic Images of Greece and Rome*. London: British Museum Publications.

von Kampen, N. (ed.), 1996: *Sexuality in Ancient Art*. Cambridge: Cambridge University Press.

Keuls, E. C., 1985: *The Reign of the Phallus: Sexual Politics in Ancient Athens*. Berkeley: University of California Press.

Kilmer, M. F., 1993: *Greek Erotica on Attic Red-Figure Vases*. London: Duckworth.

Richlin, A. (ed.), 1992: *Pornography and Representation in Greece and Rome*. New York: Oxford University Press.

Riddle, J. M., 1992: *Contraception and Abortion from the Ancient World to the Renaissance*. Cambridge, Mass.: Harvard University Press.

Winkler, J. J., 1990: *The Constraints of Desire: The Anthropology of Sex and Gender in Ancient Greece*. New York and London: Routledge.

# PART 4

## Continuity and Change

# 16 / THE CHRISTIAN MILLENNIUM

## Averil Cameron

GREECE, CONSTANTINOPLE AND
THE CHRISTIAN EMPIRE

Despite St Paul's speech on the Areopagus in Athens and his dealings with the Christian community at Corinth, Greece was slow in becoming Christian. Athens was, after all, identified with traditional culture and learning, and in late antiquity the city was one of the main 'university' towns to which the sons of the elite came to learn from such famous teachers as Libanius. By the fourth century, Christians like Basil, the future bishop of Caesarea, and his friend Gregory, who was to become bishop of Nazianzus, studied side by side in Athens with pagan fellow-pupils. Although the higher education offered in Athens was not confined to philosophy, the philosophical school identified with Plato and known as the Academy became, especially from the time of its fifth-century head Proclus, the main centre of Neoplatonic philosophical teaching (see chapter 10) in the empire until its activities were curtailed by the Christian emperor Justinian in AD 529.

Churches were late in being built in Athens, and major church buildings do not appear before the fifth century AD. The early churches in Greece, such as those at Philippi, in northern Greece, at Lechaion, the harbour of Corinth and at Thessaloniki, date from the fifth century, or at the earliest the end of the fourth; the Rotunda of St George at Thessaloniki was converted from an earlier existing building. In contrast, archaeological remains in Athens such as the so-called 'House of Proclus' have been identified as having been used by the secular teachers who flourished there; at Cenchreae near Corinth a villa was decorated with a depiction of Sokrates among the sages, and excavation of villas in Athens has revealed large quantities of classical sculpture.

In AD 267 Athens was subjected to invasion by the Heruli, in one of the many incursions by barbarian tribes in this period. The extent of damage which the city experienced is controversial; it recovered well, and its security was protected by a new fortification, known as the Post-Herulian Wall, whose building was

**Plate 16.1**  Head of Constantine the Great, *c.*AD 312

commemorated in two verse inscriptions. A local magistrate and benefactor, P. Herennius Dexippus, who was also a historian, distinguished himself in resistance to the Heruli. Greece was next to be invaded by Alaric in AD 396, but the intervening period seems to have been relatively uneventful. The province of Achaea was governed by an equestrian *praeses* under Diocletian, but was later under a proconsul; one who held this office in AD 362–4 was the prominent pagan senator Vettius Agorius Praetextatus.

With his victory over Licinius at Chrysopolis (Üsküdar/Scutari) in AD 324, Constantine (see plate 16.1) became sole emperor of the Roman world and gained control of Greece and the east. He soon began to turn the classical city of Byzantium into a typical seat of imperial rule, which he named Constantinople, 'the city of Constantine'. The inauguration took place in AD 330, a date which many regard as marking the beginning of the Byzantine empire. But although Constantine based himself at Constantinople until his death in AD 337, there was no real administrative split between east and west before the death of Theodosius I in AD 395, and the Emperor Justinian (AD 527–65) still thought of Italy and the west as properly part of his territory. To the end of the Byzantine

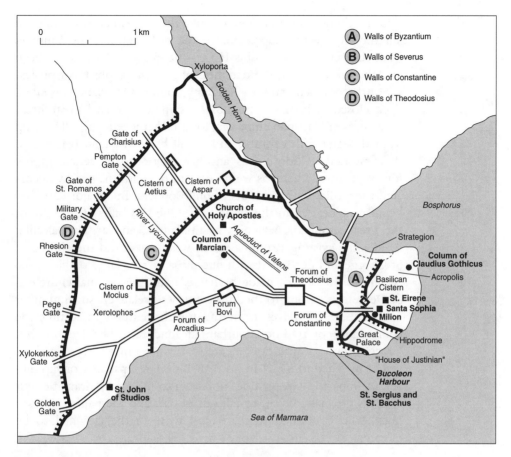

**Figure 16.1** Plan of Byzantine Constantinople

period, his successors continued to regard themselves as Roman emperors. As for religion, Constantine's buildings at Constantinople reflected his secular power at least as much they did his support for Christianity. The city of Constantinople still had relatively few churches and monasteries even at the end of the fourth century, and it was not until the sixth century at least that the eastern empire as a whole could properly be called Christian (see figure 16.1). Yet alongside imperial rule from Constantinople, the Orthodox Church was to be a defining characteristic of the Byzantine state.

At first, Greece was not significantly affected, and Athens remained a major centre of higher education. The future Emperor Julian studied there in AD 355, when Prohaeresius and Himerius were teaching, and was initiated into the Eleusinian mysteries; he left the city deeply impressed. In the fifth century, the Empress Eudocia, wife of Theodosius II (AD 408–50), is said to have been an Athenian by birth, the daughter of a pagan 'sophist', or professor of rhetoric. The famous Academy, founded by Plato, was effectively closed by Justinian in AD 529; its influence posed a real threat in the eyes of Christian emperors, for it had enjoyed a new flowering from the later fifth century, and it still boasted pagan teachers of the first rank. Corinth was another major urban centre in the fourth century, where, as we have seen, rich citizens nearby decorated their villas with portraits of philosophers. But major churches begin to appear from this period on. One was built on the site of the great shrine of Asklepios at Epidauros, and at Thessaloniki, besides the existing Rotunda which was turned into the church of St George and decorated with fine mosaics, two large basilicas, the Acheiropoietos ('Not made by hands') and the original church of St Demetrius belong to the fifth century. A relatively small number of inscriptions survives from the fourth century, indicating the continuance of traditional urban life and civic benefaction, but Greece is not a well-documented province. In theory, the laws issued by Theodosius II in AD 391–2 declared pagan worship illegal; its impact in Greece does not seem to have been dramatic, but temples gradually began to fall out of use, and the pagan philosophers who continued to teach and write in the city had to be discreet.

## INVASION AND AFTERMATH

Though further works of defence were undertaken in Athens at the end of the fourth century, all was not secure, and Greece and the Balkans remained vulnerable to invasion. This was particularly serious after the Roman defeat and the death on the field of the Emperor Valens at Adrianople in AD 378. In AD 395–6 a band of Visigoths under Alaric moved south through the pass of Thermopylae and reached Attica. By 397 the western general Stilicho had Alaric retreating to Epirus, but not before he had caused much destruction in the Peloponnese. He is said to have been deterred from entering Athens by an appearance of the goddess Athena, fully armed, but this story is likely to derive from pagan apologetic, and other sources suggest that Athens was not spared. Invasion remained a real danger. In the sixth century Justinian rebuilt the fifth-century fortifications across the Isthmus of Corinth, but although the same emperor broadly restored Roman control in the Balkans, Greece was exposed to repeated incursions by Cotrigur Huns, Slavs and Avars from the mid-sixth to early-seventh centuries. Archaeological and numismatic evidence suggests that the Slavs had reached the Peloponnese in the late 570s and that some of the inhabitants took refuge on islands in the gulf of Corinth. The extent of Slavic settlement is much disputed; nevertheless, the subsequent period was one of great insecurity, and some urban populations migrated to safer places. The medieval Chronicle of Monemvasia suggests that the rock of Monemvasia off the eastern Peloponnese came to be populated from Sparta during this process (see plate 16.2).

Little is known with certainty of conditions in mainland Greece during this period. To the north, Thessaloniki experienced repeated attacks from the 580s onwards. This gave rise to a strong belief in the power of St Demetrius as the city's protector, as can be seen in the two books of *Miracles of St Demetrius* dating from different periods in the seventh century. Constantinople itself came dangerously near to being taken when it was besieged by the Avars in conjunction with the Sasanian Persians in AD 626. During these years large areas of Asia Minor, including many cities, were severely damaged by the Persians, who also reached Palestine and took Jerusalem in AD 614, followed by Egypt, the source of much of the food supply of the capital. Though the Emperor Heraclius (AD 610–41) managed to defeat the Persians on their own ground and return home in triumph, the Arab invasions followed almost at once. The eastern provinces, including much of Asia Minor, were lost. Cyprus suffered damaging attacks, as did Rhodes and Kos. Greece itself escaped, but both military security and economic conditions in the empire fell to a low level. In many areas, while the Slavic newcomers seem to have gradually assimilated with the existing inhabitants, there seems to have been overall depopulation. Many towns, including Athens, shrank dramatically in size, and they lost the infrastructure which had supported education and culture; continuity, if any, was maintained by village settlements. Even the population of Constantinople fell from around half a million in the sixth century to below 100,000, possibly even to only half that figure. The tax system, the military organization and the administrative structure all underwent drastic change, and

**Plate 16.2** Byzantine Monemvasia on the eastern coast of the Peloponnese, founded in the later thirteenth century, one of the last fortresses to hold out against the Turks

during this period little or no control was exercised over Greece by the imperial government.

Yet the capital withstood two major Arab sieges and successfully transferred its economic and political focus to the north. A combination of diplomacy, arms, and religious and cultural colonialism based on the export of Orthodox Christianity strengthened Byzantine interests in the Balkans and later with the Rus. While in AD 811 the Emperor Nicephorus I was killed in an ambush by the

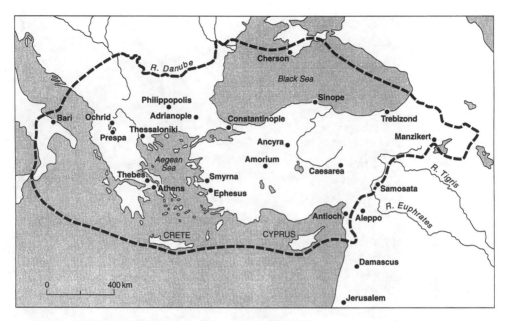

**Figure 16.2** The Byzantine Empire in AD 1025

Bulgars, by the death of Basil II, the 'Bulgar-slayer', in AD 1025, Bulgaria had been incorporated as a Byzantine province. Greece itself benefited from this change of perspective (see figure 16.2). Even in the late eighth century, during the regency of Irene, another Athenian empress, a campaign to restore Byzantine authority in mainland Greece was followed by an imperial progress through Thrace. Irene also made Athens a metropolitan city to rank with Corinth and Thessaloniki and set in motion an extension of the military 'theme' organization. The general aim of these initiatives is clear: to secure or recover the security of the area and to bring it within the control of the Byzantine state.

## THE EASTERN CHURCH

'Eastern', or 'Greek', Orthodoxy is a modern term arising from the gradual separation between Byzantium and the Western Church. In Constantine's day the church was theoretically one, and it was Constantine who called the first Ecumenical ('Universal') Council of bishops at Nicaea in AD 325. But like his successors he found unity hard to achieve. The definition of orthodoxy ('true belief')

**Plate 16.3** The Great Lavra Monastery, Mount Athos, founded in AD 963 by Athanasios

and the condemnation of heresy, whether of groups or of individuals, remained an important matter for church and state throughout the Byzantine period, and the cause of many political crises.

The Byzantine Church inherited from the early desert fathers and from Greek theologians such as Gregory of Nyssa and Basil of Caesarea in the fourth century a strong tradition of personal mysticism and communion with God. This found expression in eastern monasticism, which could take different forms, from highly organized coenobitic ('communal') monasteries, to individual anchorites. In the *lavra*, a common form of Byzantine monastic organization, the monks would live separately, coming together only weekly for a common meal and for the liturgy. These traditions are preserved today in Orthodox monasteries, for instance those on Mount Athos, the 'Holy Mountain', on a peninsula in northern Greece, where Athanasius the Athonite founded the first and most important monastery, Lavra, in the tenth century (see plate 16.3). Mount Athos is unique in its concentration of monasteries and its importance in Byzantine spiritual life. But there were monasteries everywhere in the Greek world, many of them small and relatively unimportant. Holy men, like Nikon in the Peloponnese or Luke of Stiris, both in the tenth century, or Neophytus, near Paphos in Cyprus in the early thirteenth, often gathered a nucleus of followers round them. Many surviving Greek saints' lives tell of the dedication of children to the monastic life by their parents at an early age.

The Orthodox liturgy owed much in its early stages to the practice developed by the Jerusalem church, though after the Arab conquests the main models came from Constantinople and the monastic tradition. Icons – holy pictures – are a feature of all Orthodox churches. During the period of the 'Iconoclast' controversy, in the eighth and ninth centuries, some emperors attempted to suppress icon veneration, and had existing church decoration destroyed. But the initiative failed, and the restoration of images in AD 843 is still celebrated in the Orthodox Church as the 'Triumph of Orthodoxy'. After this the interiors of Byzantine churches were even more richly covered in pictures than before, and began to look more like Orthodox churches do today.

The breach with the Papacy came only gradually (official division dated from AD 1054). The reasons centred on politics and differences of custom more than on doctrine: for instance, the Orthodox Church uses leavened bread in the Eucharist, has married clergy (though not married bishops) and does not recognize the supremacy of the Pope. In the middle period Byzantine missionaries and diplomats (the most famous were Constantine and Methodius, the 'apostles of the Slavs') brought Orthodoxy to the new peoples of eastern Europe – Bulgaria, Serbia and Russia.

Despite its close connections with the state (which were often turbulent), the Byzantine Church was not organized in a tight hierarchy. The patriarch of Constantinople (today the Ecumenical Patriarch in Istanbul) was not like the Pope. In most cases the local bishop (who would also be a monk) was the key figure.

## ECONOMIC RECOVERY

Detailed legislation provided for the financing and supply of soldiers directly by village proprietors, like the parents of St Luke the Stylite, who began life as a soldier. Monasteries also began to acquire substantial property, and together with it, dependent

**Plate 16.4**  Christ Pantokrator in the dome of Daphni Church (Attica), eleventh century AD

peasants (*paroikoi*). The extensive records of the monasteries on the rocky peninsula of Mount Athos are thus important for economic as well as religious history. Like the Great Lavra, for example, the Athonite monastery of Iviron already possessed extensive estates in the eleventh century. These monasteries possessed dependencies (*metochia*) in the town of Thessaloniki, from where the estates were administered. Another extensive landholder was the monastery of St John on the island of Patmos, founded by Christodoulos in the late eleventh century. In mainland Greece, the fine mosaics in the churches of Hosios Loukas, above Delphi, and Daphni, not far from Athens, also reflect this period of recovery (see plate 16.4). Population increase and economic growth show in increased numbers of coins found on urban sites like

Corinth, and in the development of towns. In the twelfth century, when it was visited by the Spanish Jew Benjamin of Tudela, Thebes was an important centre, famous for cloth manufacture, and especially for silk. Athens also grew in size and population from the tenth century on; indeed, these three towns – Athens, Thebes and Corinth – had become by the twelfth-century commercial centres with highly differentiated trades and production. Eustathius, archbishop of Thessaloniki in the twelfth century, writes of social and economic conditions in the city at that time. It was divided into neighbourhoods with both local churches and local officials, and its main celebration was the great fair held annually in late October on the feast of St Demetrius, which, like similar medieval fairs, was very much a commercial as well as a religious and social occasion.

Imperial patronage was responsible for some major building, including the 'New Monastery' (Nea Moni) on the island of Chios, decorated with exceptionally fine mosaics, and traditionally built by the Emperor Constantine IX Monomachos in AD 1045 as a reward to two local monks who had predicted his accession. Late in the twelfth century another emperor, Isaac Comnenus, built a great monastery of the Theotokos Kosmosotira ('Our Lady the Saviour of the World') in northern Greece. The monastery's surviving charter (*typikon*) records its extensive properties, including villages and fishing rights.

## THE IMPACT OF THE WEST

Already Greece had experienced the impact of increasing western interest in the east. In particular, Venetians were present in Greek towns and active as traders well before Alexius I Comnenus gave Venice special trading privileges throughout the empire in AD 1082. More ominously, Alexius's reign also saw the first encounter of Byzantium with the Crusaders, an uneasy alliance which was soon to turn to suspicion and hostility, and eventually to the catastrophe for Byzantium of the capture of Constantinople itself in AD 1204 by the Fourth Crusade. During the twelfth century the prosperity of the Greek towns became the direct target of the Normans, who sacked both Athens and Corinth in 1147 and besieged and captured Thessaloniki in 1185 in scenes graphically described by Eustathius, who was an eye-witness. The shock of the fall of Thessaloniki led directly to the lynching of the Emperor Andronicus

I in Constantinople. But in AD 1204 the worst happened: the Westerners turned on the capital and sacked it, carrying off its greatest treasures to the West and establishing Latin rule, with a Latin emperor and a Latin patriarch. Greece felt the effects sharply and at once. Instead of being united under Byzantine rule, mainland and islands were divided between rival powers and individual interests – Venice took the islands (including Crete) and ports essential for its sea-routes; Boniface of Montferrat seized Thessaloniki, Macedonia and Thessaly, and the French principality of the Morea sprang up in the Peloponnese. The most conspicuous result was the establishment of Frankish lords and fiefs in Greece and the building of Frankish castles like Chlemoutsi and Bodonitsa in Greece, and with them, the import of Western feudal customs. The 'Latin Empire' as such was insecure and short-lived: Byzantine rule from Constantinople was restored in AD 1261. Nevertheless, control of Greece and the islands was to remain fragmented for centuries.

Like the Empire of Nicaea in Asia Minor, where a Byzantine government in exile was set up under Theodore Laskaris after 1204, the Despotate of Epirus was established in north-west Greece, with its base at Arta, by another Byzantine family, the Angeli. The Angeli had considerable success at first, recapturing Thessaloniki in AD 1224, but rivalry with the Empire of Nicaea soon emerged, and it was the latter which recovered Constantinople. Nevertheless, the surviving churches of Arta are extremely impressive, especially the Western-influenced Parigoritissa, built in the late thirteenth century (see plate 16.5), by which time the Despotate had dynastic ties with Sicily and France. In AD 1318 the last Angelus was killed and replaced by his nephew Nicholas Orsini of Kephallonia; the latter converted to Orthodoxy and was recognized as despot by the Palaeologan emperor, Andronicus II.

## THE LATE FLOWERING AND THE END OF BYZANTIUM

Byzantium's last ruling dynasty, the Palaeologi, thus extended its influence in mainland Greece. This was a policy which dated from the first Palaeologan emperor, Michael VIII Palaeologus (AD 1259–82), and which had been gradually achieved, though it initially met with opposition from the independent principalities. The last

**Plate 16.5** The Parigoritissa church, Arta, AD 1283–1396

Byzantine emperor, Constantine XI, the brother of John VIII, had earlier been Despot of the Morea in the south-east Peloponnese, and had put an end to the Latin principality of Achaea. Constantine was aware of the need to modernize and revive the economy of his little realm. Yet the Byzantine Peloponnese, and especially Mistra, the centre of the Byzantine principality of the Morea, which looked down on ancient Sparta (see plate 16.6), was the centre of a curious late flowering of Greek culture led by the philosopher-statesman George Gemistus Plethon. The Emperor Manuel II valued these signs of vitality sufficiently highly as to build in AD 1415 the Hexamilion, yet another defensive wall across the Isthmus of Corinth on the remains of Justinian's fortifications; it had to be restored in AD 1444. Apart from the Latin citadel, the ruins of Mistra preserve traces of a substantial Byzantine town, with major churches, a palace complex and houses of prominent citizens. Not surprisingly, there are many western elements in the architecture. Mistra was also a centre of learning. As despot there, Constantine XI knew the famous Bessarion, originally from Trebizond, and later to become a Catholic Cardinal. Plethon is something of a curiosity. Like Bessarion, whose teacher he was, he had been at the Council of Florence which proclaimed the union of the churches in AD 1439,

**Plate 16.6**  Mistra, Peloponnese, fourteenth century

but at Mistra he preached a revived and idealized Hellenism for the Morea, a Platonic Utopia under a wise ruler or philosopher-king.

Plato and Aristotle were always liable to be regarded with suspicion in Orthodox Byzantium. Gregory Palamas, archbishop of Thessaloniki in the fourteenth century, was the defender of the emphasis in eastern spirituality on the possibility of mystical experience of the uncreated divine light of Mount Tabor against opposition from a Calabrian monk called Barlaam who both challenged the possibility of knowing God at all and brought specific charges against the spiritual practices of Palamas and the monks of Athos (*hesychasm*). A synod in Constantinople in AD 1341 vindicated Palamas and condemned Barlaam, but in the politically uncertain period which followed Palamas was imprisoned, and only released after being vindicated for a second time. As in the capital, a bitter civil war broke out in Thessaloniki shortly after the condemnation of Barlaam, and Palamas, whose cause was identified with that of

John Cantacuzenus, could only be installed as archbishop of the city when the latter had successfully entered Constantinople and been crowned in AD 1347. In AD 1446 the Ottoman Sultan Murad invaded the Peloponnese and destroyed the Hexamilion with his cannon and siege engines. This time the Turks retreated, allegedly having taken 60,000 prisoners. A year later, the Italian Ciriaco of Ancona visited Constantine and Plethon at Mistra and went on a tour of ancient Sparta. But the Turks came again in AD 1452, on the eve of the siege of Constantinople, and reached as far south as Messenia. The fall of the capital on 29 May, AD 1453, sealed the fate of Greece.

## GREECE: CONTINUITY AND CHANGE

The history of Greece and the islands during the many centuries of Byzantine rule is uneven, and for most of this period it was largely influenced by changes in external factors. We know most in the early period about Athens, with its vivid intellectual life and its strong pagan tradition. The Slav raids and settlement of the late sixth century hit Greece hard, and the region experienced the same economic and social changes as the remaining parts of the empire in the seventh century. However, it was to benefit later from the empire's enforced shift of emphasis away from the eastern Mediterranean. It is extremely difficult to trace the extent or subsequent history of Slavic settlers. Many will no doubt have become assimilated, while others were taken prisoner or resettled elsewhere as a result of imperial initiatives in the eighth century onwards. Material evidence permits us to see a clear growth of towns, and demographic increase, in mainland Greece, certainly by the eleventh century, partly no doubt because of its favourable position on the trading routes between the west and Constantinople. The Latins lodged themselves tenaciously after 1204 in certain areas, but, as we have seen, Greece was also the location of new Byzantine principalities. Finally, it gained from the success of the Palaeologi in restoring Byzantine influence. The new courts at Arta and Mistra stimulated building and brought patronage and cultural activity. A backwater in earlier centuries, Greece in the last days of Byzantium had become the heart of the Byzantine empire. The persistence of the Greek language was a crucial factor in making possible such continuity and revival. From an early date the spoken Greek of the medieval period ceased to observe the rules of the classical language. Yet Greek continued to be used even in those areas where there was an Arab, or later a Latin, presence. Classicizing Greek remained the language of culture throughout, and in acquiring the necessary skill in it, an aspiring scholar was put in touch with his past, whether classical or Christian. Such clerics as Eustathius of Thessaloniki or Michael Choniates, metropolitan of Athens in the twelfth century, were also accomplished scholars and writers. Greek was also, very importantly, the language of the Orthodox Church, probably the single most immediate influence in maintaining social identity. It was the church and the monasteries which as much as anything held communities together and gave them their traditions. For many parts of the period and in many individual areas of Greece the apparatus of the Byzantine state – tax collection, military provision or recruitment, legal system – was either absent or only fitfully present. Yet the ties between the Greek world and Constantinople were strong. When the city finally fell in AD 1453, Greece had lost its centre too.

## FURTHER READING

Browning, R., 1980: *The Byzantine Empire*. London: Weidenfeld and Nicolson.

Browning, R. (ed.), 1985: *The Greek World*. London: Thames and Hudson.

Castrén, P. (ed.), 1994: *Post-Herulian Athens* (Papers and Monographs of the Finnish Institute at Athens 1). Helsinki: Finnish Institute at Athens.

Frantz, A., 1988: *The Athenian Agora XXIV: Late Antiquity AD 267–700*. Princeton: The American School of Classical Studies at Athens.

Mango, C., 1976: *Byzantine Architecture*. New York: Harry N. Abrams.

Nicol, D. M., 1984: *The Despotate of Epirus, 1267–1479*. Cambridge: Cambridge University Press.

Ware, T., 1968: *The Orthodox Church*. Harmondsworth: Penguin.

Woodhouse, C. M., 1986: *George Gemistos Plethon: The Last of the Hellenes*. Oxford: Clarendon Press.

# 17 / THE OTTOMAN CENTURIES

## Malcolm Wagstaff

### INTRODUCTION

Greek-speaking Orthodox Christian communities had a wide spatial distribution in the past. They were found, for example, in southern Italy and Sicily, as well as in Asia Minor and Cyprus. This chapter, however, is concerned with the various islands and mainland territories which today compose the state of Greece. It focuses, first of all, on how these lands came under Ottoman Turkish rule and then, at varying dates, were released from it. Second, the chapter outlines the changing character of Ottoman rule in these areas, sketches the broad trends of social and economic development during the Ottoman centuries and concludes with a discussion of the legacy in the modern state of Greece of this phase of its history.

### OTTOMAN RULE: ITS RISE AND FALL

The Ottoman Empire itself began modestly around AD 1300 as the emirate of a Turkish lord, Osman, and it was from him that the imperial dynasty took its name, *Osmanlı* or Ottoman. It started as one of a number of independent Turkish-controlled principalities which emerged in Asia Minor following the break-up of the Seljuk Turkish Empire. The Seljuk Sultans, ruling from Konya, had unified Asia Minor following the defeat of the Byzantine army by Turkish forces at Manzikert (Malazgirt) north of Lake Van in AD 1071. Osman's emirate lay on the north-western frontier between Turkish domains and those of the greatly reduced Byzantine Empire. His son, Orhan, expanded the emirate to the Dardanelles and the Sea of Marmara. Civil war between claimants to the Byzantine throne brought Turkish mercenaries to Europe in the 1340s and allowed Ottoman forces to install themselves in Gallipoli (1354). Turkish raids westwards in the 1350s and 1360s led to the capture of Edirne (Adrianople). An Ottoman victory on the Maritsa river (1371) opened up the entire Balkans, including the territory of modern Greece, to Ottoman attack and conquest. By the death of Murad I in 1389 the whole of Thrace and Macedonia was under Ottoman rule (see figure 17.1). During the fifteenth century, despite defeat by Timur Leng (Tamerlane) at the Battle of Ankara (1402) and several succession crises, Ottoman power extended over the whole of mainland Greece. The capture of the Byzantine capital, Constantinople, in 1453 was almost incidental to the process, though the fall of The City was of great symbolic and emotional importance, especially in the Greek world. The islands in the Aegean passed under direct Ottoman rule in a more episodic fashion during the fifteenth and sixteenth centuries. Crete was added in 1645–69. The Ionian Islands, however, largely remained in Venetian hands until 1797 when they became briefly French and then autonomous, first under Ottoman and Russian protection and finally under that of Britain (1815–64).

Venice took the Peloponnese (Morea) from the Ottomans in 1684–7 as part of a larger war in south-eastern Europe and remained in control there until 1715 when the peninsula returned to the Empire. The effects and importance of the Venetian interlude are only now being assessed.

Numerous revolts, often encouraged from outside, challenged Ottoman rule throughout Greece (e.g. Peloponnese 1463–79, 1770; Himara 1518; Macedonia 1571; Crete 1692, 1770), but with only passing success until 1821. In that year a series of violent outbursts by the subject populations in a number of localities, especially in the Peloponnese and central Greece, coalesced into a widespread revolt and a sustained war of independence. The seeds of revolution were variously planted during the closing decades of the eighteenth century and the opening years of the nineteenth. A sense of national identity emerged with the discovery by modern Greeks resident in, or in contact with, western Europe, of the importance of ancient Greek culture to contemporary Western society. The possibility of mounting a successful popular movement to overthrow the existing order came with news of the French Revolution, but was actually witnessed when French forces occupied the Ionian Islands (1797–9, 1807–10/14). French agents toured the mainland in these years, promising support for an uprising which would have the effect of distracting the Ottoman Empire for so long as it remained part of anti-French alliances during the Revolutionary and Napoleonic Wars (1792–1802, 1803–15). Britain and Russia also had their agents in Greece, and their

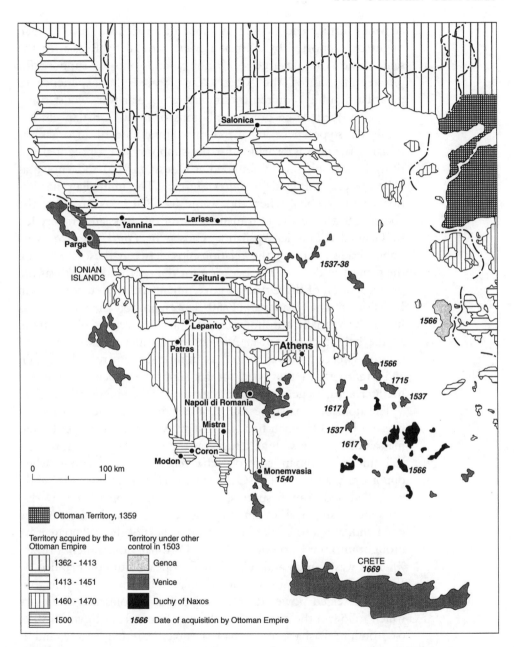

**Figure 17.1** Expansion of the Ottoman Empire in the territories which later became the state of Greece from the accession of Murad I (AD 1362) to the Treaty of Buda (AD 1503)

activities further encouraged the hope of a successful revolt which might be supported by a Great Power, particularly Russia. At the same time, the upsurge of banditry and outside support for privateering during the 'Great War' created the experience of guerrilla fighting required to conduct a popular war, whilst rising prosperity fuelled the power ambitions of local Christian elites – landlords, shipowners and merchants. Something of an organizational network was provided for the supporters of a potential uprising by a secret society founded at Odessa (1814) and known as 'The Society of Friends' (*Philiki Etairia*). The immediate inspiration of the revolts, when they came in 1821, was probably the abortive attack on the Ottoman Empire from Russian territory led by General Alexander Ypsilantis, chosen by *Philiki Etairia* as its public leader, though the relationships between these events are the subject of debate. The occasion for the northern attack was the preoccupation of the Ottoman government with the removal of Ali Pasha of Yannina (Ioannina) (1750–1822), possibly the most powerful of the virtually autonomous provincial governors of the time. At the height of his power Ali controlled much of Northern and Central Greece and was treated as an independent ruler by Britain and France when they vied for his support in their struggle for Mediterranean hegemony at the beginning of the nineteenth century.

The uprising was successful. Control of towns and villages was wrested from Ottoman hands, Muslims were driven out and often massacred as they sought refuge on the coast or in the fortresses still under Ottoman control. The reprisals were terrible when opportunity allowed. The Ottoman forces sent against the rebels were defeated. Initial success, however, was jeopardized by disagreements and rivalries amongst the revolutionary leaders, on the one hand, and also by the brutal effectiveness of the Egyptian army brought into the Peloponnese by the Ottoman government (1825–7). This was trained and officed by Europeans but commanded by Ibrahim Pasha, the son of the Albanian adventurer, Mehmet Ali, who had seized power during the period of political uncertainty which followed the expulsion of French forces from Egypt (1801–6). Ibrahim Pasha's forces had occupied Crete in 1822 and it remained under Egyptian control until 1840 when it was returned to direct Ottoman rule. On the mainland, the return of an Ottoman administration to central and southern Greece was prevented by the belated intervention of the Great Powers. Instead they sponsored the creation of a Greek state (1827–32).

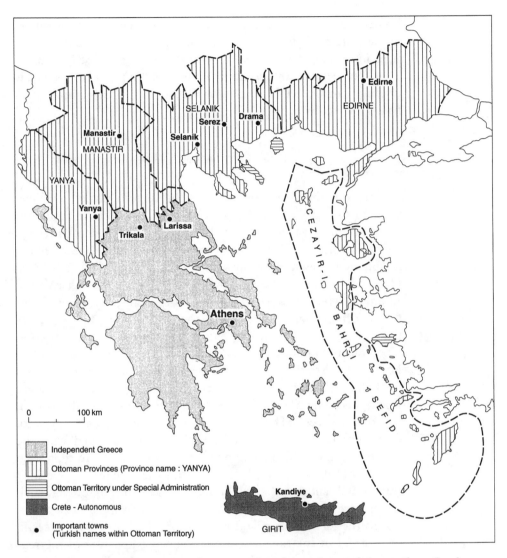

**Figure 17.2** The Ottoman provinces covering the territory of the modern Greek state *c.*1900

Despite further periodic uprisings, notably in Crete (1841, 1858, 1866–9, 1877–8), the Ottoman Empire ceded no further territory in Greece until 1880 but then, within forty years, it lost all its mainland Greek provinces and the Aegean islands, except for the Dodecanese which Italy seized (see figure 17.2). They joined Greece only in 1947. The driving force behind Greek expansion was Greek irredentism, the 'Great Idea' of restoring a Greek Christian empire in the eastern Mediterranean and uniting all Greek-speaking Christians in a single state. Following more uprisings (1888–9, 1896–7), Crete became autonomous within the Empire (1897), finally uniting with Greece in 1912. By 1923 the Ottoman Empire itself had come to an end.

## THE OTTOMAN SYSTEM

Throughout the Ottoman centuries the Aegean islands remained under the control of the Kapudan Pasha (High Admiral); the principal exception was Samos, which enjoyed a special status after the Greek Revolution. The islands were joined by the Mani, a remote mountainous peninsula in the southern Peloponnese, c.1780–1821. Mainland Greece, however, was originally part of the vast *eyâlet* of Roumeli, which covered much of the Balkans, until the seventeenth century, and came under the jurisdiction of a Beylerbey based in Sofia. It was divided into *sanjaks*, territories run as combined tax and military units by *sanjakbeys* appointed by the Sultan. Local administration was shared between a *bey*, who represented the Sultan's military force and executive power, and a *kadi* (judge) who applied the *Sheriat* (the Holy Law of Islam) and the *kanuns* (sultanic decrees). The *beys* were cavalry soldiers (*sipahis*) who, with their retainers, were obliged to go on campaign with the Ottoman armies when summoned to do so. They were supported by non-hereditary 'livings' derived from the revenues of specified agricultural lands or the exploitation of particular resources, such as fisheries and salterns. Maintenance of this support system required the identification and registration of all revenue sources in each *sanjak* at the time of conquest and the updating of the registers every twenty or thirty years to take account of any alterations.

The system changed during the seventeenth and early eighteenth centuries. Simultaneous wars on several fronts, the need for large numbers of full-time infantry armed with muskets, and the loss of valuable provinces increased the demands for direct revenue by the state. To raise it the Ottoman government progressively resorted to the device of auctioning provincial governorships and the rights to collect taxes. The two functions often merged, leading to extortion and oppression by those anxious to recoup their initial outlays. The tax collectors were often local Muslim notables

**Plate 17.1**   The Lake of Ioannina by William Page, *c.*1820

and their power increased considerably in their home districts. Strong and virtually autonomous governors emerged. Ali Pasha of Yannina (see plate 17.1) was one of the most notorious for his unpredictable, ruthless and extortionate regime and was seen as epitomizing both the general character of Ottoman rule and the erotic fantasies of the *Arabian Nights*.

Administrative reforms were introduced to the Ottoman provinces as part of the *Tanzimat* (Reformation) movement of the nineteenth century, the beginnings of which are usually dated to the Gülhane Decree of November, 1839. The reforms went through various mutations, notably in 1840, 1858 and 1864, but the overall objectives remained the same: to reduce the autonomy of the provincial rulers, to restore central authority over the provinces, to protect the subject populations and to promote socio-economic development. Although they retained wide powers, provincial governors were brought to heel, a process facilitated in due course by the development of the telegraph. Local councils, at first advisory and then administrative, were created; membership included non-Muslims, as well as Muslims. The army was reorganized along Western lines and made directly responsible to Istanbul. Modern armaments were purchased in the West. Taxes were standardized and the requisite surveys of people and revenues were revived, though tax farming remained in use. A system of large *vilâyets* (provinces) divided into *liwas* or *sanjaks* (sub-provinces) replaced the historic *eyâlets* progressively after 1864: the *vilâyet* of Selanik (Thessaloniki), for example, was created in 1867 and that of Girit (Crete) in 1871. Under pressure from the other Great Powers, special arrangements were made for Macedonia in 1903–8. The aim here was to retain the region under Ottoman control, whilst containing the inter-communal violence generated by the rival covetous intentions of neighbouring Greece, Serbia and Bulgaria for this multi-ethnic and strategic region. Selanik, the birthplace of the founder of the Turkish Republic, Mustafa Kemal, Atatürk (1881–1938), became the centre of the Turkish revolutionary movement which led to the dictatorship of the Committee of Union and Progress (1913) and ultimately to the decisions which embroiled the Ottoman Empire in the First World War and brought about its demise.

In its day the Ottoman Empire was the largest Islamic state in the world, enormously powerful at its height in the sixteenth century, and during the Ottoman centuries the provincial populations of Greece had a distinctly inferior status. This was manifest in various petty ways but most clearly in a ban on the construction of new churches (not always enforced), and exclusion from military service, as well as a consequent obligation on all non-Muslim males to pay a head tax (modified in 1856 and finally abolished in 1909). Until 1676 Christians were also liable to the *devshirme* (Greek: *paidomazoma*), the system whereby males were recruited as slaves into the imperial service, either as Janissaries (the professional infantry) or administrators.

## SOCIAL AND ECONOMIC DEVELOPMENT

Most of the Christians belonged to the Greek Orthodox Church and, as part of the *Millet-i Rum* (Greek Nation/People), enjoyed a degree of autonomy in such matters as inheritance and marriage under the supervision of their bishops. Roman law and local custom formed the basis for legal decision-making. The ultimate responsibility rested with the Ecumenical Patriarch of Constantinople. Accordingly, Gregorios V answered for the disobedience of the Greek subjects when he was hanged from the gate of the Patriarchate

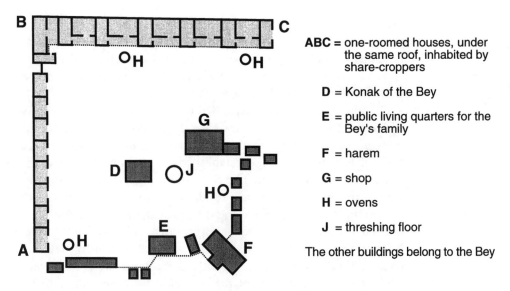

ABC = one-roomed houses, under the same roof, inhabited by share-croppers

D = Konak of the Bey

E = public living quarters for the Bey's family

F = harem

G = shop

H = ovens

J = threshing floor

The other buildings belong to the Bey

**Figure 17.3**  The *chiftlik* of Tolos in the Serres basin

in 1821 after the news of the Greek Revolution reached the capital. Certain districts, for example the Mani in the southern Peloponnese, enjoyed even greater autonomy under their own elected, though centrally approved, governor, and the vendetta was a normal part of life. Throughout Greece, communes remained responsible for local affairs and assumed collective responsibility for keeping the peace and raising taxes. They employed their own officials and in the eighteenth century some communes even formed federations, as in the Chalcidic Peninsula and at Zagori in Epirus.

Although protected as 'People of the Book' and *reaya* (subjects), the Christians under direct Turkish rule were exploited and oppressed, particularly during the seventeenth and eighteenth centuries and before the Tanzimat reforms began to take effect. They were subject to a constant stream of extraordinary and in theory emergency taxes (*avariz*) levied at the whim of local governors. Their land was often forcibly incorporated into the large estates (*chiftliks*) of powerful Muslim civilians which gradually replaced the 'livings' of the classical Ottoman system. More peasants became share-croppers. A distinctive village form emerged on the *chiftliks* of Thessaly and Macedonia, characterized by poor-quality single-storey houses arranged around an open space, sometimes containing the *konak* (residence) of the owner (see figure 17.3). The

289

expansion of brigandage was one response to the loss of land, though its socio-economic origins are complex. The exploits of the brigands (Greek: *klephtes*) became the subject of popular songs, and subsequent generations of Greeks have turned their heroes into 'freedom fighters' against Ottoman rule.

Commerce revived and expanded during the eighteenth century. There were several reasons for this. The reconquest of the Peloponnese (1715) reunited the Greek lands under a single political regime. Relative peace was established over much of the Balkans, as well as over the Levant. The circulation of goods and people was comparatively unhindered as a result. The early stages of industrialization in western Europe and the growth of population there opened up markets for food and raw materials. Merchants from Britain, France and the Netherlands, as well as nearby Italy, expanded their sea-borne trade with the coastal areas of Greece, whilst the northern parts of the mainland were brought into the commercial networks of southern Germany and the Austro-Hungarian Empire, on the one hand, and expansionist Russia, on the other. Rising demand led to the extension of cultivation which took on an increasingly commercial character. The production of cotton and tobacco increased, as did that of currants and olive oil. In the latter part of the eighteenth century Greek merchant ships took over much of the carrying trade of the Aegean basin, as well as the longer distance trade to the Black Sea and the western Mediterranean. Two events were critical in this development. The first was the Treaty of Küchük Kaynarja (1774). Under its terms Russia became the protector of the Orthodox Christian populations of the Ottoman Empire, Greek ships were allowed to fly the Russian flag and, by the modifying Treaty of Jasy (1792), the Black Sea was opened to Greek enterprise. The second critical development came with the Revolutionary and Napoleonic Wars (1792–1802, 1803–15) when Greek ships ran the British blockade to supply France and occupied Italy, whilst Thessaloniki became the great entrepôt for the whole of central Europe. The islanders of Hydra (see plate 17.2), Spetses and Psara were particularly prominent in these developments. Fortunes were made; Greek communities abroad were strengthened, proliferated and grew.

The diaspora was important in the revival of Greek intellectual life which took place in the decades before the 1821 Revolution. Its role was to build schools and libraries in the homeland, to provide Greek books printed in western Europe, and to sponsor

**Plate 17.2** View of the town and harbour of Hydra, drawn by Thomas Hope, *c*.1795

higher education at home for their compatriots. At the same time Greeks abroad maintained both the humanistic outlook and the written language of ancient Greece in a context dominated at home partly by theological tracts and service books in the learned language of Byzantium but partly also by the use of a freer vernacular in everyday life and popular poetry. The vernacular language itself changed little during the Ottoman centuries, though dialects perhaps strengthened. The use of two forms of the language, however, laid the foundations for the clash between the learned language (Greek: *katharevousa*) and the demotic which afflicted Greek education after Independence.

During the later eighteenth and early nineteenth centuries the diaspora sponsored an increasing body of secular literature which reflected, successively, the ideas of the Enlightenment, then of the French Revolution and finally of romantic nationalism. Much of this was produced by Greek scholars abroad who absorbed the fashionable ideas of the time and became aware of the reviving influence of ancient Greece on west European culture. Their publications transferred Western ideas to their fellow countrymen at home, amongst whom they helped to create a nostalgic reverence for a certain image of ancient Greece. In the increasing number of schools and colleges in Ottoman-controlled Greece, as well as amongst the diaspora itself, the rediscovery of a glorious past combined with poetical radicalism to inspire both the Revolution of 1821 and also the subsequent struggles for liberation from Ottoman rule.

## PEOPLES AND RELIGIONS

But the Greek Orthodox Christians were only one element, though numerically dominant, in the population of Greece. Some Greek-speaking people in the former Venetian islands were Latin Christians, in communion with Rome. Others, though often attending a Greek-language liturgy, belonged to other communities distinguishable on the basis of linguistic, historical and cultural identity. Albanian-speakers, for example, were widespread, not only in what is now north-western Greece but also in Attica and the Peloponnese. Vlachs, whose language is related to Romanian, were distributed over central and northern Greece, especially in the high mountains. Serbs and Bulgars were spread across Macedonia and Thrace. The numbers of people belonging to these different communities are disputed, but their admixture created the powderkeg which was exploded in the late nineteenth century by the rival ambitions of the newly independent Balkan states (see figure 17.4).

Jews also formed distinctive communities, especially in the towns. Thessaloniki had the greatest concentration. Most of the Jews came as refugees from Spain and Portugal in the reign of Sultan Bayazid II (1481–1512), and they retained a distinctive language of their own.

Then there were the Muslims, popularly described as 'Turks' because they shared their religion with the ruling elite. Some of these were Turks in the sense of being everyday users of the Turkish language. A few were administrators, of course, and others were soldiers. However, the largest concentrations of ethnic Turks, found predominantly in what is now northern Greece, originated as nomads in Anatolia. They were brought into a countryside emptied by generations of warfare and settled there during the fourteenth and fifteenth centuries to bring the land back into production. Elsewhere, many of the Albanians were Muslims and closely identified with the Empire whose governors they frequently served as soldiers. The majority of the Muslims, however, were Greek-speakers whose ancestors had succumbed to the various pressures

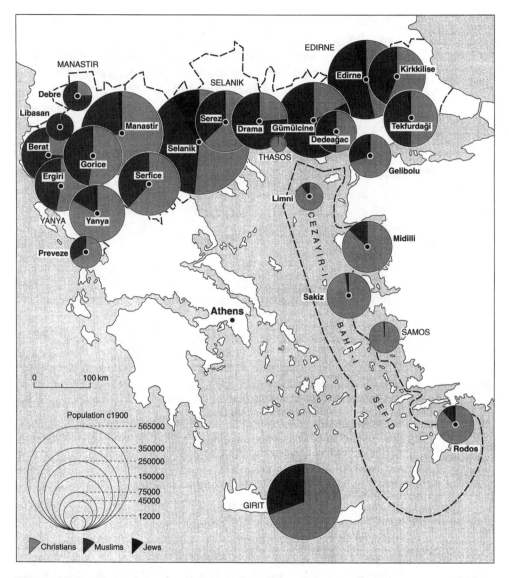

**Figure 17.4** Community composition of northern Greece and adjacent areas *c.*1900

to convert, rather than join the ranks of the neo-martyrs or be-come second-class subjects. Whilst a few were substantial land-owners, many were ordinary villagers and townsfolk. Numbers are difficult to establish, but Muslims in general reportedly formed about 9 per cent of the population of the Peloponnese before the 'ethnic cleansing' which accompanied the War of Independence.

Ottoman statistics suggest that in Crete, where the Muslim population progressively concentrated in the major towns and a limited number of villages during the nineteenth century, they formed about 30 per cent of the total population in 1894. The same sources indicate that in the same year they accounted for 46 per cent of the total population in the *vilâyet* of Selanik (Salonica/Thessaloniki) and about 45 per cent in that of Yanya (Yannina/Ioannina). By contrast, Muslims in the Aegean Islands amounted to only 12 per cent of the population. Most of the Muslims disappeared from Greece as a result of the Balkan Wars (1912–13) and the exchange of populations which followed the failure of Greece's 'Anatolian Venture' (1919–22). Only the beleaguered Muslims of Thrace now remain.

## THE LEGACY

Although the Thracian Muslims are a living survival of the Ottoman centuries in Greece, much else remains from the period. Neglected mosques and bathhouses are found in many towns, particularly in northern Greece and, on a smaller scale, in Crete. Their ground plans and built forms perpetuate some of the architectural traditions of late antiquity. Distinctive 'Turkish' houses, with blank lower walls and jettied second-storey latticed windows, survive in many northern towns. Churches were converted into mosques, normally in towns captured by siege, but the protected status of Christians allowed the Christian liturgy to be celebrated in many more, whilst the ban on new building preserved the Byzantine forms of church architecture to inspire new generations of architects after independence. Icon-painting also survived, though Western stylistic influence was often strong. The special status enjoyed by the Orthodox Church and its use of the late antique liturgies of St Basil the Great (d. 379) and St John Chrysostom (d. 407) helped to preserve the language of ancient Greece in semi-accessible form and in this regard were probably more effective than contact with the learning of the West. Vernacular vocabulary was extended by the use of loan words from Turkish, mainly substantives. Greek cooking was also influenced by Turkish cuisine. Finally, it was during the late eighteenth and early nineteenth centuries that Western travellers, scholars, artists and architects discovered the architecture and sculpture of antiquity, and made the first steps towards the archaeological study of ancient Greece.

FURTHER READING

Browning, R., 1969: *Medieval and Modern Greek*. London: Hutchinson.

Clogg, R. (ed.), 1976: *The Movement for Greek Independence 1770–1821: A Collection of Documents*. London: Macmillan.

Clogg, R., 1992: *A Concise History of Greece*. Cambridge: Cambridge University Press.

Inalcık, H., 1973: *The Ottoman Empire: The Classical Age 1300–1600*. London: Weidenfeld and Nicolson.

Mackenzie, M., 1992: *Turkish Athens*. Reading: Ithaca Press.

Mantran, R. (ed.), 1989: *Histoire de l'empire Ottoman*. Brussels: Fayard.

Plomer, W., 1970: *The Diamond of Jannina: Ali Pasha, 1741–1822*. London: Jonathan Cape.

Shaw, S. J. and Shaw, E. K., 1977: *History of the Ottoman Empire and Modern Turkey*. Cambridge: Cambridge University Press.

# 18 / AFTER INDEPENDENCE

## *Richard Clogg*

### THE REDISCOVERY OF THE PAST

One of the most pronounced features of the intellectual revival that preceded the outbreak of the war of Greek independence in AD 1821 was a recovery of a sense of the past, of the development on the part of the small nationalist intelligentsia of an awareness that the Greeks were heirs to a civilization that in the Western world was seen as the pinnacle of human achievement. For, during the dark centuries of Ottoman rule, knowledge of the ancient world had largely died out in the Greek lands themselves. It was during the first decade of the nineteenth century that Greek patriots, to the scandalized horror of the hierarchs of the Orthodox Church for whom antiquity was synonymous with paganism, began to give their children (and sometimes to adopt for themselves) the names of the worthies of ancient Greece (e.g. Sophokles and Aspasia). The nascent Greek intelligentsia, indeed, became almost intoxicated with the glories of the ancient past.

In the eyes of nationalists it became, as it remains to this day, axiomatic that the modern Greeks were the lineal descendants of the ancient. Those, such as the Austrian Hellenist J. P. Fallmerayer in the 1830s, who would challenge the notion of an unbroken continuity, racial as well as cultural – a key element in the received perception of Greek identity – were, and continue to be regarded, as *anthellines* or 'anti-Greeks'.

The early nineteenth century likewise saw the genesis of the 'Language Question', the furious, and sometimes violent, dispute as to the form of the language appropriate to a regenerated Greece, a controversy that dominated the cultural life of the independent state until very recent times. Given the time span involved, the Greek language had changed remarkably little over the near three millennia of its recorded existence. But there were those who argued for a return to the imagined purity of Attic Greek of the fifth century BC. Some sought to base the modern, written language on the spoken 'demotic' Greek of the time. Still others, among them

Adamantios Korais, one of the foremost classical scholars of his age, advocated a middle way.

It was Korais' concept of a *katharevousa* (literally 'purifying') Greek that prevailed. This was adopted as the official language of the state and education; only in 1976 was the privileged position of *katharevousa* formally abandoned, but not before generations of schoolchildren had been forced, by no means always successfully, to struggle with two forms of the modern language, as well as with ancient Greek. All countries are burdened with the past, but none more so than Greece for whom the 'Language Question' is an ever-present reminder of the way in which the legacy of ancient Greece has dominated the cultural, educational and, to a degree, the political life of the modern country.

The cultural orientation of the independent Greek state that came into existence in the 1830s was thus firmly orientated towards ancient Greece. This orientation was symbolized by the removal in 1834 of the capital from Nafplion to Athens, at that time little more than a dusty village but, as the home of the Parthenon (which nearly became the site of the royal palace), for ever associated with the splendours of the Periklean age. At this time Greek intellectuals had little interest in the medieval empire of Byzantium, which for a thousand years had held sway over a vast swathe of the Near and Middle East (see chapter 16). But in the mid-nineteenth century, Konstantinos Paparrigopoulos, a professor of history at the University of Athens, argued the case for Byzantium as the crucial link in the chain uniting the ancient and modern Greek worlds.

## THE GREAT IDEA

At a popular level, however, there were folk memories of the Christian empire of Byzantium. These were enshrined in prophecies such as that of the 'Emperor turned into marble': Constantine XI Palaiologos, the last Emperor of Byzantium, who would one day return to liberate his people. It was to the glories of Byzantium that proponents of the *Megali Idea*, the dominant ideology of the new state during the first century or so of its existence, hearkened. This 'Great Idea' aspired to gather together all the Greek populations widely scattered throughout the Near East within the bounds of a single Greek state, which would have as its capital Constantinople, the former Byzantine capital.

Most Greeks embraced the notion of the 'Great Idea' with enthusiasm. It was, however, a grandiose aspiration for a state as small and economically weak as the Greece whose existence as an independent state was formally recognized in 1830, following ten years of intermittent, and often vicious, hostilities against the Ottoman rulers of the Greek lands. For as few as a third of the Greek inhabitants of the Ottoman Empire were to be found within the bounds of the new state.

Implicit in the notion of the *Megali Idea* was territorial expansion. This in turn presupposed conflict with the Ottoman Empire, a ramshackle edifice by the nineteenth century but nonetheless one that possessed far more resources than the fledgling Greek state. Moreover, Greece's sovereignty was circumscribed by the guarantee of three 'Protecting' Powers: Britain, France and Russia, whose destruction of the Ottoman fleet at the battle of Navarino in 1827 had been instrumental in securing Greece's secession from Ottoman rule.

If most Greeks subscribed to the 'Great Idea', there were differences as to how best it might be made a reality. Some, mindful of the imbalance in the forces at the disposal of Greeks and Turks, argued that, before an expansionist foreign policy could be envisaged, a strong state should first be created. Others maintained that Greece could never be strong for as long as the largest and most prosperous Greek communities, in Constantinople itself, in Smyrna (Izmir) and elsewhere, remained outside the boundaries of the state. Still others thought in terms of strengthening and exploiting the very considerable economic, and far from negligible political, power of the Greeks of the Ottoman Empire so as to create a kind of Ottoman/Greek dyarchy that would hold sway in the Middle East, 'Our East' (*I kath'imas Anatoli*) as the expressive Greek term has it.

## STATE-BUILDING

Clearly an essential priority was to create the basic infrastructure for a state whose inhabitants had been at war for a decade. As the price of their recognition of Greek independence, the Powers had imposed the institution of monarchy, and a foreign monarch to boot, Otto of the Bavarian Wittelsbach dynasty. Otto received a warm reception on his arrival in Greece in 1833, but as he was still only 17 years old, the country was ruled by Bavarian regents until 1835.

Otto's reliance on Bavarian advisers, who showed little regard for local sensitivities as they struggled to endow the new state with western institutions, even after the ending of the regency, upset many of the protagonists in the war, who naturally felt excluded from the fruits of power. Indeed, this was one of the factors that precipitated the coup of 3 September 1843 which forced Otto to grant, in 1844, a constitution which was remarkably liberal for its time. For the first, but by no means for the last, time the military had intervened in the political process.

Whatever the formal provisions of the constitution, Otto and his ministers had little difficulty in thwarting them. Liberal political institutions had not developed organically over centuries as they had done in Western Europe but had been imported lock, stock and barrel and grafted on to a traditional society whose principles of behaviour had been profoundly influenced by the centuries of Ottoman rule. Parliamentary government did, however, prove fully compatible with the clientelism that was, and remains, such a key feature of Greek life. Deputies dispensed, and continue to dispense, patronage in return for votes, and competition for government office was furious, for the state, with its bloated bureaucracy, was one of the few means of rewarding supporters given the backward state of the economy.

King Otto was overthrown in 1862, following a further military intervention. He was succeeded by the Danish King George I who reigned until 1913. In 1864 a new and still more liberal constitution was enacted, and Britain, which had ruled over the Ionian Islands since 1815, ceded them to Greece in the vain hope of dampening irredentist fervour. A further increase in territory came with the cession of Thessaly and part of Epirus by the Ottomans in 1881. Three years earlier, at the Congress of Berlin, the predominantly Greek-populated island of Cyprus had come under British administration. The island was formally annexed in 1914 and became a British Crown Colony in 1925.

During the last thirty years of the nineteenth century political parties, hitherto fluid coalitions of place-hunting politicians, began to coalesce into two main blocs, headed by the Westernizing Kharilaos Trikoupis and the demagogic, populist Theodoros Deliyannis, whose main objective was to overthrow Trikoupis' modernizing reforms. Deliyannis was an enthusiastic champion of the *Megali Idea* and it was his support of the insurgent Cretans then engaged in one of their recurrent struggles for *enosis* (union) with Greece that led to the 'Thirty Days War' with Turkey in 1897.

Humiliating defeat at the hands of the Turks was one of the long-term factors that precipitated the army, in the form of the Military League, to mount the Goudi coup of 1909, the first of many military interventions in the political life of twentieth-century Greece. Its purpose was to sweep away the feuding politicians and make way for a rising star in the political firmament, the Cretan Eleftherios Venizelos.

## IRREDENTIST TRIUMPHS AND POLITICAL DIVISION

Venizelos launched an ambitious programme of political and constitutional reform and, having learnt the lesson of 1897, namely that even in decline the Ottoman Empire remained too formidable an adversary for single-handed challenge by Greece, worked to strengthen the armed forces and to develop alliances with the country's Balkan neighbours. This policy met with spectacular success in the Balkan wars of 1912–13, when Greece increased her territory and population by two-thirds, acquiring Thessaloniki, now the second city of Greece, a large part of Macedonia, Epirus, and many of the Aegean islands, along with Crete, from the Ottomans (see plate 18.1).

Euphoria reigned in a Greece which appeared poised to achieve the vision of the *Megali Idea* under the inspired leadership of Venizelos. But with the onset of the First World War the national unity which had underpinned the triumphs of the Balkan wars gave way to division. The roots of the *National Schism* were essentially twofold. First, there was the problem of integrating the newly acquired, and staunchly pro-Venizelos, territories of 'New' Greece with the conservative, royalist heartland of 'Old' Greece, the core of the original state. Secondly, there was the bitter dispute between king and prime minister over Greece's stance in the First World War. King Constantine I, who had succeeded his father George I in 1913, advocated neutrality, whereas Venizelos was a passionate supporter of the Entente allies.

Twice forced to resign as prime minister, Venizelos established a rival government in Thessaloniki in 1916, and in 1917 was in-

**Plate 18.1**  A band of *Makedonomakhoi* at the turn of the twentieth century

stalled as prime minister of the whole of Greece by France and Britain. He rapidly brought Greece into the war and the country's reward from the victorious allies was the right to occupy in 1919, pending formal annexation, a large area of western Asia Minor which, with its sizeable Greek population, had long been the object of Greek irredentist ambitions.

## THE END OF THE GREAT IDEA

The Greek invasion of Asia Minor, however, proved to be the catalyst for the Turkish national movement, headed by Mustafa Kemal (Atatürk). Three years of conflict culminated in catastrophic defeat in September 1922 at the hands of the Turkish army and the burning of Smyrna, home to a very large Greek population. Tens of thousands of Greek refugees fled with the retreating Greek armies to the islands and mainland (see plate 18.2). Those that remained were included in a compulsory exchange of populations, as part of the settlement reached at the Treaty of Lausanne in 1923. This resulted in more than a million Orthodox Christian refugees from Asia Minor (many of them destitute and speaking

**Plate 18.2** Refugees from Asia Minor living in boxes in the Municipal Theatre, Athens, 1923

only Turkish or the Greek dialect of Pontos (the Black Sea region) which was scarcely intelligible to mainlanders) being exchanged for four hundred thousand Muslims (many of them Greek-speakers). Thus a Greek presence in Asia Minor that stretched back three thousand years came to an end and with it the elusive vision of the *Megali Idea*.

Defeat in Asia Minor precipitated a military coup and the flight of King Constantine. In 1923 a republic was formally instituted and Constantine's successor, King George II, forced into exile. During the inter-war period the army and the refugees, whose integration into Greece, despite myriad problems, was successfully achieved, acted as effective arbiters of political life. Venizelos, who had been voted out of office in 1920, returned as prime minister in 1928. He achieved a rapprochement with Turkey, but his government was blown off course by the world slump and he fell from power in 1932. Moreover the fragility of the country's parliamentary institutions was demonstrated by an attempt on Venizelos' life in 1933 and by two unsuccessful military coups launched by his supporters in the army in 1933 and 1935. The last resulted in Venizelos' enforced exile. In a climate of increasing polarization a royalist reaction was brewing and, in 1935, King George II was restored to the throne following a patently rigged plebiscite.

The king's hopes of bridging the Venizelist/anti-Venizelist (broadly republican/royalist) divide were to be fatally compromised by the results of the elections of January 1936 which followed his return. These resulted in deadlock between the Venizelist and anti-Venizelist parties and left the minuscule communist party holding the balance of power.

## DICTATORSHIP, OCCUPATION AND CIVIL WAR

The impasse gave the chance to General Metaxas, hitherto an inconsequential political figure, to establish a dictatorship in August 1936, with the tacit acquiescence of the king. Although the Metaxas regime adopted some of the trappings of Nazism and Italian fascism, while wholly lacking their dynamism, the dictator himself remained firmly committed to Greece's traditionally pro-British orientation in foreign affairs. But he was able to give vent to his loathing of all politicians and of communists in particular. His dictatorship was deeply unpopular, but he did take a courageous stand against the Italian bullying which culminated in outright invasion in October 1940. This the Greek armies repulsed, driving the Italians far back into Albania from where the invasion had been launched. The Greek armies, and the small British and Commonwealth expeditionary force dispatched to their aid, proved no match, however, for the German forces that came to the rescue of Hitler's humiliated ally, Mussolini. Within a few weeks of the German invasion in April 1941, the whole of Greece, including the strategically important island of Crete which fell to a German airborne attack, had succumbed to German and Italian rule (see plate 18.3). The Bulgarians, a traditional foe, were permitted to occupy a part of northern Greece. The king and the government went into exile.

It was not long before resistance to the Axis occupation developed and some spectacular acts of defiance were recorded. This was spearheaded by the hitherto small communist party, which was able to exploit its experience of clandestine activity to emerge as the dominant political force in occupied Greece, controlling as it did, through the National Liberation Front (EAM), the National People's Liberation Army (ELAS). A number of small non-communist groups came into existence, but they proved to be no

**Plate 18.3**  German and Italian Troops on the Acropolis, June 1941

match for the communists' vision of radical change, allied to superior organization and a preparedness to resort to force to maintain their ascendancy. Virtually all those in the resistance opposed the return of King George II, whom they identified with the humiliations of the Metaxas dictatorship.

When the government-in-exile returned to Greece at the time of the German withdrawal in October 1944 it was unable to reach agreement with EAM/ELAS over the demobilization of resistance forces, despite the presence of communist representatives in the government. Increasing tension resulted in outright hostilities in December 1944 between the forces of the left and the government, backed up by a small British force. The communist insurgency of December 1944 was suppressed and peace of a kind negotiated between the warring groups, but the fighting proved to be the beginning of a process that culminated in late 1946 in outright civil war. This followed elections in March 1946 which resulted in victory for a right seeking revenge against the left, and a plebiscite in September of the same year which resulted in the restoration of King George II to his throne.

The communist Democratic Army enjoyed logistical support from the newly established communist regimes on Greece's northern borders, while the government forces benefited from a massive inflow of American military aid and advice. This external support proved decisive in securing the eventual victory of the government forces in 1949.

## From civil war to the European Union

Civil war was followed by the restoration of a (somewhat qualified) democratic government. When forces favouring greater demo-cratization briefly achieved office in the mid-1960s, extreme right wing and anticommunist elements in the armed forces seized power in 1967 (see plate 18.4) and misruled the country, employing methods at once ridiculous and harsh, until the regime collapsed in 1974 following an unsuccessful effort launched by the Athens junta to topple Archbishop Makarios. Makarios had emerged as president of Cyprus when the island, in defiance of the logic of self-determination, achieved on the ending of British rule in 1960 not *enosis* (union) with Greece, but independence.

In the chaos of the summer of 1974 the Greeks turned as their saviour to a veteran conservative politician, Constantine Karamanlis. He managed to defuse the crisis in relations with Turkey, which had invaded the northern part of Cyprus to protect the Turkish minority, and secured the return of the army to the barracks. He also organized a plebiscite which resulted in a decisive rejection of the monarchy, a perennial source of instability, and energetically pursued Greece's membership of the European Community.

This was achieved in 1981, the year in which Andreas Papandreou's Panhellenic Socialist Movement won a convincing victory at the polls. The smooth transition in power from a right that had monopolized power for much of the post-war period to a democratically elected socialist government appeared to indicate a new stability in the Greek political system, even if the high hopes of the electorate for radical change proved elusive.

## Xeniteia: Greeks outside Greece

The Greeks, like the Jews and the Armenians, are pre-eminently a people of the diaspora or 'dispersion', scattered in communities great and small in many parts of the world. The Greek state has

**Plate 18.4**   King Constantine II with the military junta, April 1967

never contained within its borders more than a proportion of the Greek people.

The modern Greek diaspora traces its origins to the eighteenth century, the period which witnessed the emergence of a mercantile class which was of such significance to the national movement. Greeks (and Hellenized Vlachs) achieved a dominant position in the commerce of the Ottoman Empire. Their mercantile *paroikies* (communities) were established throughout the Mediterranean, the Balkans, central Europe and southern Russia, where the Empress Catharine the Great encouraged Greeks to settle in Russia's newly acquired territories on the Black Sea and the Sea of Azov. One of the most far-flung of these merchant communities was that established in Bengal in the 1770s. Dimitrios Galanos, an early Greek settler in India, was one of the pioneers in the study of Hindu religious literature.

Greek merchants were not slow to contrast the encouragement given to commerce in the countries of western Europe with the institutionalized rapacity of the Ottoman governmental system. The fortunes they amassed were channelled into building schools and libraries in their native towns and villages and into providing scholarships for young Greeks to study in the West. If the merchants themselves remained an essentially conservative force, many of the students whose education they underwrote were attracted by the ideas of the Enlightenment and the nationalist doctrines inspired by the French Revolution. The intellectual revival of the pre-independence decades, and the publishing activity that was associated with it, were based to a considerable degree in the diaspora communities.

During the nineteenth century a new destination for Greek migrants emerged – Egypt. Greeks, mainly from the Dodecanese islands, helped make the Greek the largest of the numerous foreign communities in Egypt. Some made immense fortunes. Georgios Averoff, for instance, besides endowing schools and a hospital in Alexandria, paid for the battleship which, named in his honour, served as the flagship of the Greek navy during the Balkan wars.

During the last decade of the century mass emigration, mainly from the Peloponnese and mainly to the United States, got under way, precipitated by economic problems culminating in the bankruptcy of the Greek state in 1893. It has been estimated that as many as one in four males between the ages of 15 and 45 took the road of *xeniteia*, or sojourning in foreign parts, in the twenty years or so before the outbreak of the Balkan wars in 1912. Most left Greece with the intention of returning to the homeland after a few years, having made, if not their fortunes, then enough money to pay for dowries for their sisters (the early emigrants were very largely male) or to set themselves up in small businesses. The great majority, however, settled permanently in their adopted countries. Initially they were at the bottom of the economic pile, encountering hardship, exploitation and discrimination. In the United States, they graduated in time from peddling, shoe-shining, mining and railroad construction to running ice-cream parlours (it is claimed

**Plate 18.5**  The Politz (Politis) Candy Company, Salt Lake City, Utah, in the 1920s

that the ice-cream sundae was invented by a Chicago Greek), candy stores and restaurants (see plate 18.5).

To the second and later generations education was looked upon as the avenue for economic and social advancement. Greeks are among the most upwardly mobile immigrant communities in the United States. The many hundreds of thousands of Greek descent maintain a strong sense of Greek identity. This survives even when, as is often the case, the language or, in some cases, the Orthodox religion of the homeland has been lost, despite the high priority given from the early days to the building of churches which would act as the essential core of community life. Greeks have made their mark in most aspects of American life, not least in politics. The Greek 'lobby' is a force to be reckoned with, while the Democratic candidate for the presidency in 1988, Mike Dukakis, was a second-generation Greek-American.

Restrictive legislation in the 1920s stemmed the flow to the United States. This resumed again once quota-restrictions were lifted in the mid-1960s. Emigration continued, albeit on a more limited scale, during the inter-war period to destinations such as South Africa, central and west Africa, Sudan, Ethiopia and Latin America. Aristotle Onassis, who went on to become a shipowner and one of the wealthiest men in the world, first settled in Argentina after the Greeks were forced from his native Smyrna.

Large-scale emigration resumed after the Second World War, with as much as 12 per cent of the population leaving the country in the 1950s and 1960s. The principal destinations were Australia, where Melbourne has become one of the main centres of Greek population in the world (not excluding Greece itself), Canada and West Germany, where the inflow of Greek *Gastarbeiter* (guest-workers) was encouraged. Tens of thousands of Greek Cypriots settled in Britain. Vastly improved communications have enabled the post-war generations of migrants to keep in much closer touch with the homeland than the pioneers.

Greek migrants have generally prospered but, in focusing on the undoubted successes of the majority in their adopted countries, it is important not to lose sight of those who failed in fiercely competitive conditions, and died in poverty or returned to the homeland broken in spirit. In all immigrant communities there is tension occasioned by pressures to assimilate, especially on the later generations, and the wish to preserve a sense of Greek identity. There is also inevitable friction between the homeland and the various diaspora communities, as governments in Athens seek to mobilize Greeks abroad in support of national goals.

## FURTHER READING

Campbell, J. K. and Sherrard, P., 1968: *Modern Greece*. London: Ernest Benn.

Clogg, R. (ed.), 1976: *The Movement for Greek Independence 1770–1821: A Collection of Documents*. London: Macmillan.

Clogg, R., 1992: *A Concise History of Greece*. Cambridge: Cambridge University Press.

Dakin, D., 1972: *The Unification of Greece 1770–1923*. London: Ernest Benn.

Llewellyn-Smith, M., 1973: *Ionian Vision: Greece in Asia Minor, 1919–22*. London: Allen Lane.

McNeill, W. H., 1978: *The Metamorphosis of Greece since World War II*. Chicago: University of Chicago Press.

Mavrogordatos, G., 1983: *Stillborn Republic: Social Coalitions and Party Strategies in Greece, 1922–36.* Berkeley: University of California Press.

Mazower, M., 1993: *Inside Hitler's Greece: The Experience of Occupation 1941–44.* New Haven: Yale University Press.

Moskos, C. C., 1989: *Greek Americans: Struggle and Success.* New Brunswick: Transaction Publishers.

Mouzelis, N., 1978: *Modern Greece: Facets of Underdevelopment.* London: Macmillan.

Petropoulos, J. A., 1968: *Politics and Statecraft in the Kingdom of Greece, 1833–43.* Princeton: Princeton University Press.

Woodhouse, C. M., 1973: *Capodistria: The Founder of Greek Independence, 1821–9.* London: Oxford University Press.

Woodhouse, C. M., 1976: *The Struggle for Greece 1941–9.* London: Hart-Davis, MacGibbon.

# 19 / THE GREEK LEGACY

## Michael Greenhalgh

### INTRODUCTION

The reasons for Greece's continuing impact on the Western world up to our own day, while predicated on Greek and Hellenistic expansionism to the limits of the known world, is informed more by her intellectual and artistic, than her political, military and trading, networks. She produced a disproportionately large quantity of influential works of art, architecture, philosophy and literature.

But by the nature of things, the Greek legacy has not been unchanging, let alone constant, in its influence; rather, it has always been a moveable feast, refocused by new interpretations and perspectives over the centuries. Frequently, indeed, the legacy is far from the reality – but then traditions are often seated in illusion, because they represent visions not facts, and the vision fits the needs of the moment, rather than any objective reality. Such flexibility at first sight appears a weakness, but is in fact a strength: subsequent generations could not have measured themselves against the Greeks without reconstructing the sources according to their own ideals and horizons.

Why should there be such wide variations in the concept of Greece, the Greeks and what they meant? For two main reasons. The first is that, since 'Greek culture' covers (with the Archaic and Hellenistic periods) a time-span of nearly a millennium, followed by two millennia of reinterpretations, there is no fixed point (beyond, perhaps, Periklean Athens or the deeds of Alexander) on which to dwell. The second is the effective and much more powerful impact of Rome, who so often tried to see herself through Greek eyes, and whose material and even intellectual remains – roads, cities, monuments, artworks, laws, civil service, language – overshadowed those of Greece, whose monumental 'presence' in the West was puny by comparison. Beginning, then, with the Roman Empire, the West saw Greece through Roman eyes, and through Roman aspirations. The Turkish conquest then added another barrier to the Western knowledge of classical Greece, and knowledge of Greek art and architecture to match that of Roman begins only in

**Plate 19.1**  Marble relief of the imperial procession of Augustus' family on the Ara Pacis ('Altar of Peace'), Rome, 13–9 BC

the later eighteenth century, with the increase in travel to points east.

## ROME

Whilst some Romans clung to their own traditions, many, such as the Scipiones, were much impressed by Greek culture, which offered levels of sophistication they themselves sought to match. Some, such as Cato the Elder, admired both at the same time. Unusually, the conquerors took on many of the ideals of the vanquished, rather than vice versa. From the first century BC, the Romans imported not only her books and artefacts (sometimes even complete temples, so it seems) but also her brainpower. Plunder under the Roman Republic was a main channel of imports; and this led to the imitation of Greek statues and reliefs under the late Republic and the Empire in the form of Hellenic, and specifically Attic, revivals. The most splendid and accessible example of the vogue is the *Ara Pacis* ('the Altar of Peace'), on which the family of Augustus is presented with the same misty, semi-heroic monumentality of the Parthenon frieze (see plate 19.1, cf. plate 14.5), whilst the profusion of acanthus ornament, with its overtones of plenty and fructification, indicates that Augustus' recourse to the Greek legacy is not simply aesthetic, but political as well. There

**Plate 19.2** The Canopus at the Villa Adriana (Tivoli, near Rome). Second century AD

would have been little point in drawing such parallels had not the sources been well known, and their implications appreciated.

The importance of Rome in the promulgation of the Greek legacy is threefold. The Romans conquered and colonized all round the Mediterranean, as well as further east, so the fields to be 'sown' were far-flung. The villa built by Hadrian at Tivoli, with its numerous copies of sculptures of the age of Pheidias and later, some of which are still in place (see plate 19.2), is in part a monument to Rome's devotion to Greece. But they also had so few Greek originals, and such a thirst for them to decorate private villas as well as public areas and temples, that a veritable reproduction industry was formed. They made marble copies from the (often bronze) originals, and copied bronzes as well as making reductions and adaptations. Hence it is arguable that, without the Romans, the Greek originals would never have left Greece and Asia Minor, to be discovered only with the development of archaeological excavation little over a century ago; as it was, the Romans ensured that knowledge of Greek art was spread in numerous versions all over the Western world.

But to view Rome as simply a 'carrier' of Greek ideas and images is to underestimate the impact that Roman civilization made throughout the immense areas she conquered. The Greeks may well have left colonies around the Mediterranean, but their cultural impact was slight compared with the monuments left by the

Romans which, together with language, law, communications, technology and agriculture, defined the nature of European life for centuries. And if the city of Rome became but a poor echo of its imperial grandeur, it was and remains the seat of Western Christianity – a force for tradition equally informed by Roman civilization itself.

## THE MIDDLE AGES IN EAST AND WEST

For the Middle Ages themselves, in East or West, there was no sense of a caesura with the past – of what Panofsky has identified as a gulf, or a perception of radical 'newness', such as was sensed by the Renaissance. In predicating a decline between antiquity and themselves, Renaissance theoreticians were only partly correct. Indeed, in the West during the Middle Ages the arts did decline in quantity and perhaps sometimes in quality; art-forms such as monumental sculpture were rare indeed; and certainly, culture was at far greater a premium than it had been under the Greeks or Romans. But in the East, Byzantium was in fact, and saw itself as, the direct inheritor of the Greeks. This is demonstrated by Byzantine respect for and reworking of many areas of Greek culture, from art and rhetoric to literature and medicine. Byzantium (later Constantinople, now Istanbul, see figure 16.1) was a Greek and Greek-speaking city, and the focus of a glittering Empire which was much admired further West, where many of the most prestigious luxury goods and artworks were either imports from Byzantium, or inspired by her.

The best illustration of the West's indebtedness is provided in 1204, with the disgraceful Sack of Constantinople by the Latins, subsequent to which floods of artworks, and especially relics with their highly artistic settings, came West, including the famous quadriga on the façade of St Mark's in Venice.

But St Mark's quadriga is Roman, not Greek, for it probably came from the Circus Maximus in Rome. And what came West following the Sack was largely Byzantine, and predominantly of medieval date. There are no known examples of classical or Hellenistic Greek art, whether sculpture or painted pottery, of luxury goods, or indeed Roman copies of the same, brought to the West at this time, and only a few before the seventeenth century. For example, the famous 'Greek' vase outside the Duomo at Pisa (a copy: the original is now in the Camposanto) is indeed in Pentelic marble; but it dates from the second or first century BC, and is a Roman 'atticizing' copy of an earlier original.

## RENAISSANCE

For the Renaissance in Italy and further north, it was the material and intellectual legacy of Rome, rather than of Greece, which was more readily to hand in the Italian peninsula. But Roman culture was not necessarily the more prized, because the Renaissance often looked at antiquity through the eyes of, and hence with the prejudices and predilections of, the Romans. Hence the 'material' Renaissance in art and architecture is based on Roman, not on Greek, models: when Leon Battista Alberti builds the Tempio Malatestiano at Rimini, the first temple-fronted structure since antiquity, he turns to Roman not to Greek models, because these were what he knew and could adapt. Attempts to link anything in Renaissance art or architecture to other than literary originals are tenuous. For example, Alberti wrote three treatises (*On Painting, On Sculpture,* and *Ten Books of Architecture*) and delights in citing Greek authors; but the resultant advice is an amalgam of antique expertise, heavily dependent for appearance and examples on Rome, not Greece, and written in Latin.

Greek literature and philosophy were widely studied, although knowledge of the language remained a minority skill. Petrarch, for example, was probably not a fluent reader; and it is likely that Machiavelli knew no Greek at all. Translations therefore assumed an important place in scholars' libraries. Aristotle's works in translation (which became available in the eleventh century in Latin translations from Arabic – not Greek versions) had been a mainstay of late medieval university courses in philosophy, and Greek scholars were invited to and lionized at Italian courts. They came West to escape the advancing Turks, the more so after the fall of Constantinople in 1453. This marked the effective end of the Roman Empire in the East, when the Greek manuscripts and scholars coming West turned from a trickle to a flood. Although Latin remained the lingua franca throughout Europe, and her writers better known than those of Greece, the Greek language, and hence philosophical and literary texts in the original, were certainly widely known to scholars. To take the case of the historian, Leonardo

Bruni (1369–1444), the Chancellor of the Florentine Republic
and its historian, relied heavily for style and concepts upon Plato,
Demosthenes and Aristotle, as well as Plutarch; and with lives of
Dante, Petrarch, Boccaccio and others, he resurrected the classical
mode of biography, which had been largely dormant since antiquity. Together with Giovanni Pico della Mirandola (1463–94)
and Manuel Chrysolaros (c.1350–1415), who was the first Greek
teacher in Italy for centuries, he was responsible for the beginning
of the modern study of Plato and hence Platonism.

But Greek architecture and full-scale sculpture were unknown;
small-scale works such as coins and medals were no doubt imported, but these had no repercussions whatsoever on Renaissance
art. Etruscan tombs were routinely robbed for their jewellery and
precious metals. Thus, the Greek vases they contained must also
have been known; but, once again, they were not prized, and,
indeed, nobody realized the vases were Greek, for they were called
'Etruscan' well into the nineteenth century.

One reason for the tenuous Renaissance knowledge of Greek
culture was clearly the Turkish destruction of the Byzantine Empire, and the gradual Turkish encroachment westwards. With this
proviso, travel to the Greek mainland and islands was easy. Venetian
merchant-ships and military guard-ships had been doing so for
centuries. But travel to increase scholarly knowledge about Greece,
or the Greeks, was rare: Cristoforo Buondelmonti (with his *Liber
Insularum Archipelagi*, written in 1420; see plate 19.3) and Cyriacus
of Ancona (with his six books of *Commentaries* on his travels,
sometimes illustrated with sketches of now lost or largely destroyed
monuments, often copied), with an antiquarian streak unusual for
the fifteenth century, are the exceptions. A prime reason for this
state of affairs, flowing at least in part from Turkish hegemony, is
no doubt that there was no longer any focus to the Greek inheritance – no Eastern Empire in what was soon renamed Istanbul
(itself, ironically, derived from a Greek name), no continuing admiration for the Greek or Byzantine past, and no marble-gleaming
capital at Athens to remind visitors of the Glory that was Greece,
for Athens was only a poor, underpopulated village, and with no
entity called 'Greece' over which to rule. The reality might have
been different, had the union of Greek and Latin churches gone
ahead at the Council convened in Florence in 1439.

But lack of hard evidence about Greece did not prevent poets,
dramatists and painters and sculptors from working with 'Greek'

**Plate 19.3**   Cristoforo Buondelmonti's view of the Plain of Troy, 1420s

concepts, bolstered as they were by the literature the Greeks had left behind. In seventeenth-century France, for example, Jean Racine produced several tragedies (mainly from Euripides) on Greek topics, such as *Phèdre* (1677) or *Iphigénie* (1674). The painter Nicolas Poussin, based in Rome, produced 'philosophical' works for a circle of Stoics in France, on Greek themes such as 'The Testament of Eudamidas' (*c.*1644), which takes what is really a Roman sculptural motif of the death of a warrior, and makes it Greek. The power of the symbolism is such that it is used at least three times by Jaques-Louis David during the French Revolution (most famously in his 'Dead Marat' of 1793). The composition can also be seen in one of Flaxman's illustrations of Homer's *Iliad* (see plate 19.4) and is then used for the death of Byron who is shown with his breast heroically bared, and lying on a Greek couch.

## ENLIGHTENMENT

Fundamental to a new evaluation of Greece was a broader, supra-national view of Europe, and the place of Greece's achievement

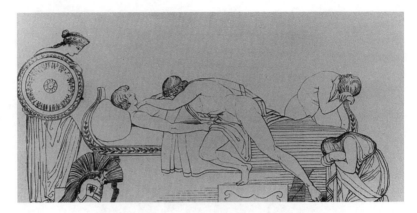

**Plate 19.4**  Thetis brings the new armour and finds Achilles lamenting the dead Patroklos (*Iliad* 19.1–11), engraving by Tommaso Pirolli after John Flaxman's drawing, 1792–3

within it. This was in part provoked by a wider interest in travel, but mainly by the writings of people such as Winckelmann, who positioned Rome as the debtor of Greece in matters artistic, thereby giving Greece an artistic primacy from which it has only recently been dislodged.

Travel in the eighteenth century was certainly easier than it had been previously; and in Britain particularly, but also in France and the German states, there developed an educational ethos which sought to 'round out' noblemen and gentlemen by having them travel to classical lands, often under the watchful eye of a tutor. Once there, the milords could match what they saw against what they had read of the classical authors, and buy and ship back to their stately homes, many of which were built partly for that purpose, any antiquities they saw, some of which were 'restored' from almost nothing. The Italian peninsula was the focus of the great majority of travellers, because it offered centuries of civilization and comfort, as well as the great art and architecture of the Renaissance, upon which contemporary achievements rested, and towards which aspirations were still frequently directed.

The eighteenth century also saw the beginnings of systematic archaeology (to be charitable; 'aristocratic treasure-hunts' better describe the earlier digs), thanks not only to what the milords had read and seen abroad and to spectacular large-scale digs such as the discovery of the buried cities of Pompeii and Herculaneum, but also because of the efforts of scholars and learned societies, mostly founded in the previous century.

Travel was combined with a thirst for antiquities, and a consciousness of the need to study and catalogue (not to mention appropriate) what was found encouraged the adventurous to go to Greece and Asia Minor, where they fought bandits, malaria and savage dogs, and the (occasionally byzantine) Turkish bureaucracy, to get drawings and trophies back to Europe. Greece and Greek monuments, totally unknown hitherto, appeared in lavish books of engravings, pre-sold on subscription to the rich and influential. Examples are James Stuart's and Nicholas Revett's *Antiquities of Athens* (1761–94); Richard Chandler's *Travels in Asia Minor* (1775) and his *Travels in Greece* (1776) resulted from a commission by a scholarly society, the Society of Dilettanti. In the preface to Richard Chandler's, Nicholas Revett's and William Pars' *Ionian Antiquities* (1769 and 1800), also funded by the Society, the purpose of this Society is described as follows: 'In the year 1734 some gentlemen who had travelled in Italy, desirous of encouraging at home a taste for those objects which had contributed so much to their entertainment abroad, formed themselves into a society under the name of the Dilettanti, and agreed upon such resolutions as they thought necessary to keep up the spirit of the scheme.' Their interests soon spread to Greece and Asia Minor.

The Dilettanti and others began to be interested in Greek works of art because they believed her art and architecture, as well as her literature and democratic ideals, were not merely still valid for their own day but, more important, offered models which provided the only means of rescuing contemporary art from what they saw as its decline. Thus James Stuart fostered the Greek Revival in the United Kingdom with buildings such as the Doric Temple at Hagley Park, Worcestershire (1758), or his Temple of the Winds at Shugborough House, Staffordshire (1775–82). The English milords, in other words, wished to create at home what they had seen abroad, with one eye on the state of the arts. It was because he believed that Greek art could improve contemporary British art that Lord Elgin took marble blocks from the Parthenon at huge personal expense, and eventually in 1816 sold them to the nation at a loss, after a Royal Commission had exposed a cross-section of preferences and prejudices about Greek and Roman art, and its utility in present circumstances. Benjamin Robert Haydon, the history painter, first saw the Marbles in 1808 'in a damp, dirty pent-house'; but 'here were the principles which the great Greeks in their finest time established.' He took Fuseli to see them, and the Swiss artist 'nobly acknowledged that he knew nothing until he saw the marbles, and bowed his venerable head before them as if in reverence of their majesty'.

However, it was undeniable that Roman models, which had been refined over several centuries in Italy by Palladio and his successors, provided better models for domestic architecture than did the Greek ones. As a consequence, a thoroughgoing Greek style (as at William Wilkins's Grange Park, Hampshire, 1809, modelled closely on the Hephaisteion in Athens) is the exception, and architects and interior designers restricted themselves to Greek motifs such as key patterns, maeanders and coupled columns and pediments. That Greek artistic ideas did not take over from things Roman as soon as illustrated publications and imported antiquities appeared in Europe is due partly to the hold which Rome and Italy, via the Renaissance, had on the culture of Western Europe, and partly to the belief of the establishment that Roman art and architecture were superior. As Sir William Chambers wrote in unpublished notes of *c.*1768, such sentiments came from 'many ingenious Men chiefly Men of Learning who accustomed to admire and to taste the Beauties of Grecian literature have easily been persuaded into the belief of Grecian Superiority in an Art of which they themselves were not Judges. . . . '

An indication of the thirst for antiquities, and of the confusion over what exactly they should look like, is provided not only by the fiasco over the Elgin Marbles, but also by trade in 'restoring' ancient statues, which was especially prosperous in the eighteenth century. The Greek and Hellenistic originals were usually in bronze, and of these the Romans made crowds of marble copies. Italian workshops, faced with an insatiable demand for whole works and a limited supply of often fragmentary pieces, sought to complete them, and often employed more imagination than knowledge. The results are to be seen in works such as the 'Diskobolos' type: in 1772, Gavin Hamilton found a torso at Ostia, and an antique head from somewhere else was also acquired – but the pieces were restored not into a 'Diskobolos' but into a 'Diomedes with the Palladion'.

## ROMANTICISM: OTHER GREECES

Of course, the Renaissance interest in travel, which grew apace during the seventeenth and eighteenth centuries, took people not only to the eastern Mediterranean, but much further afield, where commercial opportunities and even military conquest built on the great discoveries of earlier centuries – India, North America, the Far East. Europeans were alarmed to discover the existence not only of other and completely separate 'civilization nodes' – other Greeces, as it were – but also of the monuments, philosophies, literatures and legal systems which went with them. This discovery put Greece into perspective, but also presented Europe with cultures of an apparently earlier stage of development, as in the South Seas, or amongst the Indians of North America. An eighteenth-century interest in the primitive, which was to be a staple feature of Romanticism, also produced a new view of Greece to contrast with that of the 'civilized' age of Perikles: a primitive Greece, populated by people who did not act in a civilized fashion and who could not therefore have appeared in any of the plays of the French classical drama, characters such as Achilles, or Odysseus. In short, Homer came into vogue at the same period as Shakespeare – powerful, sometimes wild, often supernatural and illogical dramas of passion, which could appeal to the darker side of the so-called 'Age of Reason'.

But such primitivism was a minor strain compared with the vision of Greece as a main font of Western civilization. In art and architecture Winckelmann, Cardinal Albani's librarian and adviser on antiquities, wrote of Greek art as a vision of purity, intuiting the originals from the only works he knew, which were Roman copies. It would be difficult to overestimate Winckelmann's influence; his *Geschichte der Kunst des Altertums* (1764) was translated from German into French, Italian and English (*History of Ancient Art*).

Goethe, a man of catholic tastes, was admiring, at almost the same time as Winckelmann, the pre-classical ('primitive') Greek architecture at Paestum, south of Naples, which was very different in its rude stumpy squatness from the cadenced elegance of the Parthenon, or of its Roman derivatives on which the West has drawn for so many centuries. Indeed, the scholars and especially artists (such as Cozens and Piranesi) who visited Paestum (see plate 19.5), were sometimes also those who drew romantic land-scapes at home; so that 'the primitive', 'the noble savage', whether

**Plate 19.5** Thomas Major's drawing of one of the temples at Paestum, *c*.1764

Greek (Homer), Scottish (Ossian), Pacific (Captain Cook) or North American (Chateaubriand), shared characteristics and prestige. This naturally meant that Greek ideas and images struggled for prominence with the rest, because many Westerners found the contemporary Greeks, degraded as they were from centuries of Turkish domination, sometimes less noble than the literary concept had led them to believe. Greek art and architecture, and to a lesser extent philosophy and letters, were turned off their elevated throne, and forced to compete for survival with the ruck.

Lord Byron fulminated against what he saw as Elgin's rape of fair Greece and, when the Greek War of Independence began, went to help and to die. This tragi-comic episode underlines yet another shift in the West's focus on Greece – namely her consciousness that Greece was much degraded, and must be restored to glory so that the West could welcome her back from under the heel of the Turk into the traditions of philosophy, letters and art. The question for the West was posed emotionally by Chateaubriand in his *Notes on Greece* (1825): 'Will our century watch hordes of savages extinguish civilization at its rebirth on the tomb of a people who civilized the world?' (a sentiment similar to those which drove the Allied invasion of Greece in 1941). During the conflict, the Greeks themselves produced Periklean-style propaganda; Delacroix produced paintings which emphasize gore, sentiment and hope in equal proportions; and Byron wrote poetry about the revival of classical ideals – about the Greece of the imagination, rather than the Greece of reality. But Delacroix was not myopic: he found equal inspiration in the Arabs of North Africa – modern 'Greeks', living in a state nearer to nature than that possible in contemporary France.

## CONCLUSION: GREECE IN THE
### TWENTIETH CENTURY

Greece, often through Roman and later interpretations, held a formative position in several areas of European civilization from politics and science to culture. After Greek independence, what remained was an emotional attachment to the seat of democracy and the fountainhead of Western philosophy and literature. Thanks to the greater exposure of the Greek mainland, islands and Asia Minor through travel, Greek art and architecture finally assumed supremacy over those of Rome, and have remained on a pedestal to this day.

Indeed, to the opinion that 'What else is history than the praise of Rome?' we can add the sentiment popularized by Alfred North Whitehead and Heidigger that the whole of European philosophy is nothing but a series of footnotes to Plato. The legacy of Greece continues to our own day, but moderated by a broader, worldwide grasp of the diversities in human society, so that Greco-Roman pre-eminence in matters cultural (questioned since the eighteenth century) would no longer seriously be maintained. Nevertheless, the image of Hellenism remains as potent as it was for Bruni, Byron and Delacroix, for example in the debate around the permissible use of the term 'Macedonia', a concept with one inspiration, namely the attainments of Alexander the Great. If the West did not go to war on Greece's behalf when she was struggling against the Turks for independence, then there is good evidence that Allied intervention in Greece in World War II relied more on Churchill's sentimental vision of Greece's place in civilization than on any cold, purely military assessment – as the subsequent inglorious retreat to Crete and then North Africa underlined.

Nor is Greece forgotten today. Martin Bernal's *Black Athena: The Afroasiatic roots of classical civilization* continues the re-examination of Greece's impact via her origins, which Bernal (grandson of an egyptologist) places in Egypt. Media attention (films and videos) and scholarly reaction (largely hostile), plus discussions on the Internet, demonstrate that current preoccupations – racism, multiculturalism, black consciousness, white upper-class illusions – provide a potent cocktail for new theories, even those which attempt to undermine the comfortable assumptions of how one culture informs and influences another.

FURTHER READING

Bolgar, R. R., 1954: *The Classical Heritage and its Beneficiaries*. Cambridge: Cambridge University Press.

Chevalier, R. (ed.), 1977: *L'Influence de la Grèce et de Rome sur l'Occident moderne* (Actes du Colloque, Tours 1975). Paris: Société d'Edition 'Les Belles Lettres'.

Clarke, G. W. and Eade, J. C., 1989: *Rediscovering Hellenism: The Hellenic Inheritance and the English Imagination*. Cambridge and New York: Cambridge University Press.

Crook, J. M., 1972: *The Greek Revival*. London: John Murray.

Finley, M. I. (ed.), 1981: *The Legacy of Greece: A New Appraisal*. Oxford: Clarendon Press.

Kitzinger, E., 1976: *The Art of Byzantium and the Medieval West: Selected Studies*. Bloomington, Indiana: Indiana University Press.

Panofsky, E., 1972: *Renaissance and Renascences in Western Art*. New York: Harper Row.

Thomas, C. G. (ed.), 1988: *Paths from Ancient Greece*. Leiden and New York: Brill.

Tsigakou, F.-M., 1981: *The Rediscovery of Greece: Travellers and Painters of the Romantic Era.* London: Thames and Hudson.

Walker, S. and Cameron, A. (eds), 1989: *The Greek Renaissance in the Roman Empire* (British Museum 10th Classical Colloquium). London: The Institute of Classical Studies.

Weiss, R., 1969: *The Renaissance Discovery of Classical Antiquity.* Oxford: Blackwell Publishers.

Weitzmann, K., 1981: *Classical Heritage in Byzantine and Near Eastern Art.* London: Variorum Reprints.

Wiebenson, D., 1969: *Sources of Greek Revival Architecture.* London: Zwemmer.

# TIMELINE

The following list gives a brief selection of some significant dates in the history of Greece; it can be nothing more than an *aide-mémoire*. All indications of an approximate date are omitted: before 600 BC all the dates listed are inexact, and not a few are imprecise after that date. Events of consequence in literary, artistic and social life are given in italics.

## GENERAL PERIODS

| | |
|---|---|
| Neolithic | 7000–3500 BC |
| Bronze Age | 3500–1100 BC |
|   Early Bronze Age | 3500–2000 BC |
|   Middle Bronze Age | 2000–1600 BC |
|   Late Bronze Age | 1600–1100 BC |
| Dark Age | 1100–900 BC |
| Geometric Period | 900–700 BC |
| Orientalizing Period | 700–600 BC |
| Archaic Period | 600–480 BC |
| Classical Period | 480–323 BC |
| Hellenistic Period | 323–31 BC |
| Roman Empire | 27 BC–AD 330 |
| Byzantine Empire | AD 330–1453 |
| Ottoman Empire | AD 1300–1923 |
| Modern Period | AD 1821– |

## PARTICULAR DATES

| BC | |
|---|---|
| 1184 | Traditional date for the fall of Troy. |
| 1150 | Final destruction of Mycenae. |

| | |
|---|---|
| 1000 | Migration of Greeks from the Greek mainland to the Aegean islands and the western coasts of Asia Minor. |
| 975 | Hero's tomb at Lefkandi. |
| 776 | Traditional date for the inauguration of the first Olympiad. |
| 775 | Pithekoussai (Ischia) furnishes the earliest Greek archaeological material in the West since the end of the Bronze Age. |
| 750–700 | *The Greeks adapt the Phoenician alphabet for writing Greek.* *Homer and Hesiod active as poets.* |
| 735 | Traditional start of Greek 'colonization' of Sicily and South Italy. |
| 730–710 | The Spartans seize the neighbouring territory of Messenia. |
| 650 | The rise of Media. |
| 650 | *Archilochos of Paros active as poet.* |
| 600 | *Sappho and Alkaios of Lesbos active as poets.* |
| 594 | Solon *archon* at Athens. |
| 585 | *Thales of Miletos predicts an eclipse of the sun.* |
| 582–573 | *Cycles of Games established (582 Pythian, 581 Isthmian, 573 Nemean).* |
| 566 | *Re-organization of the Panathenaia at Athens.* |
| 550 | Cyrus of Persia conquers the Medes. |
| 546–527 | Peisistratos tyrant at Athens. |
| 546 | The Persians capture Sardis and conquer the Greeks of Asia Minor. |
| 530–490 | *Pythagoras active as a philosopher.* |
| 527 | Death of Peisistratos; his sons take over the tyranny. |
| 508–507 | The reforms of Kleisthenes at Athens. |
| 500 | *Herakleitos and Parmenides active as philosophers.* *Simonides and Anacreon active as poets.* |
| 499–494 | The Greeks in Asia Minor revolt from Persia. |
| 498 | *The earliest dated poem of Pindar.* |
| 493 | Themistokles *archon* at Athens. |
| 490 | The first Persian expedition to mainland Greece under Darius. The battle of Marathon. |

| 480 | The second Persian expedition under Xerxes. The battles of Artemision, Thermopylae and Salamis. The sack of Athens. |
|---|---|
| 479 | The battles of Plataia and Mykale. The withdrawal of the Persians from Greece. |
| 478–477 | The foundation of the Delian Confederacy by Athens. |
| 472 | *Aeschylus' tragedy* Persians *staged.* |
| 468 | *Sophokles' first prize-winning tragedy staged.* |
| 464 | Earthquake at Sparta. Revolt of Spartan Helots. |
| 461 | Reforms of Ephialtes at Athens. |
| 460 | *Zeno of Elea active as philosopher.* |
| 458 | *Aeschylus'* Oresteia *staged.* |
| 456 | *Completion of the temple of Zeus at Olympia.* |
| 455 | *Euripides' first tragedy staged.* |
| 454 | The treasury of the Delian Confederacy is moved from Delos to Athens. |
| 451 | Perikles' law to restrict Athenian citizenship. |
| 449 | Peace treaty signed between Athens and Persia. |
| 447 | *The building of the Parthenon begins.* |
| 440 | *The sculptors Pheidias and Polykleitos active.* |
| 440–420 | *Herodotos the historian active.* |
| 431 | *Thucydides begins his history.* |
| 431 | The war between Athens and Sparta begins. |
| 429 | The death of Perikles. |
| 427 | *Aristophanes' first comedy staged.* |
| 421 | The Peace of Nikias. |
| 415–413 | The Athenian expedition against Sicily. |
| 411–410 | The oligarchic revolution of the Four Hundred at Athens. |
| 404 | The capitulation of Athens to the Spartans. The oligarchy of the Thirty. |
| 403 | The restoration of democracy at Athens. |
| 399 | *The trial and execution of Sokrates.* |
| 396–347 | *Plato active as a philosopher.* |
| 386 | *Plato's Academy founded at Athens.* |
| 371 | The Thebans defeat the Spartans at Leuktra. |
| 370–330 | *Praxiteles and Skopas active as sculptors.* |
| 360–315 | *Lysippos active as sculptor.* |
| 359 | The accession of Philip II of Macedon. |

| | |
|---|---|
| *354* | *Demosthenes' first public speech.* |
| *343* | *Aristotle becomes tutor to Alexander.* |
| 338 | Philip II of Macedon wins the battle of Chaironeia and the Greeks lose their independence. A league of Greek states is formed under Philip at Corinth. |
| 336 | Assassination of Philip and the accession of Alexander. |
| *335* | *Aristotle founds the Lyceum at Athens.* |
| 334–23 | Alexander conducts a campaign against Persia. |
| *331* | *Foundation of Alexandria (Egypt).* |
| 323 | Death of Alexander. |
| *321–289* | *Menander the dramatist of New Comedy active.* |
| *310* | *Zeno of Kition founds Stoic school at Athens.* |
| *307* | *Epicurus the philosopher settles in Athens.* |
| 301 | The battle of Ipsos (Phrygia). |
| 280–275 | Pyrrhos, king of Epirus, fails to defeat the Romans in Italy. |
| *270* | *Kallimachos and Theokritos active as poets.* |
| 241–197 | Attalos I ruler of Pergamon. |
| 197 | Romans defeat Philip V of Macedon. |
| 196 | The Roman general Flamininus declares 'the Freedom of the Greeks' at the Isthmus of Corinth. |
| 167 | The battle of Pydna. The Macedonian kingdom falls. |
| 146 | The sack of Corinth and Carthage by the Romans. Macedonia becomes a Roman province. |
| 133 | Attalos III bequeaths Pergamon to the Roman people. |
| 86 | The Roman dictator Sulla sacks Athens. |
| 48– | Roman civil wars fought out in Greece. |
| 46 | Julius Caesar re-founds Corinth as a Roman colony. |
| 44 | Julius Caesar murdered. |
| 31 | Octavian defeats Antony at the battle of Actium. |
| 27 | Octavian given the name of 'Augustus'. Roman province of Achaea formed. |

| AD | |
|---|---|
| 49–52 | St Paul in Greece. |
| 67 | Nero in Greece, plans the Corinth canal. |
| *100–20* | *Plutarch active.* |
| 117–38 | Hadrian Roman emperor. |
| *132* | *Temple of Zeus Olympios in Athens completed.* |
| *170* | *Pausanias'* Guide Book *finished.* |
| 267 | The Heruli invade Greece. |
| 312 | Christianity made official state religion. |
| 324 | Constantine defeats Licinius at Chrysopolis and becomes sole ruler of the Roman Empire. |
| *325* | *First Ecumenical Council at Nicaea.* |
| *330* | *Inauguration of Constantinople.* |
| *355* | *SS Basil and Gregory Nanzianus fellow-students at Athens.* |
| 378–95 | Theodosius the Great emperor. |
| 396 | Alaric and the Visigoths invade Greece. |
| 408–50 | Theodosius II emperor. |
| 410 | The sack of Rome by Alaric. |
| 527–65 | Justinian emperor. |
| *529* | *Justinian closes the Academy at Athens.* |
| 577 | Invasions of Balkans by Avars and Slavs begin. |
| 614 | Persians take Jerusalem. |
| 633–55 | Arab conquest of Syria, Egypt and the Sasanian Empire |
| *726* | *Period of Iconoclasm begins.* |
| 823–969 | Arabs occupy Crete and raid the Aegean. |
| *843* | *Restoration of Images.* |
| *963* | *Lavra, the first monastery on Mt Athos, founded.* |
| 1025 | Bulgaria incorporated as a Byzantine province. |
| *1054* | *Official breach between the Orthodox Church and the Papacy.* |
| 1071 | The Byzantines defeated by Seljuk Turks at battle of Manzikert. |
| 1204 | The Crusaders sack Constantinople. Venice takes Crete, Corfu, etc. |
| 1261 | Byzantine rule re-established at Constantinople under Michael VIII. |
| 1402 | Ottomans defeated by Tamurlane at the battle of Ankara. |

| | |
|---|---|
| *1439* | *The Council of Florence to discuss the union of the Greek and Latin churches.* |
| 1453 | Fall of Constantinople to the Ottomans. The end of the Eastern Roman Empire. |
| 1669 | Crete added to Ottoman Empire. |
| *1734* | *Society of Dilettanti founded in England.* |
| 1750–1822 | Ali Pasha Turkish governor of Yannina. |
| *1761–94* | *Stuart and Revett's* The Antiquities of Athens. |
| *1764* | *Wickelmann's* Geschichte der Kunst des Altertums. |
| *1816* | *Lord Elgin sells the Parthenon sculptures to the British nation.* |
| 1821–31 | Greek War of Independence. |
| 1833–62 | Otto of Bavaria king of the Hellenes. |
| 1864 | George I (Prince of Denmark) made king. |
| 1864–1942 | Eleftherios Venizelos. |
| 1881–1938 | Mustafa Kemal (Atatürk). |
| 1912 | Crete becomes part of Greece. |
| 1912–13 | Balkan Wars in which Greece expands her territory by two-thirds. |
| 1919–22 | Greece's 'Anatolian Venture' fails. |
| 1923 | The Treaty of Lausanne leads to exchange of Greek and Turkish populations. End of Ottoman Empire. |
| 1940 | The Greeks make a stand against the Italians. |
| 1941 | The German army invades Greece. |
| 1944 | German withdrawal from Greece. |
| 1946 | Rhodes and Dodecanese united to Greece. |
| 1946–9 | Civil war in Greece. |
| 1967–74 | Rule of military junta ('the Colonels'). |
| *1976* | Katharevousa *ceases to be the official language of the Greek state and education.* |
| 1981 | Greece joins the European Community. |

# INDEX